The
WPA Guide
to the Minnesota
Arrowhead Country

MINNESOTA ARR

FORT FRANCES

INTERNATIONAL FALLS

LITTLE-FORK

53

CABINS 71

BIG FALLS

INDIAN RESERVATION

53

SUPERIO NATIONAL F

LUMBERING

ORR

CANOE

NORTHHOME

COOK

CHIPPEWA NATIONAL FOREST

TOWER

BLACKDUCK

46

BASS FISHING

IRON MINES (OPEN PIT)

35

EN

MOUNTAIN IRON

2

46

DUCKS

KINNEY

VIRGINIA

AUI

BEMIDJI

CASS LAKE

DEER RIVER

CHISHOLM HIBBING

GILBERT BUHL

BIWAB

EVELETH

35

4

2

BENA

COHASSET

BOVEY

KEEWATIN

MARBLE

NASHWAUK CALUMET

COLERAINE

53

GRAND RAPIDS

371

PAUL BUNYAN PLAYGROUND

WALKER

34

REMER

6

169

FISHING

SM.

LAKES REGION

65

FLOODWOOD

53

GOL

34

6

169

RESERVATION

371

EXCELLENT BATHING

STATE FORESTS

CLOQUE

CARLTC

MEGREGOR

210

61

210 AITKIN

EGGS

BARNUM

CROSBY IRONTON

IRON MINES

65

MOOSE LAKE

BRAINERD

56

61

MILLE LACS

WHEAD REGION

CANADA

PORT ARTHUR
FT. WILLIAM

61

GUNFLINT TRAIL

LAND LOCKED
SALMON

MOOSE

GRAND
PORTAGE

WASHINGTON
HARBOR

61

GRAND
MARAIS

61

LITTLE
MARAIS

DEER

DEEP SEA FISHING

LAKE
SUPERIOR

52

61

BEAVER BAY

SPLIT ROCK
LIGHTHOUSE

TWO
HARBORS

61

DULUTH

LAKE CRUISES
AND EXCURSIONS

N

W   E

S

The WPA Guide to the Minnesota Arrowhead Country

*Compiled and written
by the Federal Writers' Project
of the Work Projects Administration*

With an introduction by
CATHY WURZER

MINNESOTA HISTORICAL SOCIETY PRESS

www.mhspress.org

The Minnesota Historical Society Press is a member of the Association of American University Presses.

Manufactured in Canada

10 9 8 7 6 5 4 3 2 1

∞ The paper used in this publication meets the minimum requirements of the American National Standard for Information Sciences—Permanence for Printed Library Materials, ANSI Z39.48-1984.

International Standard Book Number
ISBN 13: 978-0-87351-634-1 (paper)
ISBN 10: 0-87351-634-6 (paper)

Library of Congress Cataloging-in-Publication Data

The WPA guide to the Minnesota Arrowhead country / compiled and written by the Federal Writers' Project of the Work Projects Administration ; with an introduction by Cathy Wurzer.
     p.   cm.
Originally published: Chicago, Ill. : A. Whitman & Co., 1941, with title The Minnesota arrowhead country.
Includes bibliographical references and index.
ISBN-13: 978-0-87351-634-1 (paper : alk. paper)
ISBN-10: 0-87351-634-6 (paper : alk. paper)
     1. Minnesota—Guidebooks.
     2. Automobile travel—Minnesota—Guidebooks.
     3. Minnesota—Description and travel.
     4. Minnesota—History, Local.
     5. Minnesota—History—20th century.
     I. Writers' Program of the Work Projects Administration in the State of Minnesota.
     II. Minnesota arrowhead country.
F604.3.W73 2008
917.7604'53—dc22
                                                                        2008027185

Contents

Part I: The General Background

Part II: National Forests

Part III: Cities, Towns and Villages

CONTENTS

Part IV: Tours

Part V: Appendices

Maps

Introduction

1941. Americans were dancing to the lush music of big bands led by the likes of Glenn Miller, the Dorsey Brothers, and Sammy Kaye. Humphrey Bogart captivated movie fans as the hard-boiled private eye Sam Spade in the film *The Maltese Falcon.* An infant by the name of Robert Allen Zimmerman was born May 24 in Duluth: many decades later, the world knew him as Bob Dylan, music legend and cultural icon. Elated Minnesotans saw the University of Minnesota Golden Gopher football team become national champions that fall, and it was front-page news when star halfback Bruce Smith was named that year's Heisman Trophy winner. (Smith is the only such honoree in school history—at least to date!) November 1 saw the publication of a regional history book that was years in the making: *The WPA Guide to the Minnesota Arrowhead Country,* a road guide for tourists that received glowing reviews in the *Duluth Herald and News Tribune.* But just a few short weeks later, its release was overshadowed by an event that changed the course of history: the horrific surprise attack on American military forces by the Japanese at Pearl Harbor.

Born of a government relief program, *The WPA Guide to the Minnesota Arrowhead Country* was part of the American Guide Series created by the federal Works Progress Administration (WPA) in the 1930s—known, after 1939, as the Work Projects Administration. The WPA was one of the programs launched by President Franklin Delano Roosevelt's administration to help the United States recover from a stock market implosion in 1929 and the economic reverberations that affected nearly every American for more than a decade after. At the height of the Great Depression in 1933, Minnesota's unemployment rate was estimated at nearly 29 percent; on the Iron Range, it was even higher. In the country as a whole, one of every four Americans was out of work. To help meet this vast need, various government-sponsored programs paid workers to build roads, bridges, and buildings. Artists, actors, and musicians were hired to create public art, plays, and concerts. Soon-to-be-famous writers like

John Steinbeck, Studs Terkel, and Zora Neale Hurston were hired in the Federal Writers' Project (FWP).

The goal for the FWP was a lofty one: to create the first comprehensive road guides to the forty-eight states that existed at the time, plus guides to U.S. cities, regions, and cultures. At least three thousand oral histories were also done with ordinary Americans, yielding records of their lives and experiences that remain valuable today. Until the FWP much of this roadside and cultural history had not been explored or recorded; without the FWP it likely would have been lost forever. History shows us that the work of the Federal Writers' Project was prolific and profound. In all, the Writers' Project churned out more than 275 books, 700 pamphlets, and 300 articles, radio scripts, and leaflets. Decades later, it fell to John Cole, director of the Center for the Book at the Library of Congress, and his staff to catalog the abundance of FWP output. In an August 2003 article in the *New York Times,* Cole depicts an amazing collection: "The Federal Writers' Project helped us rediscover our heritage in a more detailed and colorful way than it had ever been described . . . the collection offers the best examples of local history and oddball anecdotal stories ever amassed."

The job of rounding up enough writers to create *The WPA Guide to Minnesota* fell to Dr. Mabel Ulrich, a well-educated, no-nonsense woman who was a physician, a public health advocate, a bookstore owner, and a writer. In the fall of 1935, Ulrich had just ten days to find 250 writers for the Minnesota guide project. She interviewed down-on-their-luck lawyers, teachers, preachers, and small-town newspaper reporters and editors. One man wrote vaudeville skits. Other applicants had been salesmen or business executives. Very few, Ulrich later said, were "bona fide writers" except for short-story author Meridel Le Sueur and future novelist Earl Guy. Ultimately, Ulrich picked 120 "from the neediest and most promising, and praying that release from economic pressure would release talents as well, I assigned them to work."

And work they did, earning twenty to twenty-five dollars a week from the federal government for documenting the history of Minnesota's major cities and then, mile by mile, each of the towns and landmarks along every key road in the state. In a May 1939 *Harper's Magazine* article, Ulrich remembered how she sent one of her workers to verify the mileage along each route. The man packed his wife, their nine children, provisions, and a pup tent into an old sedan and traveled the routes in the guide, carefully noting the mileage. After not being heard from for nearly two weeks, the family returned with reams of notes and photos, the man saying the trip had been the greatest educational experience of his children's young lives. It remained, Ulrich said, one of her fondest memories of an often difficult time. Ulrich had quite a task as the director of the Minnesota guide. The work the writers turned in was often ungrammatical or so literal that it lacked life and color, and Ulrich ended up writing much of the guide herself. Later she said her added responsibilities didn't matter because "hopeless men and women had found hope again" in the Federal Writers' Project. *The WPA Guide to Minnesota*, published November 28, 1938, was a solid success, selling more than six hundred copies in its first month.

Meanwhile, work had been proceeding in northeastern Minnesota on a WPA guide to the Minnesota Arrowhead Country. Two accomplished Duluth women played key roles in its creation. Margaret Culkin Banning was a civic leader, active in Republican party politics, and a best-selling author, writing thirty-six novels and more than four hundred short stories and essays in her career. Banning was joined in the Arrowhead guide effort by Frieda Monger, another politically active Duluthian who also was the editor and publisher of a weekly newspaper, *Duluth Publicity.*

Banning and Monger obviously had writing and publishing credentials, but it's unclear whether many of the writers of the Arrowhead guide did. Little is known of those who participated. Many never told their sons and daughters or grandchildren about their role in the creation of the Arrowhead guide, and they are not credited in the book (nor are the writers of the Minnesota WPA guide). It is not clear why such recognition was not granted. Perhaps the writers were ashamed of being on the government dole.

Records show one gentleman, Ludwig Bodenstab of Duluth, was in the northeastern Minnesota FWP from 1936 to 1939. His son

Allan remembers him as a "man of letters" and a "dreamer" who was often unemployed, which meant the family was on public assistance during most of Allan's younger years. Ludwig was often seen hunched over a typewriter, pounding out prose and letters, and while his name isn't included in the Arrowhead guide, Allan Bodenstab says his father was likely proud of his contribution.

Though the Arrowhead guide was overseen by the WPA, the project had as a partner the Duluth-based Minnesota Arrowhead Association, a group of businessmen and civic boosters. This same group had conducted a worldwide contest in 1924 that resulted in the name of the organization and a moniker for northeastern Minnesota that remains to this day. The lucky contest winner was a man from Pittsburgh who noticed that the boundaries of the counties included in the association's territory looked much like an Indian arrowhead. Of some thirty thousand entries, his suggestion of "Minnesota Arrowhead" was deemed the best. The Arrowhead of the 1940s consisted of the following counties, in whole or part: Cook, Lake, St. Louis, Itasca, Koochiching, Beltrami, Hubbard, Cass, Crow Wing, Aitkin, and Carlton.

The Arrowhead Association underwrote the first one thousand copies of the guide and took an active role in its creation. The minutes of meetings between Margaret Culkin Banning, Frieda Monger, and others in the Duluth office of the Federal Writers' Project and the men of the Arrowhead Association in the summer of 1939 show some concern over fundraising for the book, an issue that eventually worked itself out. Notes from another meeting indicate S. Valentine Saxby, the association's executive secretary, wanted to have "certain things in the Guide to make it saleable." It isn't clear what Mr. Saxby insisted had to be in the book, but it was indeed saleable and successful. Bound in a light green cloth cover with an Indian arrowhead prominently displayed under the title, *The WPA Guide to the Minnesota Arrowhead Country* was published November 1, 1941. Nathan Cohen of the *Duluth Herald and News Tribune* wrote that the guide was "one of the most competent and comprehensive ever undertaken . . . its informal, chatty style makes it first rate reading about one of America's treasured spots—the Minnesota Arrowhead Country."

The focus of the book is straightforward, its rationale laid out in Banning's introduction: "This guidebook is published to ask people to come to the Minnesota Arrowhead Country, to tell them how to come, when to come, what they will find when they get here and how best to enrich their experience." Tourists in the 1940s had their choice of transportation options to the Twin Ports, the Iron Range, and the North Shore, ranging from cars and railroads to bus lines, airlines, and passenger steamship lines, all of them described in the guide. The book also had detailed canoe trips for those who wanted to see "nature in the raw." The Arrowhead guide included tips on accommodations, hunting and fishing laws, and even a warning that "tourists and sportsmen should be prepared for sudden changes in temperature." How true, even today.

Most striking in the guidebook are the historical stories and quirky details given for the cities and towns across the Arrowhead. Bemidji, the book says, owes its beginnings to a settler who kicked up what he thought was a diamond while walking along the shore of Lake Bemidji back in 1894. He found other glittering stones and thought he had stumbled onto a diamond field that would rival any in Africa. His friends, their eyes turned toward future prosperity, urged him to put claims in his name and theirs on large tracts of land that would surely be developed once the diamond mining began. Unfortunately, the "diamonds" turned out to be quartzite. In the end, Bemidji slowly developed into a town fueled by logging and sawmills, not precious stones.

Readers learn how ethnically diverse the Arrowhead is. The Chisholm Public Library had one of the largest collections of foreign-language books in northern Minnesota, with ten languages represented. Embarrass was called the Arrowhead's Finland and for good reason: of the 652 people in town when the book was published, only two were *not* Finns. There are stories of raucous immigrant miners' funerals in Hibbing, with bands playing and banners flying in the aisles of the church and free-flowing beer to drown sorrows and wet parched throats. Also in Hibbing, Christ Memorial Church and others in town were moved several times, some towed with pews and altars intact to other sites, as the mammoth Hull-

Rust-Mahoning Mine, one of the world's largest open-pit mines, devoured large sections of town. Very few modern-day travel guides have these kinds of amusing details.

Attention is often paid to the tip of the Arrowhead, from the forested wilderness area around Ely over to Grand Marais and, of course, along the North Shore. The guide includes, as it should, the base of the Arrowhead, that broad range of land from International Falls down to Bemidji and Brainerd, encompassing places like Aitkin, known for its turkey farms, and Deer River, home to one of the few public schools in the country to have had dormitories for its students, the costs of their living expenses paid for by the school district.

Today's readers of *The WPA Guide to the Minnesota Arrowhead Country* may find some of the language outdated and uncomfortable: Native Americans are "savages"; physically challenged individuals are "cripples." Allowances have to be given for the era in which the book was written, but it is interesting to note how such language was commonplace before efforts were made to become more sensitive when choosing words. But, you may ask, is the book still useful today? Absolutely!

Take the first tour in part IV, one of the most iconic in all of Minnesota: the drive on Highway 61 from Duluth up the North Shore of Lake Superior to the international border. Many points of interest are covered, from Gooseberry Falls State Park (which was in its infancy when the book was originally published) to the breathtaking Palisade Head, with nods to some of the many rivers that feed into Lake Superior: the Manitou, the Temperance, and the Onion. (Check out what the guide says about the origins of those last two names!) This information is still timely. The guide gives little indication, however, of the work it took to carve out a highway that meanders along some of the most beautiful terrain in the state. Many of today's motorists don't know about the heart-stopping view from the original alignment of Highway 61 outside of Two Harbors, where the road hugged the cliff with a steep drop into the lake below. Small mention is made in the guidebook of the dangerous work required to dynamite rock off the face of Silver Creek Cliff to put a highway through in the 1920s. Now motorists enjoy less of a white-knuckle ride in that area because of a tunnel that was blasted through the cliff in the 1990s.

In the early days, automobile travel was considered an adventure, something to look forward to despite the dusty, bumpy roads in the summer and the muddy, nearly impassable roads in the spring. Lodging ranged from swanky hotels in the larger cities to tent camps and motor courts that offered cut-rate accommodations for those on a budget. Often motorists would simply pull over and hunker down in their vehicle for the night. Travel in those days was as much about the trip as the destination, an opportunity to free oneself from the daily grind and explore new sights and the unique flavor of each town along the way. Small gas stations with a single pump outside, tiny cafes and lunchrooms, and oddball roadside attractions greeted early highway travelers. And despite the Great Depression, Minnesotans were taking to the road in droves, with *The WPA Guide to Minnesota* and *The WPA Guide to the Minnesota Arrowhead Country* to help them. Today's travelers find multilane interstates pockmarked by the same fast food restaurant, gas station, and motel chains. Any kitschy tourist attractions that remain are fast becoming bits of highway history.

Regarding history, the 1941 version of the Minnesota Arrowhead region's story is certainly different from what would be told today. It has to be. Time marches on, as they say, but what remains is the region's unparalleled natural beauty. Even the first sentence of the guide reflects this: "The Minnesota Arrowhead is a region of superlatives." That isn't hyperbole: northeastern Minnesota has an aliveness and a vividness that isn't found in many other places. From majestic Lake Superior to the sublime Boundary Waters Canoe Area Wilderness and the hundreds of thousands of acres of forests, meadows, and wetlands in between, with too many lakes and streams to mention—the rugged and awe-inspiring terrain is timeless and in many places still untouched. As a friend of mine from Duluth says, "Here, nature is in control. The landscape does not accommodate humans; we learn to accommodate it." Just as the land of the Arrowhead is distinctive, so are her people. Folks who live in northeastern Minnesota are tough and independent and fiercely loyal to their unique corner of the state. *The WPA Guide to the Minnesota Arrowhead Country* makes clear that these personality traits haven't changed in the years since its publication.

This book has lasting value. There is value in knowing the history of the small mining towns of the Cuyuna, Mesabi, and Vermilion iron ranges, which are strung along Highway 169 like beads on a necklace. There is value in understanding the cultural and social conventions of the many ethnic groups that settled the Arrowhead and the role the region's first residents, the Ojibwe, played in the area's history. Finally, there is value in learning about what was important to those who came before us, values made evident in this book.

I think you'll find the suggested driving tours to be fascinating. It's fun to see what is still along the highlighted highways or, if those sites are gone, to at least know what was there. You may think you know northeastern Minnesota, but I bet you'll be surprised at the things you'll learn from this guidebook that stands the test of time. The writers and editors who worked so hard on *The WPA Guide to the Minnesota Arrowhead Country* so many decades ago would be pleased. Enjoy the trip.

CATHY WURZER

Introduction

There is nothing that should give a person greater pleasure than to have his own section of the country known and appreciated, used, and enjoyed. For it is normal and sane to open the gates of your home, instead of erecting barriers around it. This guidebook is published to ask people to come to the Minnesota Arrowhead Country, to tell them how to come, when to come, what they will find when they get here, and how best to enrich their experience. Its publication is a great satisfaction to those of us who call the Minnesota Arrowhead Country home, who knew it when it was less accessible and less comfortable than it is today, and whose fathers and grandfathers have told us of previous times when to visit this region was an adventure which had real peril in it.

It is still an adventure, though the peril has reached the vanishing point. It is an adventure into country which never can lose its natural and rather wild beauty. And always it tempts the imagination to look both back and forward. We want many people to find this out for themselves.

In addition, there is something else which is satisfying in this guidebook. We are glad that this introduction to the Minnesota Arrowhead is not merely a commercial publication, nor the result of the enthusiasm of one writer. Into its making has gone a study of history and a great deal of close research which has been most interesting work and also the source of livelihood for a number of resident men and women. They have carefully studied the past and the modern relations of this section of the country, investigated its chances and capacities. They have made the Minnesota Arrowhead live in these pages, and in return the Arrowhead has given them a living, which is just as it should be.

This book is a source book, we hope. Here are the notes for hundreds of future works that may be written about the Arrowhead—biographies, adventure stories, economic analyses. It is so offered, and those of us who have been connected with the making of this book in an advisory way, or have merely offered its writers encouragement, hope that it will be a spring-board for enjoyment, education, and the furtherance and deepening of American life and self-understanding.

MARGARET CULKIN BANNING

Duluth

Preface

There are few vacation lands that can rival Minnesota's Arrowhead Country in sheer diversity of interest. Almost literally, the region has everything—rockbound lakes and lakes surrounded by grassy meadows, tranquil and turbulent rivers, hill farms and level plowland, industries large and small, luxuriously appointed summer resorts and isolated beauty spots that are accessible only to the hiker with pup-tent. Among its rock outcroppings, the oldest geological formations known to man, have arisen some of the Northwest's newest settlements. Men and machines, clawing out its rich pockets of ore, have scarred the surface of the Iron Range with huge, almost terrifying chasms—and built beside their waste heaps some of the finest school buildings in the world.

It is strange, in view of all this, that so little has been written about the Minnesota Arrowhead Country. Such a region deserves to be widely known, and strangers, equally with its residents, can enjoy reading its story.

In THE MINNESOTA ARROWHEAD COUNTRY, that story has been written by those who know it best because they are a part of it. The book, from beginning to end, is the work of Arrowhead people. The illustrations are not merely typical of the region—they are actual Arrowhead pictures.

For the supplying of up-to-date information on Arrowhead communities, we are indebted to chambers of commerce and other local civic organizations. We are grateful to the St. Louis County Historical Society and its secretary, Otto Wieland, and to Librarian Jane Morey and the staff of the Duluth Public Library for their generous cooperation. Thanks are due especially to Mrs. Frieda J. Monger, who supervised the writing of the final text, to Mrs. Margaret Culkin Banning for the Introduction, and to all the other members of the co-sponsor's advisory committee. The roster of the committee, serving under Mrs. Banning as chairman and Mrs. Monger as co-chairman, is as follows: Miss Jane Morey, Messrs. S. Valentine Saxby,

J. R. Pratt, J. H. Jordan, Lewis G. Castle, V. E. Fairbanks, W. E. Culkin, Otto E. Wieland, J. H. Darling, Dwight E. Woodbridge, Eugene W. Bohannon, A. W. Taylor, G. A. Andresen, George J. Barrett and W. A. Putman.

Much helpful information and advice was given by officials of the Oliver Mining Company, by the U. S. Engineer's office in Duluth, and by representatives of the United States Forest Service stationed in the Minnesota Arrowhead.

For maps and jacket design, we are indebted to the Minnesota WPA Art Project.

Roscoe Macy, *State Supervisor*
Minnesota WPA Writers' Project

General Information

Railroads: Big Fork & International Falls; Chicago, St. Paul, Minneapolis & Omaha; Duluth, Missabe & Iron Range; Duluth, South Shore & Atlantic; Duluth, Winnipeg & Pacific (Canadian National); Great Northern; Minneapolis, Red Lake & Manitoba; Minneapolis, St. Paul & Sault Ste. Marie; Minnesota, Dakota & Western; Minnesota & International; Northern Pacific.

Bus Lines: Northern Transportation Co.; Northland Greyhound Lines; Triangle Transportation Co.

Passenger Steamship Lines: Canadian Steamship Lines; Chicago, Duluth, & Georgian Bay Transit Co.; H. Christiansen & Sons.

Air Lines: Northwest Airlines, Inc.

Highways: US 2 through Duluth to northwestern part of State; US 53 through Duluth to International Falls on the Canadian border; US 61 from Minneapolis and St. Paul through Duluth to Canadian border at Pigeon River; US 71 from International Falls on the Canadian border through Bemidji to southern part of State; US 169 from Minneapolis and St. Paul through the Cuyuna Range and the Mesabi Range to connect with State 1; US 210 from Duluth through Cuyuna Range to connect with US 10; US 371 from US 10 at Little Falls through Brainerd to connect with US 2 at Cass Lake; State 23 from Duluth through Fond du Lac to connect with US 61 as Sandstone. (All main highways are kept open throughout the winter.)

Traffic Regulation (digest): Maximum speed, 60 miles per hour in day time; 50 m. p. h. at night or at any time when persons and vehicles on the highway at a distance of 500 feet ahead are not clearly discernible;

30 m. p. h. in any municipality. Nonresident may operate motor vehicle 3 months on out-of-state license. Minimum age for drivers, 15 years. "No Passing" zone barrier lines are marked by solid yellow stripes paralleling the center line of pavement. Driver's license must be carried at all times and exhibited on official demand. Headlights must be depressed when approaching an oncoming vehicle.

Accommodations: The Minnesota Arrowhead has good, year-round hotels in the larger communities. There are resorts with modern facilities in all parts of the region, some open throughout the year, others only in season. Tourist homes and tourist camps dot the highways, and attractive wilderness campsites are to be found throughout the forest areas.

Information Services: Minnesota Arrowhead Association, Hotel Duluth, cor. 3rd Ave. E. and Superior St., Duluth, maintains an all-year bureau and two summer bureaus; Duluth Chamber of Commerce, Medical Arts Building, 324 W. Superior St., Duluth, maintains an all-year bureau and a summer bureau; West Duluth Business Men's Club, Ramsey St. bet. 56th and Grand Aves., in cooperation with the Minnesota Arrowhead Association, maintains a summer bureau; West End Business and Civic Club, Curtis Hotel, 2001 W. Superior St., in cooperation with the Minnesota Arrowhead Association, maintains a summer bureau. For other Arrowhead communities, see *Cities, Towns and Villages.*

Hunting and Fishing: Following is a digest of Minnesota hunting and fishing regulations:

Fishing Laws: The Arrowhead region is in the northern fishing zone of Minnesota. Game fish are designated as wall-eyed pike, sand pike or saugers, great northern pike or pickerel, muskellunge, crappies, bass, sunfish, catfish, trout, lake trout (landlocked salmon). Rough fish are bullheads, whitefish, carp, dogfish, redhorse, buffalofish, suckers, sheepshead.

Open Season: Wall-eyed pike, sand pike or saugers, great northern pike or pickerel, muskellunge, May 15 to Feb. 15; crappies, June 21 to Feb. 15; bass (large-mouth, small-mouth, and yellow), June 21 to Dec. 1; sunfish, rock bass, catfish, June 21 to Jan. 1; trout (except lake trout), May 1 to Sept. 1; lake trout (landlocked salmon), Dec. 1 to Sept. 15 (except Lake Superior, Oct. 1); bullheads, whitefish, carp, dogfish, redhorse, buffalofish, suckers, sheepshead, May 1 to Mar. 1.

Licenses: Nonresident, 16 years of age or over, $3.00; resident, 18 years of age or over, $1.00. Two-coupon shipping license, fee $1.00, permits non-resident to ship to himself up to 20 pounds of game fish, dressed weight— 10 pounds or less per coupon.

Limits: Wall-eyed pike, 8 per day, 12 in possession; sand pike or saugers, 8 per day, 12 in possession; great northern pike or pickerel, 8 per day, 12 in possession; perch (yellow), no limit, but subject to restrictions by commissioner to fix limits of 25 per day; muskellunge, 2 per day, 2 in possession; crappie (black and white), 15 per day, 25 in possession; bass (large-mouth, small-mouth, and yellow), 6 per day, 12 in possession; trout (except lake trout), 15 per day, 25 trout or 20 pounds in possession; lake trout (landlocked salmon), 5 per day, 10 in possession; sunfish, rock bass, and all other kinds of fish for which a specific limit is not provided, and excluding those kinds with no limit, 15 per day, 30 in possession; bullheads, 50 per day, 50 in possession; no limit to carp, dogfish, redhorse, sheepshead, suckers, eelpout, garfish, whitefish (not less than 16 inches), buffalofish (not less than 15 inches).

Unlawful: To take fish by means of explosives, drugs, poisons, lime, medicated bait, fish berries, or other deleterious substances, or by nets, trot lines, wire strings, ropes, and cables. To have in possession fish nets (except minnow nets, landing nets, and dip nets), unless tagged and licensed by the Game and Fish Director; legel nets in possession of licensed commercial fishermen excepted. To fish with more than one line or more than one bait, except that 3 artificial flies may be used. To fish within 50 feet of a fishway. To deposit sawdust or refuse or poisonous substance in waters containing fish life. To buy or sell game fish, except fish taken under commercial license. To retain game fish after April 1 in the year following the open season. To take or possess, at any time, rock or lake sturgeon. To take shovel-nose or hackle-back sturgeon, spoonbill, or paddlefish from inland waters. To take fish in any manner other than by angling, except as spearing or netting of certain kinds is expressly permitted. To take fish from public water closed by order of director.

Small Game Hunting Laws: Summary of small game hunting regulations:

Open Season: Shooting of prairie chicken, grouse, partridge and pheasant permitted during fall in areas defined yearly. No open season on spruce grouse or wild turkey. Hunting of migratory wildfowl subject to Federal and State regulation. Seasons established each year for taking of gray and fox squirrel, cottontail and snowshoe hare.

Licenses: Nonresident, $25; resident, 16 years of age or over, $1.00, which must be purchased in the county in which the applicant resides.

Limits: Bag limits on migratory birds and upland game are subject to annual change. Shooting dates are not printed on licenses, but are prescribed in press releases issued by Federal and State authorities shortly before opening dates.

Unlawful: To use a hunting license or coupon of another person; to hunt in any State park or game refuge; to take migratory game birds with rifle or pistol or in any other way than with shotgun not larger than 10-gauge fired from shoulder, or with bow and arrow; to take migratory game birds with automatic or hand-operated repeating shotgun holding more than 3 shells; to shoot game from a motor vehicle or to carry firearms therein unless taken apart or contained in a case, unloaded in both barrels and magazine; to bait hunting grounds for taking migratory waterfowl and mourning doves; to use live decoys for migratory waterfowl; to transport protected game without official tags.

Big Game Hunting Laws: Summary of big game hunting regulations:

Open Season: Deer, bear (only in even-numbered years), Nov. 15 to Nov. 25, inclusive; with bow and arrow only, Itasca County only, Nov. 1 to Nov. 5, inclusive. No open season for moose, caribou, elk.

Licenses: Nonresident, $50.25; resident, $2.25, which must be purchased in the county where applicant resides.

Limits: One bear and one deer of any age or of either sex.

Unlawful: To use artificial lights in taking deer; to use snares, traps, set or swivel guns; to employ salt lick or other devices to entice or entrap deer; to shoot deer from any artificial platform higher than 6 feet; to use dogs for hunting of deer; to keep dogs about hunting camp in deer hunting area; to keep or transport deer if not tagged with license tag "B" and sealed with metal lock seal immediately after killing; to keep deer more than 5 days after close of season if not tagged by proper official.

Border Regulations: United States Customs Offices at International Falls are open day and night; at Pigeon River they are open from 6 a.m. to 11 p.m. between May 15 and Sept. 30, and from 7 a.m. to 12 midnight between Oct. 1 and May 14. No passports are required. United States citizens, native-born as well as naturalized, should carry identification papers. (Temporary restriction: Former subjects of enemies of Great Britain are not permitted, at the present time, to enter Canada unless they have received special permission from Canadian authorities in advance.) Purchases in Canada up to $100, if for personal use, may be brought back duty-free provided the resident has remained outside the territorial limits of the United States for 48 hours. The $100 exemption may include cigarettes, tobacco, foodstuffs, not more than 100 cigars, and not more than one wine gallon of alcoholic beverages.

Climate: Spring arrives late in the Arrowhead, especially along the shores of Lake Superior. Summers are comparatively cool. Autumn is prolonged by the moderating influence of the lake. Winters, as a rule, are severe. Tourists and sportsmen should be prepared for sudden changes in temperature.

Prohibited: Picking of the moccasin flower (*Cypripedium spectabile*) and the trillium.

Poisonous Plants: Poison ivy, a climbing plant with trifoliate leaves, and poison oak (poison sumac), usually prevalent in swamps, are found in the region. Laundry soap may be used both as a preventive and as a first-aid remedy.

(*Note:* There are no venomous snakes in the Arrowhead region.)

PART I

The General Background

Past and Present

THE MINNESOTA ARROWHEAD is a region of superlatives. It contains the State's most rugged topography, lowest and highest altitudes, its only three-way watershed, and richest iron ore deposits; its finest trout streams and best deer hunting; greatest national forest, the Superior; longest and wildest canoe trips; its most elaborately equipped schools; its largest county, St. Louis, one of the most extensive in the nation, covering 6,611.75 square miles and having, in addition to the courthouse in Duluth, two full-time auxiliary courthouses, at Hibbing and Virginia, and one part-time courthouse, at Ely.

In 1924, the Northeastern Minnesota Civic and Commerce Association sponsored an international contest for naming the area. An observing Pittsburgher, Odin MacCrickart, noted that the boundaries outlined by the association roughly suggested the form of an Indian arrowhead. His proposed name, "Minnesota Arrowhead," was adjudged best of the 30,000 letters submitted.

A glance at the map will show that the tip of the Arrowhead is marked by Pigeon Point, one side by the Canadian boundary of rivers and lakes, the base by a curving line from International Falls, through Bemidji, Brainerd, Aitkin, Moose Lake, and Carlton, to Duluth, and the other side by the north shore of Lake Superior. The air-line distance from east to west, Pigeon Point to Bemidji, is about 260 miles; from north to south, International Falls to Malmo, it is about 160 miles. The area approximates 20,500 square miles, or more than 13,000,000 acres. Included are all or parts of the following counties: Cook, Lake, St. Louis, Carlton, Itasca, Aitkin, Koochiching, Beltrami, Crow Wing, Hubbard, and Cass.

Altitudes range from 602 feet, the level of Lake Superior, to 2,230 feet in Cook County, the average being about 1,400 feet. The "Saw-

3

tooth Range," (*see Arrowhead Tour 1*), just back of the north shore of Lake Superior and paralleling it from about Beaver Bay to Grand Marais, has an abrupt elevation of from 500 to 900 feet above lake level. Only the smaller part of the Arrowhead is prairie land, and that is in the western section.

Of the region's population of about 350,000, nearly two-thirds live in Duluth and the other municipalities. The majority of the remaining one-third is engaged in farming.

GEOLOGY

The geological setting of the Minnesota Arrowhead region is linked to the very earliest period in the life of the earth—the Archean. It is, of course, not possible to trace the long procession of events during this period. However, scientists usually are agreed that it was in the seas of this geologic age that the iron formations of the Vermilion Range accumulated.

Although many theories have been advanced to account for the iron in the Arrowhead ranges, it generally is believed that the iron formations (iron oxide, silica, etc.) were discharged into the sea water by either deposition or seepage, or both. The fact that the Minnesota ranges are similar in age and general character to certain iron formations in all other continents seems to indicate they are but part of a more or less continuous metalliferous zone, here exposed by volcanic action and by streams and glaciers.

Eons followed the accumulation of the iron formations; then something manifested itself that was to change the area. From the depths of the earth a gigantic mass of molten rock (batholith) had been rising, pushing aside or melting and assimilating the rocks above it. As it neared the surface, it domed the earth's crust into a mountain range; lava belched forth, the roof collapsed, and the resulting chasm became the basin of Lake Superior.

On the northern highlands of the continent, during the most recent glacial period, a huge ice cap slowly formed, and gradually moved southward until the entire area was covered by a vast sheet of ice. Under its weight, the continent sank. With the melting of the glacier, waters collected over the sunken land to make Lake Agassiz, probably the largest fresh-water lake the world has ever known, and smaller lakes, among them Lake Duluth, which occupied the western part of the Lake Superior basin.

As the ice sheet receded, it left extensive deposits. Some of these, spread thinly across the surface, became the till plain; others, piled up, appeared as hills, moraines, or the gravel ridges called eskers. Some of the glacial deposits were rich in pulverized granite, slate, lava, sandstone, and limestone, and these produced the soil that today makes up the better agricultural areas of the region. Other glacial deposits bore the great forests that were destined ages later to become a nation's playground—the Minnesota Arrowhead.

FIRST INHABITANTS

The time of arrival in this region of the first inhabitants, as well as their racial stock, is hidden in the obscurity of prehistoric time. They may have been the ones who worked the ancient copper mines on Isle Royale (*see Arrowhead Tour 1*), leaving traces of an engineering skill far surpassing that of the natives found by the explorers.

The Dakota (Sioux) are supposed to have been the earliest of the Indian tribes in this area, as evidenced by fragments of pottery and other artifacts (*see Arrowhead Tour 3*). They were superseded by the Ojibway—or Chippewa, as the white man interpreted the Indian name. These were of Algonquian stock and when first encountered by white explorers early in the seventeenth century were living in the Lake Superior region. In the course of westward migration, they occupied the territory around Sault Ste. Marie, being called Saulteurs. Later they established a settlement along Chequamegon Bay and on Madeline Island (La Pointe), north of Ashland, Wisconsin. By successive contests against the warring Sioux, they gradually extended their domain, until in the eighteenth century they were in control of all of northern Minnesota.

THE WHITE MAN COMES

The identity of the first white men to set foot in Minnesota is still a subject of dispute, but most historical records give credit to Pierre d'Esprit, Sieur de Radisson, and Médard Chouart, Sieur des Groseilliers. Born in France, these brothers-in-law came adventuring to the Arrowhead between 1655 and 1660, when Radisson was little more than a boy. For their joint ventures in trail blazing and fur trading they must have been admirable partners, as the young Radisson's thirst for adventure was complemented at every turn by the mercenary shrewdness of Groseilliers.

The first flotilla of furs they took to Quebec from the Northwest was valued at 200,000 livres ($40,000); the second, which was confiscated, has been estimated to have been worth as much as $300,000. Their success in fur trading aroused the envy of their greedy superiors in eastern Canada, and they were proscribed as *coureurs de bois,* or unlicensed traders. Groseilliers was thrown into a Montreal prison, despite repeated protests that all their activities were motivated solely by patriotism, and that it was only when they refused to share their spoils with the governor that their trading licenses were withheld. Outraged by their own country's ingratitude, they turned to England and there published the narrative that was responsible, at least in part, for the chartering of the Hudson's Bay Company in 1670.

Their various voyages covered a quarter of a century. It has been inferred, chiefly on the evidence of an old map, that between 1655 and 1663 they came twice to Minnesota and traded at Fond du Lac, French for "end of the lake," as the entire region at the head of the lakes was called.

Although many of the stories carried to Europe were fantastic exaggerations, the Northwest had proved that it contained furs enough to meet the exorbitant demands of greedy courtiers, and potential wealth vast enough to tempt even monarchs. Nicolas Perrot was dispatched to the Upper Lakes, and he persuaded the tribal chiefs to assemble at the Sault, where on June 14, 1671, Simon François Daumont, Sieur de St. Lusson, took formal possession for France "of all countries discovered or to be discovered between the Northern, Western, and Southern Seas . . ." Father Claude Allouez, a Jesuit already at home on the inland rivers (he had visited the place where Duluth now stands), enjoined the Indians' allegiance to the French King.

Jean Baptiste Talon, Intendant of New France (Canada), in 1673 chose Louis Jolliet and Father Jacques Marquette to explore the region of the Mississippi. Marquette, who was familiar with several Indian tongues, died before completing the journey, but Jolliet's reports on the potentialities of the fur trade so delighted the Governor General, Louis de Buade, Comte de Frontenac, that he immediately planned a new trade expedition into the area. After dispatching his engineer, Hugues Randin, to the head of the lakes to distribute gifts, he bestowed official approval upon Daniel Greysolon, Sieur du Lhut, the choice of the Montreal merchants, as leader of the new trading venture.

Du Lhut, or Du Luth, born about 1636 in St. Germain-en-Laye,

France, was the most striking of all the Arrowhead's explorers. He had renounced an enviable position in the Royal Guard of Louis XIV to go to New France. In September, 1678—for reasons unknown—he turned his back on cities and civilization, and embarked from Montreal upon the first of the voyages that were to result in breath-taking dangers, romance, and fame. Pushing farther and farther west, he claimed for his mother country all the territory he visited. Wherever he went, his fearlessness and tact won the friendship and admiration of even the most hostile Indians.

In 1679, he was wintering at the Sault; by June 27, he had reached Little Portage, the base of Minnesota Point; by midsummer, he had visited Mille Lacs (*see Arrowhead Tour 3*). On September 15, he called a council of all the northern tribes to meet with him near the site of the present Duluth, for the purpose of establishing peace and pledging friendship. His dramatic meeting with the Franciscan missionary, Father Louis Hennepin, who had accompanied an expedition sent to the upper Mississippi by Robert Cavelier, Sieur de la Salle, occurred in 1680. When the priest and his two companions were made "enforced guests" by a band of Sioux, Du Lhut set out to rescue them. He came upon them somewhere below the mouth of the St. Croix, on the Mississippi, and secured their release by claiming Hennepin as his brother. Du Lhut and his augmented party returned to the lakes where he pursued his fur trading.

Records are few, but it seems likely that rival jealousies were responsible for Du Lhut's incarceration in Quebec in 1681 as an unlicensed trader. Challenging his accusers, he went to France to clear his name, and returned in triumph to resume his adventurous life. In 1679, he or his brother Claude built Fort Kaministiquia near the present Fort William (*see Arrowhead Tour 1*), where Jacques de Noyon may have stopped, about 1688, when he traversed the border lakes and rivers.

The supremacy of the French became definitely established in the Indian mind when Du Lhut, in 1683, informed of the murder of two fellow-countrymen on Lake Superior, set out with a mere handful of men for the camp where the slayers had been given shelter. In the presence of a seething tribe that outnumbered his men ten to one, he arrested, tried, and executed the pair. His amazing courage, when ranging through unbroken wilderness, running uncharted rapids, or waging hand-to-hand conflict with savages, made him the most colorful figure in this part of the country. That all this time he suffered acutely from gout would pass belief, were there not documented evidence. Retired to Montreal at last by ill health, he died in 1710 and was buried at the little church of the Recollects.

Pierre Gaultier de Varennes, Sieur de la Vérendrye, gallant gentleman and "Columbus of the Old Northwest," haunted day and night by his dream of finding a northwest passage to the Pacific Ocean, did more than any other man to lay the foundation for the Arrowhead's great fur trade empire. His voyages were made between 1731 and 1742. With a party that included three sons and a nephew, he built a loose network of forts along the lakes and rivers that now are a part of the international boundary, and thus made possible the rapid expansion of the trade. He and his Indian aide, Ochagach, drew what is considered the oldest map of this border region, a rough sketch, but one that was to prove of great assistance to later explorers. No fur trade, however lucrative, could divert him from his dream of a waterway to the Pacific. A brave but tragic figure of westward exploration, dogged by one misfortune after another, Vérendrye was destined to receive the Cross of St. Louis but, after his death, to lie in an unmarked grave.

EARLY FUR TRADING

In the seventeenth and eighteenth centuries, the decrees of European fashions increased the demand for furs. It was the wealth to be had from the backs of animals, particularly the beaver, that opened this territory to the outside world. Companies were formed to handle the extensive fur trade that developed, and, as the territory changed hands, the control of the industry passed from one nation to another.

In barter with Indians the French excelled, intercepting, even in the remotest interior, pelts intended for the Hudson's Bay Company. They dominated the trade in the area from the time Radisson and Groseilliers took out the first cargo in 1656 until France ceded Canada to Great Britain in 1763. After this, rivalry grew so bitter between the English company and the Montreal and Quebec traders, and among the traders themselves, that a group of the latter organized for self-preservation what in 1784 formally became the Northwest Company.

The Hudson's Bay Company eventually gained supremacy, largely through its taking over and buying the loyalty of many of the French traders and half-breed interpreters. In the Arrowhead, however, the

Northwesters were hard to uproot. So firmly had they established themselves that even as late as 1805, 22 years after this had become American territory, the visit of Lieutenant Zebulon M. Pike to acquaint the traders and Indians with their new allegiance was received coldly. In fact, his departure was followed by a rehoisting of British flags. Although other companies sprang up from time to time, the Hudson's Bay, the Northwest, and the XY (a dissident group that split off from the Northwest Company) were the most important in the building up of the Arrowhead's commerce in furs until after the War of 1812. Congress then excluded all foreigners from trading in United States territory, and John Jacob Astor's American Fur Company took over the entire domestic field.

Under British control the industry, with headquarters in Montreal and Quebec, reached its greatest height. As the fur traders penetrated deeper and deeper into the labyrinth of lakes and rivers, a trade so extensive, complex, and profitable developed that before long an inland trading post was required. The logical site for such a post was Grand Portage, the Lake Superior terminus of the Grand Portage Trail, which long had been used by Indians and *voyageurs* to avoid the falls and rapids of the lower Pigeon River. The Arrowhead's first and most colorful white settlement, as well as Minnesota's, was this fur trading post. The thousands who came to it for business went back to spread far and wide rumors of the country's riches. Traffic between Grand Portage and Montreal and Quebec became so great that several hundred white traders and *voyageurs* with thousands of Indians were engaged in this part of the fur trade.

The inland transportation of furs to Grand Portage was carried on by *voyageurs* over the waterways of the region in light canoes of about one and one-half tons capacity. The rivers and lakes were linked by portages, over which the canoes and the cargo had to be toted. The furs were packed in bundles of 90 pounds each, and two such bundles, occasionally even three, was the average load for a man.

Wild life seemed inexhaustible, but through over-exploitation and waste, the region soon became almost depleted of furs. Trade waned, companies consolidated, Astor withdrew (1834). Ramsay Crooks, who since 1809 had been connected with Astor, took control and inaugurated new policies.

In 1837 came a country-wide panic, and for the succeeding five depression years the American Fur Company, a dominant factor in world trade, fought to survive. In 1842, the vast organization collapsed. Pierre Chouteau Jr. and Company of St. Louis took over the industry but discontinued operations here in 1847.

Bringing the first white men into the region, the fur trade, ironically enough, delayed settlement, for the fur companies well knew that, once their wilderness was overrun by prospectors or settlers, the source of their profits—the fur-bearing animals—would vanish.

COPPER AND GOLD EXPLORATION

With the disappearance of the fur trade as an organized enterprise, there came a virtual standstill in the economic life of the region. This situation did not change until there was a new influx of people. These newcomers were El Dorado seekers rather than settlers, interested, not in what the land might produce, but in what it might possess. They were hunting for copper.

Rumors of vast and varied mineral wealth in the wilderness beyond the north shore of Lake Superior had long been current. Tales of copper mines on Isle Royale, worked and abandoned by an unknown earlier race, had been familiar to Indians and fur traders. In 1746, it was recorded by a *voyageur* that "there were found, north of Lake Superior, several large lumps of the finest virgin copper." The finder wrote: "In the honest exultation of my heart at so important a discovery, I directly showed it to the company [Hudson's Bay Company], but the thanks I met with may be judged by the system of their conduct. The fact, without any inquiry into the reality of it, was treated as a chimerical illusion, and a stop arbitrarily put to all further search into the matter, by the lords of the soil."

Benjamin Franklin heard of the rumors in France and insisted, in the Treaty of Paris, 1783, that Great Britain cede to the United States all the shore of Lake Superior from Pigeon Point to Fond du Lac and including Isle Royale. Franklin regarded the securing of this region as one of his greatest achievements.

In 1826, the Chippewa granted the United States the right to explore any part of their country for metals or minerals. Oddly enough, however, there was no rush for the advantages of the grant, even though prospectors were returning from the wilderness with proof of the alleged rich deposits. Some of these men obtained licenses to trade with the Indians. They built shelters, hoping that the Government soon would abrogate the Indians' title to the land, open the region to white settlement, and legalize their claims. The Government delayed action, so their hopes faded and finally died.

In 1848, an official exploration of the north shore from Fond du Lac to the Pigeon River revealed a vein of copper at French River and veinstone and further indications of metal at several other points. Thereupon, mining interests in Michigan, across the lake on the south shore, brought influence to bear toward the opening of the area for white settlement. The Treaty of La Pointe ceding the "triangle" north of Lake Superior was signed by the Chippewa chiefs in September, 1854. Then the boom started. Before the treaty could be ratified and confirmed, the miners and settlers avid to reach the promised wealth rushed into the area. Shacks and shanties were built, and, when the territory was opened officially, claims were established by preemption. The Reverend James Peet, a Methodist missionary who arrived at the head of the lakes in 1856, describes what he saw when journeying in a rowboat from Fond du Lac to Grand Portage: "Along the North Shore of Lake Superior for 30 miles . . . nearly all the land is claimed and a shanty built nearly every half mile. Some of the 'town sites' have one or two families on them, others a few single men, others are not inhabited at all."

In 1856, the Government established a land office at Buchanan, a forest-covered wilderness offering not even a place to land a boat. John Whipple, the receiver, viewed the site with dismay, then opened his office in 1857 in an abandoned house two miles distant, in the deserted Montezuma, which thereupon became Buchanan (*see Arrowhead Tour 1*). Here the mouth of the Sucker River provided at least a good beach. Whipple's recorded experiences with the newly created Northeastern Land District of Minnesota vividly exemplify conditions as they then existed. Plat books containing records of the district's land surveys had been lost in transit from the surveyor general's office at Dubuque, Iowa. After tracing them from Dubuque to Chicago and back again, Whipple finally located them at Taylors Falls, Minnesota. As far as Deer River (Pine River), he was able to convey them by team over the Minnesota Trail (Military Road). At this point the road became impassable, and he and a packer, the precious books on their backs, were obliged to trek for four days through mud and water to Superior.

The copper boom was short-lived. No paying ore having been found, and with the panic of 1857 imminent, the prospectors, who a few short months before could not get in fast enough, now stampeded out by ox team over rude trails, by rowboat, or on foot with pack and blankets.

Other attempts, less dramatic than this one, have been made to locate the metal in profitable quantities, one coming as late as 1929. None has met with commercial success.

A few of the copper locations yielded traces of more precious metals. Old residents of Beaver Bay tell of an Indian who used to appear during the summer with dazzling specimens of silver, but who never could be induced to reveal the location of his mine.

Spectacular gold rushes twice have enlivened the area. In 1865, the yellow metal was reported near Lake Vermilion, and hopeful prospectors again poured into the region, but this boom, too, collapsed. In 1893, the same dream lured many to Rainy Lake, Canadian border, when the precious quartz was discovered on little American Island (*see Arrowhead Tour 3*). After a brief period of intensive mining in 1894, the Bevier Mining and Milling Company, organized to operate the claim, abandoned the venture, and the mines remained undisturbed for 42 years. In 1936, gold mining was resumed temporarily on the islands.

SAW LOG IS KING

In their search for gold and copper, the treasure-seekers of 1854-55 overlooked the wealth before their eyes—the towering pine that covered the hinterland. As the dreams of underground wealth did not materialize, most of the disillusioned left the region. Those who remained, not being able to get away, began to cut the pine, and it was thus that the lumber industry was started in the Minnesota Arrowhead.

The first sawmill in the region was built in Oneota (1855) at the site of the present Duluth, Missabe and Iron Range ore docks. Many others followed in quick succession, among them one at Burlington Bay, opened in 1857-58 by Captain J. J. Hibbard, and another at Beaver Bay, in 1859, by the Wieland brothers. In 1870, a railroad had reached Duluth, and a year later the Duluth Ship Canal was opened—two events that gave a heartening impetus to lumbering.

Waves of lumbermen now began to surge in. The lumber industry of Minnesota, which was to become by the turn of the century the leading producer in the Union, first attracted New Yorkers and New Englanders, particularly "Maine-ites," as those from Maine were called. They were augmented by French and Scotch from eastern Canada and by some Irish and Germans. Later came thousands upon thousands of Scandinavians, Finns, Slavs, and other Europeans, many of them known for their skill as woodsmen. In the first decade of the twentieth century, the industry reached its peak in the Arrowhead region.

The lumberjacks were colorful figures in the pageant of America's making. They were a homogeneous group, bound together by the type of work they followed. Canny, dexterous, and skilled in their work, they were hard-living, hard-fighting fellows, with amazing disregard of danger and a seeming vanity for whiskers. All had seen occasions when a slight slip on the drives plunged men into icy waters or to a mangling death beneath the onrushing log boom. On the tote-road the snapping of a weak link in the log-sled chain might release a load of logs, endangering the lives of drivers and horses.

Very few of these men who went into the timber saved their money or bought land. Many were "rolled" for their wages when in town on periodic drunks. They reigned supreme in the area as long as lumbering was the chief livelihood. Their prowess in log-rolling, jam-breaking, and raft-piloting was the wonder of the settlers, and today their feats are commemorated annually in Arrowhead community celebrations (*see Brainerd; Bemidji*).

In Duluth, the center of the lumber industry was for many years on Rice's Point and St. Louis Bay, and between 1875 and 1880 a sawmill operated in what now is Lincoln Park, for cutting the timber along the hills of the West End. Duluth mills reached their highest mark of production in 1902, when more than 435,000,000 feet were cut. After that there was a steady decline, until by 1915 the total output did not exceed 80,000,000 feet.

The Virginia and Rainy Lake Lumber Company was formed when a group of operators pooled their interests; and in its first 20 years it produced more than 2,000,000,000 feet. Its single mill developed quickly into what was claimed to be "the largest white pine lumber mill in the world," turning out 225,000,000 feet during its peak year. From 1910 to 1925, the company employed annually between 1,700 and 2,500 men and used 900 horses and 13 locomotives.

Great changes have taken place in lumbering since the days when it was in its "hand-tool period," especially with regard to transportation. In early days, timber was cut only along the banks of streams and lakes, water serving as the means of transportation. Even from the mills, finished products were sent to market by water.

River drives and rafting, however, were discarded, to a great extent, when railroads were built in the region. Sleighs, drawn by oxen or horses, were then used to bring logs to the railroads, whence they were taken to the mills.

But even this mode of transportation gradually gave way to the motor truck, which, eliminating the necessity of reloading, has in the last two decades become an important factor in Arrowhead lumbering activities.

THE IRON ORE RANGES

In the first quarter of the nineteenth century, Dr. John McLaughlin, a trader on Lake Vermilion who became famous in the Oregon country, wrote in a short sketch of the area: "The only mineral I have seen in the Country is Iron which though very common I never saw in any large quantity." Iron was not in demand. It was copper and gold that drew prospectors to the region. The search for gold, though fruitless, led to the discovery of iron ore on the Vermilion Range.

In 1864, the State legislature authorized Governor Swift to appoint a competent person to make a geological survey of the region north of Lake Superior in search of metals. Dr. Augustus Hanchett was appointed and turned the field work over to Thomas Clark, a civil engineer and one of the first settlers at the head of the lakes. In their reports, they stated that beds of copper, iron, and slate had been observed in their examination of a portion of the north shore. The meager appropriation limited the extent of the survey.

In 1865, Governor Miller appointed State Geologist H. H. Eames to continue the survey for minerals on the north shore of Lake Superior. Eames, with his brother Richard, penetrated to Vermilion Lake, where he found iron ore exposed from 50 to 60 feet in thickness in two parallel ridges near the mouth of a stream known as Two Rivers. From that time, the locality was called Vermilion Range.

In those days, rumors of the presence of gold on Vermilion Lake overshadowed all other events, and Eames was one of many who was struck with gold fever. This fact probably delayed iron ore mining for nearly 20 years.

The following description by a contemporary sheds new light on the Eames expedition, new because it is not incorporated in official records. Henry P. Wieland wrote two letters, in February, 1932, to the St. Louis County Historical Society, where they are on file. The substance of these letters is as follows:

> In the summer of 1865, Dr. Eames (probably H. H. Eames) and two other men came to Beaver Bay, on the north shore of Lake Superior. Eames asked for Christian Wieland, uncle of Henry and well-known civil engineer, and a long conference ensued. Two days later they started on an expedition to Lake Vermilion, led by Christian Wieland.
>
> At a point near the present site of Babbitt, St. Louis County, Christian Wieland called attention to indications of iron, but Eames' mind was set on gold. "To hell with iron, it's gold we're after," he said.
>
> After their arrival at Vermilion, Wieland was soon convinced that the gold excitement was a false alarm. He therefore left Eames at Lake Vermilion and returned to Beaver Bay with samples of the iron ore that he had discovered on the eastern end of the Mesabi Range. Later in the same year, Wieland succeeded in interesting an Ontonagon (Michigan) capitalist in his discovery, and they decided to build a road from Beaver Bay to Babbitt. In preparation for this work, Christian Wieland and his brothers Henry and Ernest hauled a considerable quantity of supplies out to Greenwood Lake, Lake County, during the winter of 1865-66. Soon after this was done, the financier died, and the plans had to be abandoned.
>
> Henry P. Wieland, then a boy of thirteen, was sent to Greenwood Lake the following winter to dispose of the supplies, by trading them to the Indians for furs. This incident later gave rise to a story about a trading post at Greenwood Lake.

Another man, George R. Stuntz, started an expedition of his own, in 1865, to prospect for gold at Lake Vermilion. He was spoken of by contemporaries as the "pioneer of pioneers" at the head of the lakes, and was well acquainted with the topography of the region. He searched for gold and, incidentally, discovered the location of the first bed of iron ore to be worked in Minnesota, the Breitung Mine, near the present city of Tower. From this mine the first shipment of iron ore was made by rail in the summer of 1884.

In the early 1870's, Peter Mitchell, from the Ontonagon Syndicate of Michigan, began explorations of the ore body discovered in 1865 by Christian Wieland on the eastern Mesabi. Samples of the ore were taken by Stuntz to George C. Stone, who forwarded them to Charlemagne Tower of Philadelphia. Tower was so thoroughly convinced of the region's wealth that he sent two exploring parties in 1875 and 1880, under Professor Albert H. Chester, and began buying up land around Lake Vermilion.

The reports of Chester led directly to the opening of the district. The Minnesota Iron Mining Company was organized in 1882. Among its officers were Tower and Stone. The company took over the charter of the Duluth and Iron Range Railroad, which, although organized in 1874, had not advanced beyond incorporation. Tracks were laid between Agate Bay on Lake Superior and the Soudan Mine (originally called the Breitung Mine). When the first ore train was loaded in 1884, every man present threw a lump into the leading car for good luck. The reign of Arrowhead iron had begun.

The Vermilion Range was the initial step in the area's great iron industry, but the Mesabi, to the southwest, was to furnish the rungs to the top of the ladder. Location of the first iron ore on the Mesabi Range was made on the eastern end (near Babbitt, a few miles south of Birch Lake), but it was not considered of sufficiently high grade to warrant mining.

Leonidas Merritt, however, and some of his relatives, all timber cruisers, thought otherwise. In 1890, he took out 141 leases, and test pits definitely established the fact that here was a second iron range. Mining operations on the Mesabi began in 1891. The first ore was shipped in 1892, and five years later 20 mines were producing nearly 3,000,000 tons.

Unlike the Vermilion Range, where shafts have to be sunk, the Mesabi Range is mined primarily by the open-pit method. The ore bodies are near the surface on the Mesabi, and the overburden (mostly glacial drift) can therefore be easily removed by steam and electric shovels (*see Buhl*). The largest of the latter load a 50-ton ore car with about three scoops.

The Mesabi ores are, generally speaking, softer and more friable than those dug on the Vermilion. Because of this characteristic of the deposit and of its easy accessibility, there is a tremendous output on the Mesabi, which in turn brings down the costs of production. The Mesabi ores, because their friability acts as a clog, necessitated a remodeling of blast furnaces. But after the initial difficulties were overcome, the output, to keep abreast of the rapid strides being made in the industrial world, increased at a rate unsurpassed theretofore in iron-ore mining. The ores mined on the Mesabi have formed the broad base of the American steel industry for several decades.

The discovery of Minnesota's third iron range, the Cuyuna (about 100 miles west of Duluth), was made in 1904 by Cuyler Adams, a prospector. Aware of the strong magnetic attraction in the area, he chose a likely spot, set drills in motion, and discovered ore. The Cuyuna was worked first in 1911 at the Kennedy Mine (now exhausted). Both open-pit and underground methods are used. This range differs from the others in that its ore carries varying amounts of manganese, a metal comparatively scarce in the United States.

During the World War, approximately 90 per cent of the country's supply of manganese came from the Cuyuna Range.

In the early days of iron mining in the Arrowhead, it was held that ores must contain from 60 to 65 per cent iron, a standard later lowered to 51.50. As exhaustion of the richest ore threatened, it became necessary to improve (concentrate) those of lower grade. This is accomplished by washing, drying, crushing and screening, fusion, and magnetism. In mining parlance, these processes of improvement are termed "beneficiation." In recent years, as high as 40 per cent of the total output has been beneficiated. At first ore was identified by the name of the mine that produced it, but before long, to simplify shipping, it became known by the grade of its composition, which often was obtained by mixing ores. Today, in the ore's course from mine to furnace, samples are analyzed repeatedly, not only for iron, but also for phosphorus, silica, manganese, and the percentage of moisture.

Railroads were built to transport the ore from the mines to the ports of Duluth-Superior and Two Harbors. The steadily increasing output of the mines necessitated improved loading facilities for lake shipments to eastern furnaces. In order to transfer the millions of tons from the trains to the ships, docks of new design were required. These, so characteristic a feature of Duluth and Two Harbors, are specially constructed piers equipped with pockets, into which the hopper-bottomed cars drop the ore. From these pockets, with capacities of 300 to 400 tons, an average of 10,000 tons can be dumped into a vessel's hold in six hours.

The story of the struggle for possession of the mines is crowded with drama. The panic of 1893 brought disaster to many, forcing them to sell for almost nothing holdings they knew were worth millions. The owner of the Fayal Mine at Eveleth (now inactive) sold out for $30,000, well aware he was sacrificing a fortune, and, as it proved, the mine later yielded $10,000,000. Another, hard-pressed, deeded his tract to a relative to protect it from creditors and could get it back only by giving the relative a tenth interest, for which the latter eventually received about $500,000. When the banks demanded more collateral from one Duluthian, he could offer only a second mortgage on his barn; yet ten years later his income from minimum royalty was $1,000 a day. Many valuable and interesting accounts of the search for iron ore, with its hardships and disappointments, its speculations and litigations, have been preserved in the annals of history. Paul de Kruif's *Seven Iron Men* presents the generally accepted account of the Merritt-Rockefeller controversy.

The taxing of mining properties long has been a controversial issue between the State and the mining companies. Valuations are set by the State Tax Commission. As the towns grew, they exercised their right of local taxation. In some of the communities, the mining companies pay more than 95 per cent of all taxes levied. The volume of mining-tax moneys has made possible civic improvements that would do credit to much larger and older cities in the nation. In fact, the most elaborate public schools in the country are to be found in this area. Hibbing, for example, expended $3,800,000 for its high school and junior college.

Few mines are operated by the fee owners (property owners), because of the great outlay of capital required. The properties usually are leased to operating companies. They pay the fee owners a royalty on each ton produced and shipped and are responsible for all taxes. The State of Minnesota is the greatest fee owner. At the time of its establishment, it was given two sections of land in each township for school purposes, all ungranted swamp land, and scattered tracts for the State university. In 1935, there were 58 mines on State properties, among them the Missabe Mountain, the Leonidas, the Hill Annex, and the Mesabi Chief. The royalties from these are placed in their respective trust funds—school, swamp, university.

The question of how long the Arrowhead's iron-ore deposits will hold out is often propounded. A rough estimate in 1911 placed the reserve at 173,000,000,000 tons. The mining companies have not as yet felt the threat of scarcity. Indications are that higher-grade ores should last well into the final quarter of the century, while low-grade and mixed ores may last for many centuries. The United States Bureau of Mines and the University of Minnesota are now experimenting successfully with utilization of the lower-grade ores.

Of Minnesota's wealth, about $100,000,000 a year comes from the Arrowhead's three iron ranges, which produce annually some 40,000,000 tons of ore. More than 25 iron range communities owe their existence to the mines. Thousands are employed in the mining and transporting of the ore, while it is estimated that 100,000 persons rely on the industry for their livelihood.

FROM CANOE TO AIRPLANE

For centuries, the only highways in the area were the maze of foot trails and water courses traversed by moccasined feet and birchbark canoes. The trails and portages are still to be found in the fastnesses of the Superior National Forest.

At the head of the world's greatest inland waterway, the Arrowhead's first advance in transportation was, as a matter of course, made on water. Small sailing vessels were adequate for a time. With the development of the Arrowhead and the rapidly expanding markets for lumber, iron ore, and dairy products, and also for western wheat, the need for larger and better ships was constantly growing, until today carriers on the Great Lakes are as fine as any on the high seas. The importance of Lake Superior shipping to the nation's economic life can best be indicated by figures which show, for instance, that in 1938, one of the lake's poorest shipping seasons, 40,042,739 tons passed the locks at Sault Ste. Marie, while, by comparison, 34,418,000 tons passed through the Suez Canal, and 26,227,268 tons through the Panama Canal. For both the Suez and the Panama canals, 1938 was one of the best years.

"The two canals [at Sault Ste. Marie, connecting Lake Huron with Lake Superior], with their five great locks (four on the American side, one on the Canadian), are the greatest ship highway in the world. An average of 100 ships a day pass through during the navigation season of eight months, and the total traffic in 1925 amounted to 81,875,108 tons, valued at $1,117,817,292. The Davis and the Sabin locks (1,350 feet long and 80 feet wide) are the longest in the world."

While water transportation was developing, other modes of transportation also were improved and increased. The first overland route to connect the Arrowhead with the outside world was the Military Road, cut from St. Paul to Superior in the 1850's. The Vermilion Trail was blazed through the wilderness between Duluth and Tower in 1865 to accommodate the gold seekers. Finally came the highways of today, providing easy access to the beautiful rivers, lakes, and forests of the Arrowhead region.

The first railroad ran its tracks into Duluth from St. Paul in 1870. That year also saw (at Carlton) the beginning of the Northern Pacific's construction westward. Steel rails now penetrate almost every part of the Arrowhead. Only one county, Cook, has no railroad service.

The need to transport workers from their homes to the mines was met by a bus system that formed the nucleus of the far-flung Northland Greyhound Lines. Today, most points in the Arrowhead can be reached by bus.

The larger municipalities have excellent airports. Many lakes provide good landings for seaplanes and amphibians. Air service reaches a new height of modern convenience by allowing time-pressed fishermen to be taken to and from the fishing grounds.

AGRICULTURE

As the forests were cleared and the railroads completed, many of the lumbermen and laborers turned to farming. Nature provided good soils in many parts of the region, and, although clearing the land and cultivating the soil was slow and arduous work, eventually it bore fruit.

In 1911, twenty varieties of Arrowhead potatoes won first prize at a show in Madison Square Garden, and a year later St. Louis County's entry took the L. W. Hill Great Northern cup. Itasca County now features the "Arrowhead brand" of baking potatoes, which rival those grown in Idaho. As the remoter sections were settled, other crops became highly successful. The fertile bed of glacial Lake Agassiz proved to be one of the best clover- and alfalfa-producing areas in the country, and the till plains of the south and west produce excellent grain and hay. Today, the largest proportionate farm acreage is found in Carlton, Crow Wing, Aitkin, and Cass counties.

Throughout the area, potatoes, oats, and hay are the major crops. Because feed can be grown so easily, dairying and livestock-raising have come to the fore, in 1930 contributing more than half the total farm income. The number of creameries, both cooperative and independent, has increased. In recent years, small fruits have been grown profitably in the sandy districts. Many poultry farms have been developed, supplying chickens and turkeys to both home and Eastern markets. Aitkin is now known as the "turkey capital," because of the fine quality of turkeys marketed there.

University farm schools at Duluth and Grand Rapids conduct experiments and study local farming problems. The North Central Agricultural School and Experiment Station (Grand Rapids) became a branch agricultural school in 1926. The North East Experiment Station (Duluth) was established in 1913. On the 253-acre farm have been developed new cold-resistant fruits and vegetables, the disease-free Arrowhead rutabaga, and the Arrowhead sunflower. Among the numerous successful varieties tried, the potato seedling, 19-9-c, set a production record.

PRESS AND RADIO

The Arrowhead's first press was a gift and served Indians who could neither read nor write. Described as "complete . . . portable . . . of unique pattern . . . one of several that had been built as compact as possible, and designed for use on shipboard," it had been presented by Oberlin College and Ohio Sunday School students to the Reverend Alonzo Barnes in 1849, when he accepted a post in a Chippewa mission at Cass Lake. He used it as an aid in his Christian endeavor.

As the communities along the north shore of Lake Superior developed, a need for newspapers was felt. The first to be established was *The North Shore Advocate* at Buchanan in 1857-58, but in 1859, when the land office was moved to Portland, the newspaper ceased to advocate. The second, which was the first in Duluth (April, 1869), was the *Duluth Minnesotian,* a weekly, written, edited, printed, and perhaps even delivered by Dr. Thomas Foster. At birth it was only a five-column, four-page sheet, yet it was well-edited and under the doctor's good care, prospered. In 1878, it was merged with the *Duluth Tribune,* whose quarters since founding in 1870 had been so limited that type was set up out-of-doors. That year also saw the appearance of the *Weekly Lake Superior News,* which in 1881 became a daily and in 1892 was consolidated with the *Duluth Tribune,* to form the *Duluth News-Tribune.*

From these beginnings, several newspapers sprang into being, and today there are 69 in the area, 59 of them weeklies. The development of the nine dailies has paralleled that of the region. *The Brainerd Daily Dispatch* appeared in 1881, the year Brainerd was reincorporated as a city. Two years later, it was followed by the *Duluth Herald,* which was consolidated under one ownership with the *Duluth News-Tribune* in 1929. The discovery of iron ore on the Mesabi Range accounted for the appearance of two others: the *Virginia Daily Enterprise* and *The Hibbing Daily Tribune,* founded in 1899. *The Bemidji Daily Pioneer* was established in 1903. Four years later, *The Daily Journal* in International Falls began publication. Two Finnish dailies are also published in Duluth.

On page 22 is a complete list of the 69 newspapers currently published in the Arrowhead region.

The Arrowhead's first radio station, WEBC, affiliated with the National Broadcasting Company, was established in Duluth-Superior in 1924 by the Head of the Lakes Broadcasting Company, which since has opened two other stations, WMFG in Hibbing in 1935, and WHLB in Virginia in 1936. Duluth's second station and the region's fourth, KDAL, which broadcast its first program in 1936, is an affiliate of the Columbia Broadcasting System. In 1939, a third network service was added when the Mutual Broadcasting System's affiliate, WDSM, started to broadcast from studios in Superior and Duluth.

ARROWHEAD NEWSPAPERS: 1941 LIST

Aitkin . . . . Independent Age
Aitkin . . . . Republican
Aurora . . . . Aurora News
Barnum . . . . . . Barnum Herald
Bemidji . . . . Bemidji Daily Pioneer
Bemidji . . . . Bemidji Sentinel
Bemidji . . . . Northland Times
Big Falls . . . . . . Big Fork Compass
Big Fork . . . . . . Itasca Progressive
Biwabik . . . . Biwabik Times
Blackduck . . . . . Blackduck American
Bovey . . . . Bovey Press
Brainerd . . . . Brainerd Daily
            Dispatch
Brainerd . . . . . . Brainerd Journal Press
Brainerd . . . . . . Brainerd Tribune
Brainerd . . . . . . Crow Wing County
            Review
Buhl . . . . Buhl-Kinney Herald
Carlton . . . . Carlton County Vidette
Cass Lake . . . . . Cass Lake Times
Chisholm . . . . . Mesaba Miner
Chisholm . . . . . Tribune Herald
Cloquet . . . . . . Pine Knot
Coleraine . . . . . Coleraine Iron News
Cook . . . . Cook News Herald
Crosby . . . . Crosby Courier
Deer River . . . . Deer River News
Deerwood . . . . . Deerwood Enterprise
Duluth . . . . Duluth Free Press
Duluth . . . . Duluth Herald
Duluth . . . . Duluth News-Tribune
Duluth . . . . Duluth Publicity
Duluth . . . . Industrialisti (Finnish)
Duluth . . . . Labor World
Duluth . . . . Lakeview Times
            Reminder
Duluth . . . . Midwest Labor
Duluth . . . . Päivälehti (Finnish)
Duluth . . . . Skandinav
            (Norwegian-Danish)

Duluth . . . . Steel Plant News
Duluth . . . . Weekly Herald
Duluth . . . . West Duluth Budgeter
Duluth . . . . West End News
Ely . . . . Ely Miner
Eveleth . . . . Eveleth Clarion
Eveleth . . . . Eveleth News
Floodwood . . . . . Rural Forum
Gilbert . . . . Gilbert Herald
Grand Marais . . . Cook County News-
            Herald
Grand Rapids . . . Grand Rapids
            Independent
Grand Rapids . . . Herald-Review
Hackensack . . . . Hackensack
            Independent
Hibbing . . . . Hibbing Daily Tribune
Hibbing . . . . Independent
Hill City . . . . . . Hill City News
International
  Falls . . . . The Daily Journal
International
  Falls . . . . International Falls
            Press
Ironton . . . . Ironton Ranger
Littlefork . . . . . Littlefork Times
Moose Lake . . . . Star-Gazette
Nashwauk . . . . . Eastern Itascan
Northome . . . . . Northome Record
Pequot . . . . Pequot Chronicle
Proctor . . . . Proctor Journal
Tower . . . . Weekly News
Two Harbors . . . Lake County Chronicle
Virginia . . . . Virginia Daily
            Enterprise
Virginia . . . . . . Queen City Sun
Virginia . . . . . . Range Facts
Walker . . . . Cass County Pioneer
Walker . . . . Walker Pilot

FOLKLORE AND FESTIVALS

It is but natural that such a region as the Minnesota Arrowhead, with its Indians as well as its other inhabitants from many different places and countries, should have numerous legends, folk customs, and festivals.

Kitchi Gummi and its hinterland play a vivid role in Indian legends, most of which are woven around the bitter warfare between Chippewa and Sioux. Science has explained the formation of Minnesota Point, but the Chippewa believe the sand bar was created to save a young brave who was trapped by the Sioux on the south shore of Lake Superior. Surrounded on three sides, he had turned to flee, only to find his escape blocked by icy water. There was death before and behind. The Great Spirit urged him into the water, then caused land to form in front of him. As the Sioux started to follow, part of the newly formed land sank, and this channel became the Superior Entry.

Wild-rice harvesting is a time of many Indian ceremonial dances. In early evening, the roll of the tom-tom calls, and Indians carrying packs and bundles make their way toward the building in which the dance is held. Before the hall, serious-faced braves, surrounding a bonfire, are drying and stretching a drumhead. The inside of the hall is a dimly lighted octagon; in the center stands a raised platform for the drummers, whose measured beat accompanies a chorus of voices swelling into a fascinating musical story of war and victory. Out of the darkness at the edge of the room, colorfully dressed girls appear and form a circle. To the rhythm of the tom-tom they dance a halting step, bending the right knee at each inflected beat and shuffling to the left, to continue the circling with a swaying motion. The tempo increases as youths, their suits trimmed with beads, feathers, and fur, and headdresses partially covering their faces, rush into the room, stepping lightly on their toes, and thumping the floor with their heels twice to each beat of the music. Their muscular bodies twist and turn sinuously, sometimes almost touching the floor. The dancers are extremely skillful, and their ceremonial performance is of great interest to visitors.

Although the Paul Bunyan legends relate to the lumber camps of the entire country, some belong exclusively to the Arrowhead. Paul's blue ox, Babe, measuring, when only a tyke, 42 axe handles and a plug of chewing tobacco between the eyes, reached his full size at the time Paul logged northern Minnesota. Once when Paul's camp was the headwaters of the Mississippi, Babe broke into the cache and ate 80 hogsheads of salt pork. This made him so thirsty he went to the river to get a drink. Now Paul's drive had nearly reached the mills at New Orleans, but, when Babe began to drink, the logs started upstream faster than they had been floating down. Not until a log six feet in diameter tickled his nose did the blue ox stop drinking. With a snort that sent the logs southward again, he turned toward camp. All true woodsmen know that Minnesota's ten thousand lakes are Babe's hoofprints.

While the Indians have their legends and the lumberjacks their Paul Bunyan stories, so, too, have the region's diverse racial elements their own quaint customs and their own peculiar celebrations. The French-Canadians have their annual "Mulligan" each fall, and, just previous to the beginning of Lent each year, they hold their well-known Mardi Gras. The Scotch, who have their Clan Stewarts, observe Robert Burns Day, January 25, and St. Andrews Day, November 30.

One of the largest affairs held by any racial group is the Midsummer Festival of the Scandinavians in Duluth every year. As Midsummer Day occurs on June 24—a holiday in northern Europe— the celebration is held on the Sunday nearest that date. The Norwegians celebrate their Independence Day, May 17, known as *Syttende Mai.*

The Finns, among the region's larger racial groups, also celebrate Midsummer Day. Their festivities, however, differ from those of the Scandinavians in that the day is celebrated in a different town or city each year on the week end nearest June 24. They have also their *Laskiainen* festivities—corresponding to the Shrovetide—to which increasing attention has been given in recent years.

The Poles have their Independence Day on May 3, and Pulaski Day is held on October 8.

The Arrowhead's Serbian population, adhering to the Julian calendar in their religious rites, celebrates its Christmas on January 7 and its New Year's Day on January 14. Their Christmas is a very colorful affair.

The Yugo-Slavs—the largest Slavic group in the Arrowhead— have their own organizations, their festivities, and their traditional customs.

The Italians in the region, comprising the greater part of the State's

total number of this nationality, also observe their own celebrations
and customs.

THE ARROWHEAD TODAY

The Minnesota Arrowhead is one of the major melting pots of the
nation. Its fur trading, lumbering, mining, shipping, and railroading
have attracted adventurous, enterprising, and hard-working people
virtually from the four corners of the earth.

Frenchmen and French-Canadians were the first pale faces to
penetrate the Lake Superior region. They were in control of the
country and also masters of its first industry—the fur trade—for more
than a century. With the advent of the British régime, Anglo-
Saxon, Scotch, and Irish immigrants came and gradually gained the
upper hand in the fur trade.

The fur trade was followed by lumbering, but iron-ore mining
eventually became the dominant economic factor in the Arrowhead.
These activities, together with the building of railroads and the development of Lake Superior shipping, attracted thousands upon thousands from Eastern States and from foreign countries.

In the Arrowhead melting pot may be found French-Canadians,
other Canadians, Anglo-Saxons, Scots, Irish, Swedes, Norwegians,
Danes, Finns, Finland-Swedes, Germans, Russians, Poles, Czecho-
Slovaks, Rumanians, Austrians, Yugo-Slavs, Greeks, Italians, Swiss,
and several other nationalities.

Today side by side with the Old World stands the ultramodern
New World. Some of the schools in the region are among the most
elaborate in the country; yet many of the pupils return to homes
in which foreign tongues are still spoken and foreign customs observed. Almost within the shadows of majestic educational institutions, Slovenian hoeing bees are held with no loss of their naïveté.
Recreation is often found in racial clubs.

Assimilation of these many peoples has been effected largely by
the schools, together with cooperating local organizations. The com-
plexity of the undertaking is indicated by the report of an iron range
school that the year's regular enrollment included representation of
30 nationalities. In Duluth alone, during the 1936-37 term 488 nat-
uralization enrollees were of 27 distinct nationalities. The English
courses developed in Americanization work are outstanding in the
State.

Within the region today, there is an Indian population of 4,464, all Chippewa, whose affairs are administered by the Consolidated Chippewa Indian Agency, the third largest unit in the United States Indian Service. In the Arrowhead are five of the seven reservations under the Agency's jurisdiction—Grand Portage, Vermilion, Fond du Lac, Nett Lake, and Cass Lake—two hospitals, at Fond du Lac and Cass Lake, and the Indian section at Ah-Gwah-Ching Sanatorium.

These Chippewa Indians claim they are the most highly assimilated group in the country. There has been no serious trouble between them and what is, perhaps, the most varied group of nationalities to which American Indians have had to adapt themselves. Intermarriage has been considerable, and educational privileges are identical with those enjoyed by whites. Most of the Indians are self-supporting.

Many of the towns founded by the early settlers were laid out in haphazard fashion. Newer ones have been planned more carefully and built with an eye to civic beauty, health, and efficiency. Just outside the mining towns, and grouped about the mines themselves, are the "mine locations," residential sections built by the mining companies for their workers.

In costly public buildings the Arrowhead excels. Probably nowhere else within an equally limited area are there so many elaborate schools as on the Mesabi and Vermilion iron ranges. Taxes paid by the mining companies have given the ranges these schools, and it is not only in outward appearance that they are superlative. They are splendidly equipped in practically every detail, having gymnasiums, swimming pools, auditoriums, recreational rooms, libraries, and study halls.

Because of the isolation of some of the rural sections, school districts have been consolidated and bus systems installed, and one district, Deer River, has even built a dormitory. Smith-Hughes instruction (industrial work) is offered in both rural and urban schools.

RECREATION AND SPORTS

The Minnesota Arrowhead region affords an ideal setting for recreation and sports of almost every description. Its temperate climate and its varied topography have made it one of the major playgrounds of the nation. Each season of the year brings widely differing games and sports activities.

Inland lakes and streams and the cool waters of Lake Superior offer opportunities for such sports as brook trout fishing, deep-sea fishing, swimming, sailing, yachting, and canoeing. Other summer sports gaining favor are golf, tennis, cycling, archery, baseball, diamondball, and horseback riding.

In the autumn, football, hiking along scenic trails, and hunting —which draws nimrods from large sections of the country—are great favorites in the region.

Winters of crispy coldness and abundant snowfall make the Arrowhead country unexcelled for such sports as snowshoeing, dog-team sledding, sleigh riding, sliding, and tobogganing. Skiing, for which the hills of the region are ideal, skijoring and curling—one of the major sports in Duluth—reflect the spirit of peoples from European countries. Ice boating is increasing in popularity, especially in Duluth where Superior and St. Louis Bays and the St. Louis River are sheltered. Another highly favored winter pastime is hockey. Bowling also shares the spotlight with basketball in winter sports.

A winter-sports center recently developed at Fond du Lac bids fair to challenge, both in magnitude of activities and in scenic beauty, the fame of such well-known places as Lake Placid and Sun Valley.

Swimming is fostered by the schools, some of which are equipped with excellent tanks. Anne Govednik, the Olympic swimming star, was coached at Chisholm. As for skating, Lois Dworshak and Anne Haroldson, nationally known stars in that sport, received their training in Duluth. Bobby and Ruby Maxon and several other young skaters who also had their early training in Duluth are attracting the eyes of the nation.

Completely equipped recreational buildings that serve as community centers are more common than uncommon in the area, and most districts have recreational boards that supervise year-round programs.

SOCIAL WORK

Social service in the Arrowhead, where there is only one large industrial center, numerous small cities and villages, and an overbalancing rural area, has presented many problems, but the last few years have seen seven-league strides made through the consolidation of public agencies and their close cooperation with private endeavors. Most of the municipalities maintain school doctors and nurses, and rural schools are visited regularly. All but the most isolated sections have easy access to hospitals, and, whereas formerly only the employees of large industrial units enjoyed hospitalization, now this health service is available to the general public.

The Duluth Lighthouse for the Blind, located in the Moore Memorial Building, 312 West Superior Street, is the only organization of its kind in the Arrowhead. It aids the blind in the teaching of handicrafts and sale of products. The Lighthouse welcomes visitors who may, if they wish, make purchases of a variety of handmade products.

A welcome arrival in the homes of many cripples is the visiting teacher of the Homecrafters Project, developed by the Minnesota Association for Crippled Children and Disabled Adults and at present sponsored by the State department of education. This service provides educational, recreational, and sheltered-employment facilities for the permanently disabled homebound adults. The project operates only in Minnesota.

ARTS AND LETTERS

The Arrowhead has contributed much to the field of fine arts. Among those who have attained national recognition are: Margaret Culkin Banning and Florence Jaques, authors; Rose Tentoni and Estelle Lenci, opera stars; Paul Le May and Luigi Lombardi, conductors; Ernest Lachmund, composer; Francis Lee Jaques, bird illustrator; David Ericson, Knute Heldner, and Birney Quick, painters, and Sidney Buchman, scenario writer. Many have gained prominence in radio, stage, and screen work, including Warren William, Richard Arlen, Judy Garland, Elinor Harriot, Merna Pace, Dorothy Arnold, and Rod La Roque.

Great Unsalted Sea

LAKE SUPERIOR is truly magnificent. It is the largest body of fresh water in the world, being 383 miles long, 160 miles wide, and reaching a depth of 1,290 feet. Its area is 32,000 square miles, its maximum tide 3 inches. The Chippewa knew it as Kitchi Gummi (*great water*), and poets have immortalized it in verse and song. Its waters vary in temperature only a few degrees throughout the year; thus it has a decided effect on climate, shortening the spring, cooling the summer, tempering and prolonging the fall, and moderating the winter. The western end freezes for 20 or more miles from shore, and ice was recorded as 38 inches thick in the winter of 1904-05.

The lake attracts thousands of tourists each year to motor along its scenic north shore, to fish for trout in its cold plunging streams, and to view the interesting and exciting business of commercial fishing. In tranquillity, Lake Superior is impressive, in the fury of a storm it is awe-inspiring.

Artifacts found along lakeshores and rivers attest that, long before white men knew of the existence of the Great Lakes, Indians from as far away as Saskatchewan and the Rocky Mountains made trips to Lake Superior. The first authentic accounts of the lake reached the civilized world through Samuel de Champlain, who in the early seventeenth century was stationed at Quebec as New France's governor and lieutenant general.

Fired by the dream of a Northwest Passage to the Pacific, he attempted to explore the region several times. In 1623 or 1624, he sent out Stephen Brule (Etienne Brûlé), who, it is said, traversed the whole length of the great inland sea. From the information Brule brought back, and items gleaned from the Huron Indians, Champlain in 1632 drafted a crude map of the region. Father Charles Raymbault and Father Isaac Jogues attempted to repeat Brule's voyage in

29

1641 but got only as far as the Sault. Then, for nearly 20 years, French and Indian fighting stopped all Northwest exploration.

After Radisson had demonstrated the fortunes to be had from furs, fur trading became even more alluring than exploring. Until the end of the Indian War in 1763, expeditions were made to the Upper Lakes by young Frenchmen. Many of them became past masters in the art of persuading the Indians, through gifts and cajolery, to loot the forests of pelts.

Du Lhut established trading posts along the north shore of Lake Superior, from 1679 to 1683. Pushing westward, Noyon paddled the border lakes in 1687-88, it is claimed. Zacherie Robutel, Sieur de la Noue, completed the buildings and stockade at the mouth of the Kaministiquia River in 1717, and was in command of the fort until 1721. After Vérendrye established a chain of forts along the inland waterways between 1731 and 1742, quantities of furs were shipped annually to Grand Portage. They were transported by canoe or sailboat to Montreal and other Eastern ports for shipment to European markets.

In 1762, a party of English traders with a military escort arrived at Grand Portage—the first voyage on the lake under a British flag. It was not until three years later that English trade on the lake began in earnest. In 1765, Alexander Henry started trading operations at Chequamegon Bay on the south shore of Lake Superior, and soon British traders were operating at many points on the lake.

Among the last of the outstanding French explorer-traders was Jean Baptiste Perrault, who in 1793 built Fort St. Louis, the Northwest Company's first trading post at the head of the lakes. His map indicates the presence of two other posts, on Connor's Point and Rice's Point, both on the Duluth-Superior Harbor.

GRAND PORTAGE

Although no more than a primeval wilderness, the Arrowhead boasted a port before the Declaration of Independence was signed at Philadelphia. This port, Grand Portage, was the metropolis of the fur country, and it enjoyed flourishing trade, shops, French fashions, drinking places, and even law enforcement. The story of the settlement and the trail that runs nine miles from Lake Superior to the upper Pigeon River is one of the most spectacular and colorful in all frontier history (*see Arrowhead Tour 1*).

By 1792, the Northwest Company maintained its central depot here, where each July accounts were settled with its wilderness employees. The traders arrived from Montreal and Quebec in flotillas of lake canoes bringing the next year's supplies and goods for barter, and the fur-laden river canoes of *voyageurs* filtered in from the wilds. In 1798, the post consisted of sixteen log buildings surrounded by a high stockade, with lodging for officers and clerks, a huge mess hall, and room for storage. Beyond the enclosure were the camps of the *voyageurs*, tepees of the Indians, and a canoe yard that accommodated 150 canoes.

The *voyageurs*, mostly French-Canadians from the region of the St. Lawrence, were dramatic figures. All excelled as boatmen, performing the amazing feat of crossing and recrossing from Lake Superior's Grand Portage to the Pacific's Columbia River, their trips timed with surprising precision.

Usually, the lake canoe carried a cargo of more than five tons and was manned by fourteen *voyageurs*, while those on the interior lakes and rivers carried one to two tons and could be handled by two men.

FROM SAIL TO STEAM

To bring schooners, sloops, and brigs to the greatest of the lakes, the fur traders, long accustomed to portaging canoes around barriers, dismantled the larger craft before the falls of the St. Mary's River at Sault Ste. Marie and reassembled them on Lake Superior. The first sailing vessel built on Lake Superior was the *Ottawa,* launched in 1731 by a French officer, Louis Denis de la Ronde, at a shipyard near the Sault.

For more than a hundred years, sailing vessels were built and portaged. Then, in 1845, came the first steamboat, the *Independence,* a propeller craft of 280 tons, whose maximum speed in good weather was four miles an hour. In 1846, another steamboat, the *Julia Palmer,* also of 280 tons, appeared. In that year sails listed in the census of Lake Superior were ". . . three of 70 tons, *Algonquin, Swallow, Merchant;* four of 40 tons, *Uncle Tom, Chippewa, Fur Trader, Siskowit;* one of 50 tons, *Whitefish.*" Among the early steamer passengers were the elder Merritts and their seven sons, also their cow Betsy, coming from Ohio. Arriving at the head of the lakes, they established a home at Oneota, near the harbor.

More boats of both sail and steam came into demand with the

beginning and development of mining activity on the south shore of Lake Superior. It was not until the ship canal at the Sault was completed in 1855 that larger vessels were able to make their way up from the other lakes.

With the development of iron-ore mining on the Arrowhead ranges came the problem of its shipment to Eastern furnaces. The shortness of the Lake Superior shipping season (usually April 15 to December 1) demanded larger bottoms and more speed. Ore docks were improved to such an extent that soon a new type of lake carrier was required, one with greater carrying capacity and ease of loading and unloading.

The need was filled in 1889 when Captain Alexander McDougall of Duluth introduced his lake freighter—a radical departure in shipbuilding, as its engine was in the stern instead of in the middle. His first freighters were called whalebacks, or "pigs," as they were dubbed by salt-water sailors. Resembling huge cigars, their distinguishing feature was the steel deck rounded at the sides over cylinder-shaped holds. Within five or six years, 45 whalebacks of varying sizes were built at Duluth. Some were tried for a brief period along the Atlantic Coast. Their seaworthiness was demonstrated by the *Charles W. Wetmore,* which carried a cargo of corn from New York to Calcutta, India, and returned by way of Cape of Good Hope.

Only one was a passenger steamer. This vessel, the *Christopher Columbus,* 362 feet long and the largest of its type, was one of the sights at the World's Fair in 1893 in Chicago. It was used for short trips between the city and the Fair Grounds, since its construction permitted disembarkation of 5,000 passengers in five minutes.

Structural changes in the ore docks sounded the death knell of whalebacks on the Great Lakes, and no more were built. Modern lake freighters, 600 x 58 x 70 feet (called 600-footers), carry from 15,000 to 16,000 tons of cargo and draw only 18 to 20 feet. The largest iron-ore carrier in the world is the *Harry Coulby,* built in Ohio at a cost of $1,250,000. On one trip, in 1929, it carried 16,371 tons.

At several points along the north shore of Lake Superior, navigation is difficult and hazardous because of magnetic deflection of the compass. When visibility is poor, captains estimate their distance from land by the time required for the echo of the ship's whistle to return. Shore depths still are uncertain, although soundings become more reliable as the charting of the lake bottom progresses.

Human imagination is taxed, in these days of modern transportation facilities, to understand how the early navigators dared, with their crude and primitive craft, to sail a body of water as large and, at times, as treacherous as Lake Superior. Today, navigation makes use of such modern devices as the radio beam and improved meteorological instruments. These, combined with more rigid safety rules, make a lake trip comparatively safe, as well as a most interesting and enjoyable experience.

DULUTH-SUPERIOR HARBOR

Of natural harbors, the best on the Great Lakes and one of the best in the world is the Duluth-Superior. It has dominated the growth and development of the head of the lakes from the time the first native sought shelter within it. Although open but eight months of the year, it is second in tonnage only to New York Harbor.

The Duluth-Superior Harbor has an area of 19 square miles, frontage of 49 miles, 17 miles of dredged channels, and 99 docks. The total capacity of its 25 grain elevators is 46,925,000 bushels. The coal docks, with a capacity of 13,013,000 tons, are among the largest in the world.

Average yearly commerce is more than 48,000,000 net tons, and in 1929 it exceeded 60,000,000. In 1937, vessels arriving and departing numbered 10,271, many of which were from distant ports. The Minnesota tonnage tax is the lowest in the country, and Duluth demands no enrollment fee.

After the last glacier had melted, the counteraction of the St. Louis River and Lake Superior caused a nine-mile long deposition of sand and gravel between the north and south shores of the lake. This finger of land, Minnesota Point, whose width is about that of two city blocks, forms the Duluth-Superior Harbor's natural breakwater. There are two entries: one natural, the Superior Ship Canal, cut by the St. Louis River; the other, man-made, the Duluth Ship Canal.

With the opening in 1855 of the Sault Ste. Marie Canal—now the greatest sea-highway in the world—connecting Lake Huron and Lake Superior, interlake shipping was made possible. The first Government improvement was the building of a lighthouse at the Superior Entry in 1857. It proved a useless construction, as, shortly after its completion, the entry shifted nearly half a mile south. Development was begun on the new Superior Entry, but, before the work was completed in 1875, Duluth had dug its own canal and was in the midst of its classic row with the State of Wisconsin. Superior, although it had the only harbor facilities in the 1850's, watched with envy the rapid growth of the Minnesota settlement across the bay.

Both cities built their hopes on the harbor, but to derive full benefit from it, they realized that they must have railroads to the interior. By 1857, Duluth had secured charters for a railroad and a ship canal, but the Panic and the Civil War delayed all enterprise for ten years. At last, during 1868, construction of the Lake Superior and Mississippi Railroad was begun at St. Paul.

With the coming of the railroad, agitation increased in Duluth for a harbor of its own. The citizens decided to cut a canal through Minnesota Point. Dredging was begun in the fall of 1870 and almost completed by the following spring. Then Superior, convinced that such a canal would damage its natural entrance, prevailed upon the United States Circuit Court to issue an injunction restraining further operations.

On a Saturday afternoon in 1871, Sidney Luce, a prominent Duluthian, received word that this order would be served the following Monday. Early Sunday morning, fifty grimly resolute men went to work with pick, shovel, and wheelbarrow. By noon a narrow stream began to trickle through from the bay, whose waters, six inches higher than the lake, then rapidly widened the channel. By midafternoon, a rowboat passed through, and the following morning Captain Sherwood's tug *Fero* steamed from bay to lake, its tied-down whistle tooting defiance. Ten days later the injunction was dissolved, but only on condition that Duluth build a dike from Rice's Point to Minnesota Point (across the bay) to prevent currents being turned from the Superior Entry. This dike later had to be removed, and today only a few pilings remain.

In 1893, after much jealous antagonism and litigation, Duluth and Superior agreed to bury the hatchet and develop their joint interests. Three years later, Congress designated the landlocked waters of the two cities as one, the Duluth-Superior Harbor, appropriating $3,000,000 for its development. New and longer piers were constructed, channels were improved, the Duluth Ship Canal was widened, and new lighthouses were built.

The Duluth Ship Canal now has two 1,734-foot piers, 300 feet apart, and is spanned by a lift-bridge erected by Duluth in 1930; the Superior Ship Canal has one 1,584-foot pier and one 2,096-foot, 500 feet apart, and two converging breakwaters. Both are equipped with lighthouses, fog signals, and radio beacons. Their piers are electrically lighted

promenades. Jurisdiction is vested in the War Department, with the
Corps of Engineers in charge. Customs, steamboat, and immigration
inspection, and patrol and coast guard services are maintained. The
United States Weather Bureau issues reports daily, and a Navy
Department hydrographic office issues ice bulletins and other aids to
navigation.

COMMERCIAL FISHING

The waters of the Minnesota Arrowhead have been, from the
earliest days, one of the dependable sources of food. Fish has always
been plentiful in the rivers and lakes, particularly in Lake Superior.
For the Indians and early settlers, fishing was a necessity, a matter
of subsistence. The fish had, strictly speaking, no commercial value in
the days when the region was but sparsely settled and fish could be
had by everybody with little effort. There was, furthermore, no outside demand, owing to the lack of transportation facilities. Most of
the early settlers in this region would have faced starvation many
times, had it not been for the abundance of fish in the "pond" at their
doorsteps. When food supplies were low, they lived on fish—fish
three times a day for weeks on end. It is small wonder that in other
parts of the country they were spoken of as the "fish eaters" at the
head of the lakes.

It was in 1836 that the American Fur Company decided to market
Lake Superior whitefish on a commercial scale. A fishing station
was established at Grand Portage, where only a few warehouses remained from fur-trading days, and soon this was followed by others
at Isle Encampment and Isle Royale, and later at La Pointe and
Fond du Lac. From 300 to 500 barrels, mostly whitefish and trout,
were shipped annually from Grand Portage alone, and in 1839 the
company owned at least three large fishing schooners.

With the collapse of the American Fur Company, the industry
as big business came to an end, not to be revived for many years.
Nevertheless, individuals here and there continued the trade, and during the panics of 1857 and 1873 fishing was all that kept many settlers
alive, for Lake Superior fish were legal tender in almost any market.

Today, commercial fishing along the north shore of Lake Superior
is a profitable industry. More than four-fifths of the yearly catch of
almost 8,500,000 pounds are herring, with trout, whitefish, ciscoes,
and suckers making up the balance. Most are caught with gill nets

at night, though for lake trout setlines sometimes are stretched between two anchor buoys, from which 50 to 60 supplementary lines are
suspended, baited with small fish called shiners. There is no closed
season for lake trout, and fishermen may ply their trade even in the
spawning season, on the condition that they bring the spawn to the
French River Hatchery (*see Arrowhead Tour 1*). The fishermen's
homes—some of the older ones log structures—hug the shore along
bays and inlets.

PART II

National Forests

Chippewa National Forest

WHILE THE point of the Minnesota Arrowhead region—between Lake Superior and the chain of border lakes—embraces the Superior National Forest, the broad western base of the Arrowhead includes another Federal Reserve—the Chippewa National Forest, so named for the Chippewa Indians, one of the main tribes of Algonquian stock.

Under an act of Congress, the forest was established by President Theodore Roosevelt on June 27, 1902, as a Federal Reserve. On May 23, 1908, the Minnesota National Forest was proclaimed, and on June 22, 1928, the present name was adopted. Additions were made, and on December 29, 1936, the entire area of 1,312,824 acres was proclaimed Chippewa National Forest.

The region, in geological times, was invaded by ice lobes from the north and from the northwest, as evidenced by lateral and terminal moraine deposits. The recession of the glaciers also left depressions, many of which are now filled with water, forming the lakes of the forest. The northeastern section drains through the Big Fork River to the Rainy River and thence to Hudson Bay, but the main area of the forest is drained by the Mississippi to the Gulf of Mexico.

The Chippewa National Forest is located in Itasca, Cass, and Beltrami counties. The topography varies from very flat or undulating in some parts to very hilly in others. The average elevation is about 1,300 feet above sea level. The soil varies from flat sand plains to heavy clay and stony soil in the more hilly portions.

Approximately 460 lakes are distributed over the area, some of the larger being Leech Lake, Lake Winnibigoshish, Cass Lake, Bowstring Lake, Sand Lake, Ball Club Lake, Island Lake, Mud Lake, Boy Lake, Turtle Lake, Squaw Lake, Cut Foot Sioux Lake, Big Rice Lake, Round Lake.

Until the middle of the nineteenth century, trapping and fur trading were the only means of making a living in the area. It was not until the 1890's that logging operations were begun in the forest. Gradually the major part of the original growth of timber was removed.

With the advent of the railroad came the first settlers. Farming on a small scale began, and the first village came into being. The region attracted the attention of the Federal Government—resulting in the creation of the Federal Reserve—and early recreationists spread the fame of its scenic beauty.

From an Indian point of view, the area now embraced in the Chippewa National Forest must come very close to their conception of our Garden of Eden—Happy Hunting Grounds—with plenty of fish, plenty of game, and plenty of wild rice. Along the shores of its many lakes, thousands upon thousands can find recreation, and hunters and fishermen will seldom be disappointed.

Star Island, in Cass Lake, is the location of one of the outstanding public camping sites of the forest, namely, Star Island Campground. Three other camping sites on Cass Lake are: Knutson Dam Campground, on the northern part of the east shore; Norway Beach Campground, with its beautiful, mature red-pine stands, on the southern part of the east shore and immediately north of US 2, where it approaches Cass Lake from the east; Ojibway Campground, south of US 2, on a road circling Pike Bay, leading through an area of ten sections of virgin Norway pine, that has been permanently reserved for recreational purposes by the Federal Government.

About five miles (airline distance) due south of Ojibway Campground, on the south shore of a small lake, is Lake Thirteen Campground; seven miles farther south, on the east shore of the northern arm of the westernmost bay of Leech Lake, is Squaw Point Campground; another five miles south, on the east shore of Walker Bay, three miles northeast of Walker, is Walker Bay Campground.

Near Walker, the Forest Service has built a Winter Sports Area, with toboggan slide, ski runs, ski trails, shelter, and parking spaces.

The above-named seven public campsites are located near the western edge of the forest. Near the southeastern corner of the forest, on State 34, eight miles west of Remer, is Mabel Lake Campground; about 18 miles due north of Mabel Lake, near US 2, is Six Mile Lake Campground; six miles due north from there, on a road connecting US 2 and State 46, is Idlewild Campground; nine miles north-

northeast from there, between State 46 and the east shore of Cut Foot Sioux Lake, is Williams Narrows Campground; three miles northwest from there, at the northern tip of Cut Foot Sioux Lake, is Seeley Point Campground; and 15 miles southwest from there, on the south shore of Lake Winnibigoshish, 16 miles east from the village of Cass Lake on US 2, is Richards Townsite Campground. The last five campsites are clustered around Lake Winnibigoshish, in the central part of the forest.

Caribou Lake Campground is near the eastern edge, on State 38, 22 miles north of Grand Rapids. The Forest Service has built a modern forest camp on small Rugby Lake, three miles southeast from Caribou Lake. This new camp—called Organization Camp—was established especially for the purpose of providing camping facilities for such organizations as church groups, Boy and Girl Scouts, 4-H Clubs, and others.

There are about 360 privately owned summer resorts within the area of Chippewa National Forest, 157 tourist homes under permit, and many more on privately owned land.

The District Headquarters of the United States Forest Service are at Cass Lake. Ranger stations are at Bena, Blackduck, Cass Lake, Cut Foot Sioux, Dora Lake, Marcell, Remer, and Walker. For fire detection, 21 permanent lookout stations are distributed in the forest. From the lookout towers, visitors may obtain excellent views of the area.

Federal highways 2 and 371 traverse the forest, and State highways 34, 6, 46, and 38 afford easy access to all parts of the region. In addition, there are 642 miles of Forest Service truck trails winding through the forest, many of which make delightful drives.

The upper Mississippi, born in near-by Itasca State Park, flows through Lake Bemidji and then winds its way from west to east through the central part of the forest, crossing Cass Lake and Lake Winnibigoshish and, incidentally, marking here the line between Cass County and Itasca County.

The Mississippi—from the Algonquian, meaning "Great River"—the chief river of North America, the Father of Waters, the dividing line between East and West, figuratively the spinal cord and literally the backbone of the United States in more than one respect, had been one of the main objects of attraction from the time of the earliest explorers of the New World to the days of Henry R. Schoolcraft, the discoverer of its source in 1832 (see Cass Lake).

"It was first made known by name to Europeans in the Jesuit Relation of 1666-67, published in Paris in 1668, which mentions 'the great river named Messipi.'" Louis Jolliet and Father Marquette arrived in 1673 at the confluence of the Wisconsin River with the Mississippi; they are considered the discoverers of the upper reaches of the great river. Jonathan Carver, in 1766, first described and mapped the river with its present spelling, "which was followed by Pike, Cass and Schoolcraft, Long and Keating, Beltrami, and all the later writers."

The Mississippi enters Chippewa National Forest about one mile west of small Long Lake, crosses its southern tip, and then flows through the northern part of adjoining Cass Lake—so named by Schoolcraft in honor of Governor Cass of Michigan, the head of the great expedition of 1820. A narrow channel—bridged by US 2—connects the main body of Cass Lake with its southern part, Pike Bay, named for Lieutenant Zebulon M. Pike, the commander of an expedition "sent to the upper Mississippi in 1805-06 by the United States War Department."

In the northwestern corner of Cass Lake, not far from the mainland, is Star Island—so called for its shape—an old Indian domain. When Schoolcraft, in 1832, was on the island with his guide, Chief Ozawindib, there was a village—bearing the name of the chief—of 157 persons, and he saw "small fields of corn and potatoes, cultivated by the women."

Eight miles (airline distance) east of Cass Lake, the Mississippi enters a large and shallow body of water, Lake Winnibigoshish, which covers 77 square miles in the heart of the forest. Bena, a tourist center, lies at its southern tip and Seeley Point Campground near its northern shore. The Mississippi flows through the lake from southwest to northeast, and, from the point where it leaves the main body of the lake, it runs in a general southeast direction to the eastern border of the forest, crossing US 2 at the small village of Ball Club.

From Bena it is four miles to the northernmost tip of Leech Lake, where the small settlement of Portage Lake is located. Leech Lake, with its 173 square miles of surface, the third largest body of water within the State, has "a very irregular outline, with numerous bays and projecting points, and it contains several islands."

The Leech Lake region is of unusual historic interest. William Morrison, a widely known fur trader, was stationed here in 1802 in the service of the X Y Company, while his younger brother, Allan, had charge of a fur-trading post at Leech Lake after 1820. Morrison County was named in honor of these two brothers.

Lieutenant Pike, explorer of the upper Mississippi, visited, in February, 1806, a trading post of the Northwest Company, which was "about two miles distant to the northwest from the North Narrows—opposite to Goose Island."

In 1833, the Reverend William Thurston Boutwell established a mission "on or near the isthmus that connects the Peninsula with the mainland of the present Leech Lake Agency," where he remained for four years.

In 1836, the famous geographer and cartographer, Joseph N. Nicollet, had his camping place, for a week, on Otter Tail Point. "On Nicollet's return from Lake Itasca, by way of the Mississippi and Cass Lake, he again camped on Otter Tail Point during the first week of September, visited with Boutwell, and had long interviews with Flat Mouth, the very intelligent, friendly, and respected chief of the Pillager Ojibways." A village of these Chippewa Indians was located on the north end of the Peninsula, at the North Narrows, when Schoolcraft visited there in 1832, and east of this village was a trading house of the American Fur Company.

"Flea Point, called Sugar Point on Schoolcraft's map of Leech Lake," was, in 1898, the site of the last battle between Indians (Chippewa) and white soldiers in Minnesota. In this battle, Major Melvin C. Wilkinson lost his life.

With the advance of white men, the Indians were forced to retreat, and, through a number of "Indian treaties," they were confined to Indian reservations. Much of the Chippewa National Forest was formerly an Indian reservation, but, under the Act of May 23, 1908, the Indians ceded part of their reservation to the Government, including the virgin timber around Cass Lake and Pike Bay. The rest of the timber was sold by the Indians, the cutting being completed in 1923. The cutting policy reserved five per cent of the stand for seed trees during the period from 1902 to 1908, and ten per cent of the stand from 1908 until the logging was completed. Ten sections of virgin Norway pine were permanently reserved. The remaining stands of merchantable timber—about 100,000 acres in 1940—consist largely of jack pine, red pine, white pine, aspen, birch, balsam, and mixed hardwoods.

The land and resources of the forest are managed so as to bring the greatest value to the largest number of people. Constant improvement is being planned and accomplished for the protection of the forest from fire, insects, and disease. Valuable timber is being increased by reforestation at a rate of approximately 5,000 acres annually. Second-growth timber stands are being improved by giving the necessary release to crop trees, by the cutting out of dead and diseased trees, and by pruning. The mature stands are being utilized by selling the timber to local people on a sustained-yield basis, at the rate of approximately 20,000,000 board feet per year. Land-use plans have been prepared to classify all areas of the forest.

Superior National Forest

THE SUPERIOR NATIONAL FOREST, beginning with an initial grant of 36,000 acres in 1909, is one of the great wilderness areas of the United States. Lying entirely within the tip of the Arrowhead, it covers a total of 3,725,849 acres, of which 1,830,977 are Federal; 612,754, State; and 1,282,118, private property.

To the north is a similar Canadian territory, a part of which is known as the Quetico Provincial Park, and together they form a matchless canoe country, where cold waters, teeming with fish, sparkle in lakes and streams often separated by mere strips of land or united by tumbling rapids.

The forest contains more than 5,000 lakes, ranging in size from a few acres to 70 square miles. Great glaciers carved its countless valleys and ridges. Most of the northern portion drains into Hudson Bay through Rainy River and Lake of the Woods; the southern part, including the extreme eastern tip, drains through numerous swift streams into Lake Superior.

A State game refuge of 1,175,040 acres offers a wide variety of game fish, from salmon trout to muskellunge—commonly called "muskies."

For centuries in this great wilderness area, the Indians in birchbark canoes skimmed quiet waters and shot treacherous rapids, hunted and fished, picked berries, harvested wild rice, walked the trails with moccasined feet. To this Arrowhead region came the fur traders, shouldering their heavy burdens as they crossed the portages. Here the Hudson's Bay and Northwest companies fought for trade supremacy. Here the romance of the past is preserved for the enjoyment of all who visit the region.

Camps and picnic grounds in the Superior National Forest are made ready for summer visitors by the National Forestry Department.

Development of these public facilities has been accomplished by the Forest Service during the last few years, in order that visitors to the Arrowhead region may enjoy the full benefits of the national forest. Rustic and simple in design, they provide the necessities of good water and sanitary facilities, safe open fireplaces, tent sites, tables, and rough firewood, in a natural setting where the cares of everyday life may be forgotten.

For the convenience of wilderness travelers, there are also 30 improved canoe campgrounds located along the portage routes. Improvements at these locations have been held to a minimum to preserve the naturalness of the territory and yet provide the necessities for fire prevention and sanitation.

Along the Sawbill Road out of Tofte are the Oxbow and Poplar River campgrounds, both located on good trout streams, and the Sawbill campground at the end of the road and the edge of the Superior canoe country.

Between Finland and Ely are three developments, at Dumbell Lake near Isabella, on the Little Isabella River, and at the South Kawishiwi River southeast of Ely. The South Kawishiwi Camp and Picnic Ground is a major development, including facilities for auto trailers and a large community building and grounds for the accommodation of large picnic parties.

The Federal Government, since assuming control of the Superior National Forest, has instituted an intensive program of conservation through its Forestry Department. The 1940 spring planting program included 4,304,300 trees planted on 3,850 acres. The trees planted consisted of red pine, white pine, jack pine, white spruce, and northern white cedar. In addition, 5,500 acres were prepared during the summer of 1940 for planting in the fall and the spring of 1941, the Knife River Nursery at Two Harbors and the Eveleth Nursery at Eveleth being equipped to furnish 6,000,000 trees for these plantings.

Slash and other hazards have been removed from 40,400 acres; 550 miles of roads have been built; 101 miles of portages have been improved; and 81 miles of trails added. From 25 Federal and 7 State lookout stations, all strategically placed, foresters watch for smoke. Each Civilian Conservation Corps and work camp is a fire-fighting unit.

A seaplane is used for forest fire patrol when visibility is low, and for initial attack on fires in areas not accessible by road. It accommodates three men besides the pilot, and carries hand fire-fighting equipment. Planes are also used for observation of going fires. Under emergency conditions, local commercial planes are also used for patrol or fire observation on other national forests throughout the region.

Fire prevention in this wilderness area has reached a state of efficiency little dreamed of a few years ago. It has become more and more a public responsibility, with the forest's increasing use as a recreational area, for most of the fires are caused by careless campers.

Game and fish specialists and recreational engineers are cooperating in the protection of wild life in the forest. Each year, waters are restocked. Fish are planted in the lakes and streams in cooperation with the United States Bureau of Fisheries and the Minnesota Conservation Department.

During the spring of 1940, 500,000 brook trout were planted in feeder streams and suitable cold-water lakes, and 354,000 lake trout, 30,000 brown trout, and approximately 7,000,000 wall-eyed pike were planted in interior lakes already stocked with these species. The Forest Service is also cooperating with the State Conservation Department at the Tower Hatchery in the transportation of the pike to lakes where they are to be planted.

The Cascade rearing ponds near Grand Marais were stocked with 150,000 brook, rainbow, and brown trout during the first week in June. These fish are held in the ponds until fall, when they average three to six inches in length. They are used to stock lakes and streams within the forest.

In cooperation with the United States Bureau of Fisheries, the Forest Service assisted in tagging 1,000 wall-eyed pike on Everett and Twin Lakes. As the tagged fish are caught by fishermen during the summer, they are reported to local game wardens. In this way, records are kept of the movements and rate of growth of the fish.

By careful and continued restocking of streams and lakes, the Forest Service and the Minnesota Conservation Department maintain good fishing in the waters of the Superior National Forest.

Trout streams have been improved with dams, deflectors, shelters, better banks and bottoms. Houses for wood ducks have been built, and wild rice and duck potatoes have been planted in many lakes. Birch and cedar slashings are fed to deer at their yarding areas. Game censuses are taken, and stream and lake surveys made. The water table created by beaver dams is to be preserved where necessary by man-made structures.

Superior National Forest is constantly gaining in popularity as a vacationland. Increasing emphasis is placed upon its recreational value. Within it is a primitive area, a 1,079,430-acre tract, increased from the 786,284 acres set aside in 1925 to be preserved in its natural beauty. Logging, confined to the interior, is prohibited on lake shores. Portages, rivers, and streams are left in their original state.

Accessible only by canoe, hydroplane, or on foot, its towering forests and interweaving lakes and streams form a sportsman's paradise. Nearly all the forest's lakes are in the primitive section. These are the starting points of well-marked canoe routes with divergent side trips. Like the Indian and fur trader of a bygone day, the modern canoeist paddles through long, narrow lakes in a land of ever-changing beauty. And like the Indian of old, he packs his boat and duffle over the portages. Beaver, muskrat, grouse, porcupine, bear, fox, deer, and moose may be seen, but only occasionally a road, resort, or permanent camp. A two-day jaunt or extended journey, a lazy fishing trip or back-bending voyage of exploration—any or all may be arranged.

There is even a lure attached to the names of the lakes. The charm and originality of the Indian nomenclature has been perpetuated in such lakes as Kekekabic, Kawasachong, Cherokee, Gabimichigami, Maniwaki, and Mukooda. Because there are countless "long" lakes, Ely was wise enough to discard the English for the original "Shagawa." Although historian and romanticist alike deplore the loss of Indian names, it cannot be denied that the ordinary traveler often stammers over those remaining, to the point where he readily would surrender their picturesque and musical qualities for forthright Yankee words.

CANOE TRIPS

(The canoe trips described in the following pages cover but a small segment of the Arrowhead country.)

In a setting of unbelievable beauty and tranquillity, a gigantic network of interlocking rivers and lakes spreads over the Arrowhead region, from Bemidji in the west to Pigeon Point in the east, from International Falls in the north to Mille Lacs in the south—an area of more than 20,000 square miles.

There are no railroads or highways in the wilderness area of the Minnesota Arrowhead—it actually is "nature in the raw." Yet only a few minutes by air takes the visitor to the starting points of canoe routes.

INFORMATION FOR CANOEISTS

Seasons: Lakes usually are ice-free by May 10; freeze-up begins as early as October 10, and most lakes are covered with ice by November 1. May, June, September, and October are the best months for fishing, and July and August for camping.
Climate: Generally cool.
Transportation: Starting points can be reached by motor and hydroplane.
Accommodations: Except for resorts and lodges on privately owned land, there are no accommodations in the "primitive area" other than campgrounds maintained by the Federal Forest Service, which afford tables, benches, fireplaces, and water.
Information Service: Complete information obtainable from Minnesota Arrowhead Association, in Duluth, and from Federal and State Forest Service stations.
Guide service: Experienced guides may be had at the starting points.
Clothing and equipment: Hiking and camping outfit; be sure to take a compass along. (For further particulars contact Minnesota Arrowhead Association, Duluth.)
Caution: Rapids in strange waters should not be run, since they may lead to falls or impassable water; rapid and treacherous currents are so marked in text; note warnings in regard to submerged rocks.
Portages: Portages are trails between bodies of water; portages in Canadian waters usually are marked only by a blaze on a tree, or a Forest Service sign warning campers to put out their fires.
Liftovers: Liftovers are water portages not navigable when water is low.
Distances: In computing distances traveled, the canoeist may estimate the rate of two men's paddling as three miles per hour. (With few exceptions, distances are given in rods; one rod equals 16½ feet; 320 rods a mile.)

CANOE TRIP 1

INTERNATIONAL BOUNDARY ROUTE

McFarland Lake—Mountain Lake—Rose Lake—Gunflint Lake—Saganaga Lake—Cypress Lake—Big Knife Lake—Prairie Portage—Upper Basswood Falls—Table Rock or Skull and Crossbones Campgrounds—Crooked Lake—Iron Lake—Shortiss Island (Lac La Croix)—Coleman Island (Lac La Croix)—Group of Islands (on northwest end of Lac La Croix)—South end of Lac La Croix—Loon Lake—Crane Lake; 17 days.
235 miles of paddling; 9 of portaging.

Excellent fishing of all kinds.
Guides available at Grand Marais, McFarland Lake, Crane Lake.
Most of the portages are marked by signs showing names of lakes and distances.
Currents vary, and are rapid and treacherous at lower end of Basswood River.

Following the international boundary, this route is one of exciting scenery, primitive portages, and numerous rapids, falls, and narrows. The Picture Rocks on Lac La Croix (*see Arrowhead Tours 3; 4*), of unknown origin, painted with dull red ochre, appear five feet above the water's edge and measure from six to eight inches in height. They represent a moose, goat, hands, bear paws, deer, a circle, and a man holding a spear.
Starting point MCFARLAND LAKE (*resort, undeveloped campground*).

First day. North across McFarland Lake (*see Canoe Trip 2*) and paddle into LITTLE JOHN LAKE; N. on Little John into JOHN LAKE;

N. on John and portage 80 rods to EAST PIKE LAKE; N. across East Pike and portage one mile to MOOSE LAKE; W. across Moose and portage 172 rods to LILY PONDS; W. across Lily Ponds and portage 26 rods to MOUNTAIN LAKE (*partially developed campground*).

Second day. West across Mountain and portage 85 rods to WATAP LAKE; W. across Watap and paddle into ROVE LAKE (*to reach Canoe Trip 2, paddle S. via Daniels Lake*); W. on Rove and portage N. W. 560 rods to ROSE LAKE (*partially developed campground; landlocked salmon; to reach Canoe Trip 2, paddle S. via Stairway Portage and Duncan Lake*).

Third day. South on Rose and portage one rod to RAT LAKE; W. on Rat and portage 80 rods to SOUTH LAKE; N. W. on South and portage N. 80 rods to NORTH LAKE (*entry into Canada*); N. and W. on North and portage five rods to LITTLE GUNFLINT LAKE; paddle W. on Little Gunflint into GUNFLINT LAKE (*resort, partially developed campground; landlocked salmon; another starting point at extreme west end, see Arrowhead Tour 1*).

Fourth day. Northwest on Gunflint and paddle into MAGNETIC LAKE; N. on Magnetic and paddle into GRANITE RIVER (*downstream*); portage six rods (*rapids*) from Granite to Granite; N. on Granite and portage 80 rods (*rapids*) to COVE LAKE; N. W. on Cove and portage 240 rods (*rapids*) to Granite River; three short portages (*rapids*) from Granite to GNEISS LAKE; paddle W. and N. on Gneiss into MARABOEUF LAKE; N. across Maraboeuf and portage 12 rods (*rapids*) into Granite River; 2½-rod portage (*rapids*) from Granite to SAGANAGA LAKE (*resort, partially developed campground; landlocked salmon, walleyed pike; another starting point, see Arrowhead Tour 1; Canoe Trip 5; entry into Canada*).

Fifth day. Southwest on Saganaga and portage five rods to SWAMP LAKE; 93-rod portage from southwest end Swamp to CYPRESS LAKE (*partially developed campground*).

Sixth day. Portage three rods from west end Cypress to LITTLE KNIFE LAKE; paddle W. into and to the west end of KNIFE or BIG KNIFE LAKE (*partially developed campground; wall-eyed pike; see Canoe Trip 13*).

Seventh day. Portage 74 rods (*rapids*) from Knife to KNIFE RIVER (*downstream*); four-rod portage (*rapids*) from Knife to SEED LAKE; 24-rod portage (*rapids*) from Seed to Knife River; 12-rod portage (*rapids*) from Knife to CARP LAKE (*entry into Canada*); 44-rod portage (*rapids*) from Carp to BIRCH LAKE (*see Canoe Trip 13*); W. across Birch and into SUCKER LAKE; W., skirting north end Sucker to PRAIRIE PORTAGE (*partially developed campground; falls*).

Eighth day. Portage 33 rods (*falls*) to BASSWOOD LAKE (*land-locked salmon, wall-eyed pike, northern pike; see Canoe Trips 9, 10; entry into Canada*); N. and W. across Basswood to UPPER BASSWOOD FALLS (*partially developed campground*).

Ninth day. Portage 275 rods (*falls*) to BASSWOOD RIVER (*downstream*); 24-rod portage (*rapids*) from Basswood to Basswood; 40-rod portage (*rapids*) from Basswood to Basswood; 12-rod portage (*Lower Basswood Falls*) from Basswood to CROOKED LAKE (*Indian Picture Rocks; Forest Service cabin; partially developed TABLE ROCK or SKULL AND CROSSBONES CAMPGROUND; see Canoe Trip 10; entry into Canada*).

Tenth day. Paddle five or six miles from east end Crooked to a point three miles E. of CURTAIN FALLS at W. end of lake (*partially developed campground*).

Eleventh day. Portage 116 rods (*Curtain Falls*) to IRON LAKE (*partially developed campgrounds on islands; wall-eyed pike; ample time to enjoy scenery of Rebecca Falls*).

Twelfth day. West across Iron and short liftover (*rapids*) to BOTTLE LAKE; W. across Bottle and portage 90 rods to LAC LA CROIX (*Indian Picture Rocks; excellent fishing; 861 islands; see Canoe Trips 11, 12, 14; entry into Canada*); paddle N. on Lac La Croix to SHORTISS ISLAND (*partially developed campground northwest end of island*).

Thirteenth day. Paddle N. around east side Shortiss to north end COLEMAN ISLAND (*partially developed campgrounds on several islands in vicinity*).

Fourteenth day. Paddle due west of Coleman 12 miles to group of islands at northwest corner Lac La Croix (*partially developed campgrounds on some islands*).

Fifteenth day. South on Lac La Croix to 30-rod portage to LOON LAKE (*partially developed campground*).

Sixteenth day. West across Loon to 50-rod portage (*canoes and luggage conveyed on small-railed, narrow-gauge flat car*) around LOON DAM FALLS to LOON RIVER; N. W. (*downstream*) on Loon to LITTLE VERMILION LAKE; N. across Little Vermilion and through LITTLE VERMILION NARROWS (*partially developed campground*).

Seventeenth day. Paddle from Little Vermilion Narrows into SAND POINT LAKE; N. and S. across Sand Point and S. through KING WILLIAM'S NARROWS into CRANE LAKE; paddle across south shore of Crane (*resorts, cabins; boating, swimming; fishing; outfitting; motor transportation; see Canoe Trip 15*). Retrace to starting point.

CANOE TRIP 2

East Bearskin Lake—Clearwater Lake—McFarland Lake—East Bearskin Lake; 3 days.
38 miles of paddling; 5 of portaging.

Average fishing for pike and trout.
Guides available at Grand Marais, East Bearskin Lake.
Portages are marked by signs showing names of lakes and portage distances.
This route passes through excellent scenery with rugged shores and high cliffs.

Starting point EAST BEARSKIN LAKE (*lodges, housekeeping cabins, campground, summer homesites; boating, fishing; outfitting*).

First day. From west end East Bearskin Lake portage 104 rods to SEED LAKE; N. across middle of Seed and portage 112 rods to FLOUR LAKE; across west end Flour and portage 155 rods to west arm of HUNGRY JACK LAKE; N. on Hungry Jack to eight-rod portage to WEST BEARSKIN LAKE (*to reach Canoe Trip 1, paddle N. via either Daniels Lake, or Duncan Lake and Stairway Portage*); from West Bearskin portage one mile (*motor transportation*) to CLEARWATER LAKE (*lodges, meals; swimming, boating; outfitting; trout fishing*).

Second day. Paddle to east end Clearwater and portage 214 rods to WEST PIKE LAKE; from east end West Pike portage 122 rods to EAST PIKE LAKE; from southwest end East Pike portage 160 rods to McFARLAND LAKE (*unimproved campground; see Arrowhead Tour 1*).

Third day. Cross west end McFarland; if water is low, portage five rods S. to PINE LAKE (*when water is high, channel is passable; submerged rocks*); from southwest end Pine portage 240 rods to CANOE LAKE; from southwest end Canoe portage 22 rods to ALDER LAKE (*submerged rocks*); portage from northwest end Alder 48 rods to East Bearskin; paddle W. to starting point.

CANOE TRIP 3

Poplar Lake—Winchell Lake—Brule Lake—Cherokee Lake—Long Island Lake—Henson Lake—Poplar Lake; 6 days.
47 miles of paddling; 5 of portaging.

Good fishing for pike and trout.
Guides available at Grand Marais, Poplar Lake.
Portages are marked by signs showing names of lakes and portage distances.
Current in Long Island River is negligible.
This route passes through several burned and cut-over areas, but the lakes are beautiful.

Starting point POPLAR LAKE (*lodges; boating, swimming; outfitting*).

First day. South across Poplar Lake to 50-rod portage to LIZZ LAKE; S. on Lizz to 75-rod portage to CARIBOU LAKE and through narrows (*submerged rocks*); S. from narrows to 23-rod portage to HORSESHOE LAKE (*submerged rocks*); 92-rod portage from southwest end Horseshoe to GASKIN LAKE; 51-rod portage from southwest end Gaskin to WINCHELL LAKE (*undeveloped campground; trout fishing*).

Second day. Portage 15 rods from southwest end Winchell to TRAP LAKE; 325-rod portage from south end Trap to MULLIGAN LAKE; 32-rod portage from Mulligan to LILY LAKE; 60-rod portage from south end Lily to BRULE LAKE (*undeveloped campground; landlocked salmon*).

Third day. Paddle W. across Brule and portage six rods to SOUTH TEMPERANCE LAKE; 52-rod portage from north end South Temperance to NORTH TEMPERANCE LAKE; 103-rod portage N. W. from North Temperance to SITKA LAKE; 130-rod portage N. W. from Sitka to CHEROKEE LAKE (*undeveloped campground*).

Fourth day. Portage 14 rods from north end Cherokee to GORDON LAKE; 25-rod portage from north end Gordon to LONG ISLAND RIVER; paddle N. on Long Island River (*downstream*), portaging twice (*rapids*) to LONG ISLAND LAKE (*undeveloped campground*).

Fifth day. Portage 17 rods from east end Long Island to MUSKEG LAKE; cross Muskeg and portage 187 rods to KISKADINNA LAKE; 37-rod portage from east end Kiskadinna to ONEGA LAKE; 32-rod portage from east end Onega to HENSON LAKE (*undeveloped campground*).

Sixth day. Portage 40 rods from east end Henson to PILLSBERY LAKE; short portage E. from Pillsbery to SMALL LAKE; 96-rod portage N. from Small Lake to MEADS LAKE; 300-rod portage from east end Meads to Poplar Lake; paddle N. E. to starting point.

CANOE TRIP 4

Round Lake or Cross River—Tuscarora Lake—Little Saganaga Lake—Frazer Lake—Kekekabic Lake—Sea Gull Lake; 5 days.
56 miles of paddling; 6 of portaging.

Fair fishing for landlocked salmon, speckled trout, wall-eyed pike, and black bass.
Guides available at Grand Marais, Round Lake or Cross River, Sea Gull Lake.
Portages are unmarked except between starting point and little Saganaga Lake and from Ogishkemuncie to Sea Gull Lake, where names and distances are given.
Current in rivers is sluggish.
This route passes through a very wild and scenic region.

Starting point ROUND LAKE or CROSS RIVER (*lodges, housekeeping cabins; boating, swimming, fishing; outfitting*).

First day. Northeast (*upstream*) on Cross River and portage 96 rods (*rapids*) from Cross to Cross; follow Cross through several small PONDS and portage 30 rods to HAM LAKE; S. E. on Ham and portage 30 rods to Cross River; liftover (*beaver dam*) from Cross to Cross; paddle S. on Cross and take small STREAM to the R.; upstream from point shown on map as Cross Bay and portage 60 rods (*rapids*) to SNIP LAKE; S. on Snip and portage 60 rods to COPPER LAKE; 160-rod portage from extreme west end Copper to TUSCARORA LAKE (*undeveloped campground; land-locked salmon*).

Second day. From west end Tuscarora portage twice and cross two small ponds to OWL LAKE; short portage from west end Owl to CROOKED LAKE; S. W. across Crooked and portage 80 rods to MORA LAKE; W. across Mora and portage 30 rods to LITTLE SAGANAGA LAKE (*undeveloped campground; wall-eyed pike; numerous islands delightful for camping; see Branch Route from Little Saganaga Lake to Ogishkemuncie Lake*).

Third day. Portage 18 rods from southwest end Little Saganaga to BEAVER POND; S. on Beaver Pond and portage nine rods to ELTON LAKE; one-rod liftover (*rapids*) from south end Elton to BEAR LAKE (*mountain trout*); 70-rod portage from west end Bear to HOE LAKE; W. across Hoe and portage 60 rods to SMALL LAKE; W. across Small Lake and portage 40 rods to V LAKE; 152-rod portage from west end V to LEDGE LAKE; W. across Ledge and portage 202 rods to CAP LAKE; 72-rod portage from west end Cap to ROE LAKE; W. across Roe and portage 33 rods to LITTLE SAGUS LAKE; 65-rod portage from west end Little Sagus to FRAZER LAKE (*undeveloped campground; wall-eyed pike*).

Fourth day. Portage 16 rods from north end Frazer to GERUND LAKE; 30-rod portage from north end Gerund to AHMAKOSE LAKE; 97-rod portage from north end Ahmakose to WISINI LAKE; ten-rod portage from north end Wisini to STRUP LAKE (*black bass*); 86-rod portage from north end Strup to KEKEKABIC LAKE; cross to east shore Kekekabic (*undeveloped campground; landlocked salmon; to reach Canoe Trip 1, see CANOE TRIP 13*).

Fifth day. Northeast on Kekekabic and make short portage to EDDY LAKE (*to reach Canoe Trip 1, portage 37 rods from northwest end Eddy to Knife Lake*); E. on Eddy and portage 32 rods to a POND; E. across Pond and portage 10 rods to second POND; 50-rod portage from east end second Pond to OGISHKEMUNCIE LAKE (*see Branch Route from Little Saganaga Lake to Ogishkemuncie Lake*); N. E. across Ogishkemuncie and portage 50 rods to a POND; N. E. across Pond and portage 50 rods to JASPER LAKE; 37-rod portage from northeast end Jasper to ALPINE LAKE; 60-rod portage from east end Alpine to ROG LAKE; E. across Rog and portage 17 rods to SEA GULL LAKE (*wall-eyed pike, northern pike*); N. E. across Sea Gull (*resorts, cabins; outfitting; boating, fishing, swimming; motor transportation*). Retrace to starting point (*five days*); or to Ogishkemuncie Lake, thence to starting point (*three days*).

BRANCH ROUTE

From Little Saganaga Lake to Ogishkemuncie Lake: via Little Saganaga Lake; one day; 5.5 miles of paddling; 0.5 of portaging.

Good landlocked salmon fishing.

Paddle to north end Little Saganaga Lake; short portage from Little Saganaga into RATTLE LAKE; N. across Rattle and portage 40 rods into GABIMICHIGAMI LAKE (*landlocked salmon*); N. W. across Gabimichigami and portage 30 rods into AGAMOK LAKE; paddle W. across Agamok and portage 60 rods to a POND; N. W. across Pond and portage 50 rods into Ogishkemuncie Lake. Retrace to Little Saganaga Lake (*one day*).

CANOE TRIP 5

Sea Gull Lake—Red Rock Lake—Sea Gull Lake; 2 days.
23 miles of paddling; 0.5 of portaging.

Good fishing for pike and lake trout.
Guides available at Sea Gull Lake.
Portages are marked by signs showing names of lakes and portage distances.
Current in Sea Gull River is sluggish.
This is one of the finest scenic routes, passing many beautiful islands and skirting rugged shores.

Starting point SEA GULL LAKE (*lodges, housekeeping cabins, meals; boating, swimming, fishing; outfitting*).

First day. Southwest across Sea Gull Lake and portage 17 rods to ROG LAKE; 60-rod portage from west end Rog to ALPINE LAKE; N. across Alpine and portage 51 rods to RED ROCK LAKE (*undeveloped campground*).

Second day. Portage eight rods from north end Red Rock to BIG SAGANAGA LAKE (*see Canoe Trip 1*); paddle along south shore Big Saganaga to extreme southeast end and S. into SEA GULL RIVER; S. (*upstream*) on Sea Gull, portaging twice (*rapids*) to Sea Gull Lake; E. to starting point.

CANOE TRIP 6

Sawbill Lake—Polly Lake—Little Saganaga Lake—Snip Lake—Cherokee Lake—Sawbill Lake; 5 days.
62 miles of paddling; 5 of portaging.

Good fishing for wall-eyed and northern pike.
Guides available at Sawbill Lake.
Portages are marked by signs showing names of lakes and portage distances.
River currents are sluggish, except in Kawishiwi River.
This route offers beautiful scenery, with many beaver dams.

Starting point SAWBILL LAKE (*lodge, campground; excellent fishing for wall-eyed and northern pike; boating, swimming; outfitting*).

First day. West across Sawbill Lake to 27-rod portage to ALDON LAKE; from southwest end Aldon portage 144 rods to BETH LAKE; from west end Beth portage 232 rods to GRACE LAKE; from south arm Grace W. to 14-rod portage to GRACE RIVER (*downstream, jagged submerged rocks*); two short portages (*rapids*) from Grace to east side PHOEBE LAKE; W. across upper half Phoebe to PHOEBE RIVER (*downstream*); 120-rod portage (*rapids*) to HAZEL LAKE; N. W. across Hazel to 51-rod portage (*falls*) to Phoebe River (*submerged rocks*); three portages (*rapids*) on Phoebe to 108-rod portage to POLLY LAKE (*undeveloped campground*).

Second day. Northwest across Polly and portage 17 rods to KA-WISHIWI RIVER (*downstream*); 50-rod portage (*rapids*) and then 157-rod portage (*rapids*) from Kawishiwi to KOMA LAKE; N. across Koma to 20-rod portage (*rapids*) to Kawishiwi River; portage 40 rods from Kawishiwi to KAVENDEBA LAKE; portage between and cross two PONDS to 26-rod portage from Kavendeba to PAN LAKE; N. across Pan portaging between two PONDS to 43-rod portage to south shore BEAR LAKE (*mountain trout*); N. across Bear to one-rod portage to ELTON LAKE; N. to nine-rod portage from Elton to BEAVER POND; across Beaver Pond to 18-rod portage to LITTLE SAGANAGA LAKE (*undeveloped campgrounds; wall-eyed pike, lake trout; see Alternate Return from Little Saganaga Lake to Sawbill Lake*).

Third day. Paddle to southeast end Little Saganaga and portage 30 rods to MORA LAKE; E. then curve N. W. in Mora to 80-rod portage to CROOKED LAKE; E. by N. E. across widest part of Crooked and short portage to OWL LAKE; from Owl cross two small PONDS and short portage to TUSCARORA LAKE; E. across Tuscarora to 160-rod portage to COPPER LAKE; N. E. on Copper and portage 60 rods to SNIP LAKE (*undeveloped campground*).

Fourth day. Cross length of Snip E. and portage 180 rods to CROSS BAY LAKE; S. on Cross Bay and portage 50 rods to RIB LAKE; S. on Rib and portage 30 rods to KARL LAKE that narrows into LONG ISLAND LAKE; S. W. on Long Island into LONG ISLAND RIVER (*upstream*); S. on Long Island, making two short portages (*rapids*) to 25-rod portage to GORDON LAKE; 14-rod portage S. from Gordon to CHEROKEE LAKE (*undeveloped campground; landlocked salmon*).

Fifth day. Across to southwest end Cherokee and W. into CHER-OKEE RIVER (*upstream*) for short distance; from south bank Cherokee portage 192 rods to SKOOP LAKE; S. across Skoop and 12-rod portage to ADA LAKE; W. on Ada and portage 75 rods to ADA CREEK (*downstream*); portage 75 rods from Ada to north end Sawbill Lake, and paddle S. to starting point.

ALTERNATE RETURN

From Little Saganaga Lake to Sawbill Lake: via "Little Sag Route"; 2 days; 15 miles of paddling; 4 of portaging.

Rigorous traveling over Great Laurentian Highland Divide; fair pike fishing; docks at some portages.

First day. Portage 30 rods from southeast end little Saganaga Lake to MORA LAKE; from south end Mora portage 96 rods to HUB RIVER; S. (*upstream*) on Hub and portage 13 rods (*rapids*) from Hub to Hub; 301-rod portage (*rapids*) from Hub to HUB LAKE; from south end Hub portage 12 rods to MESABA LAKE (*unimproved campground*).

Second day. Southeast across Mesaba and portage 109 rods to HUG LAKE; S. across Hug and portage two rods to DUCK LAKE; portage 80 rods from south end Duck to ZENITH LAKE; S. W. across Zenith and portage 270 rods to KELSO RIVER (*downstream*); 84-rod portage (*rapids*) from Kelso to Kelso; liftover (*beaver dam, rapids*) from Kelso to Kelso; S. from Kelso into KELSO LAKE; S. and E. on Kelso into Kelso River; portage 17 rods from Kelso to Sawbill Lake; S. E. on Sawbill to starting point.

CANOE TRIP 7

Lake One—Lake Three—Hudson Lake—North Kawishiwi River—Polly Lake—Parent Lake—Isabella Lake—Isabella River—Bald Eagle Lake—South Kawishiwi River—Lake One; 11 days.
83 miles of paddling; 9 of portaging.

Good fishing for wall-eyed and northern pike.
Guides available at Ely, Winton, Lake One, or Fernberg Landing.
Portages are marked by signs showing names of lakes and portage distances.
Currents vary.
This route takes the canoeist through wild country, with beautiful scenery and lakes dotted with numerous islands.

Starting point LAKE ONE or FERNBERG LANDING (*resort, housekeeping cabins; forest lookout station; developed campground; boating, swimming; outfitting*).

First day. Southeast across Lake One; portaging 36 rods to a POND; from Pond portage 89 rods to LAKE TWO; E. and S. across Two through narrows into LAKE THREE (*developed campground*).

Second day. Paddle E. across Three through narrows into LAKE FOUR; paddle E. and N. across Four into NORTH KAWISHIWI RIVER (*upstream*); portage 17 rods (*rapids*) from North Kawishiwi to North Kawishiwi; portage 23 rods (*rapids*) from North Kawishiwi to North Kawishiwi; portage five rods (*rapids*) from North Kawishiwi to HUDSON LAKE (*developed campground*).

Third day. From east end Hudson portage 90 rods to INSULA LAKE; paddle to east end Insula (*developed campground*).

Fourth day. Paddle from Insula into North Kawishiwi River; portage 17 rods (*rapids*) from North Kawishiwi to North Kawishiwi; paddle from North Kawishiwi into and skirt south end LAKE ALICE, then into North Kawishiwi River; 17-rod portage (*rapids*) from North Kawishiwi to North Kawishiwi; 81-rod portage (*rapids*) from North Kawishiwi to North Kawishiwi; 19-rod portage (*rapids*) from North Kawishiwi to North Kawishiwi (*partially developed campground*).

Fifth day. Portage 71 rods (*rapids*) from North Kawishiwi to MULBERG LAKE; S. E. across Mulberg and into North Kawishiwi River; 24-rod portage (*rapids*) from North Kawishiwi to KOMA LAKE; S. across Koma and portage 157 rods (*rapids*) into North Kawishiwi River; 50-rod portage (*rapids*) from North Kawishiwi to North Kawishiwi; 17-rod portage (*rapids*) from North Kawishiwi to POLLY LAKE (*partially developed campground*).

Sixth day. South across Polly and portage 82 rods to TOWNLINE LAKE; across Townline and portage 179 rods to KAWASACHONG; S. across Kawasachong and liftover (*beaver dam*) into North Kawishiwi River; liftover (*beaver dam*) from North Kawishiwi to North Kawishiwi; paddle from North Kawishiwi into SQUARE LAKE; liftover (*rapids*) from Square to North Kawishiwi River; paddle from North Kawishiwi into KAWISHIWI LAKE; portage 582 rods from Kawishiwi to PARENT LAKE (*partially developed campground*).

Seventh day. West across Parent and portage 57 rods (*rapids*) to PARENT RIVER (*downstream*); 24-rod portage (*rapids*) from Parent to Parent; 32-rod portage (*rapids*) from Parent to Parent; 39-rod portage (*rapids*) from Parent to Parent; 22-rod portage (*rapids*) from Parent to Parent; 39-rod portage (*rapids*) from Parent to Parent; 26-rod portage (*rapids*) from Parent to Parent; 19-rod portage (*rapids*) from Parent to Parent; 40-rod portage (*rapids*) from Parent to Parent; 22-rod portage (*rapids*) from Parent to Parent; 15-rod portage (*rapids*) from Parent to Parent; 26-rod portage (*rapids*) from Parent to Parent; 15-rod portage from

Parent to Parent; 27-rod portage from Parent to ISABELLA LAKE (*partially developed campground*).

Eighth day. West across Isabella and portage 22 rods (*rapids*) to ISABELLA RIVER (*downstream*); 12-rod portage (*rapids*) from Isabella to Isabella; 106-rod portage (*rapids*) from Isabella to Isabella; 27-rod portage (*rapids*) from Isabella to Isabella; 15-rod portage (*rapids*) from Isabella to Isabella (*partially developed campground*).

Ninth day. Portage 40 rods (*rapids*) from Isabella to Isabella (*Forest Service cabin*); portage 36 rods (*rapids*) from Isabella to Isabella; 16-rod portage (*rapids*) from Isabella to Isabella; 156-rod portage (*rapids*) from Isabella to Isabella (*Forest Service cabin*); 158-rod portage (*rapids*) from Isabella to BALD EAGLE LAKE (*partially developed campground*).

Tenth day. Paddle N. W. across Bald Eagle into GABBRO LAKE (in low water, it is necessary to make a short portage between these two lakes because of rapids); 148-rod portage (*rapids*) from northwest end Gabbro to SOUTH KAWISHIWI RIVER (*downstream*); paddle on South Kawishiwi for one mile and turn N. E. (*upstream*), portaging 27 rods (*rapids*) from South Kawishiwi to South Kawishiwi (*partially developed campground*).

Eleventh day. Portage 22 rods (*rapids*) from South Kawishiwi to South Kawishiwi; seven-rod portage from South Kawishiwi to South Kawishiwi; paddle from South Kawishiwi into NORTH KAWISHIWI RIVER (*upstream*); eight-rod portage (*rapids*) from North Kawishiwi to North Kawishiwi; 24-rod portage (*rapids*) from North Kawishiwi to North Kawishiwi; 16-rod portage (*rapids*) from North Kawishiwi to North Kawishiwi; 12-rod portage (*rapids*) from North Kawishiwi to LAKE ONE; paddle N. E. to starting point.

CANOE TRIP 8

White Iron Lake, or Silver Rapids—Clear Lake—Birch Lake—White Iron Lake, or Silver Rapids; 3 days.
30 miles of paddling; one of portaging.

Good fishing for wall-eyed pike.
Guides available at Ely, White Iron Lake, or Silver Rapids.
Portages are marked by signs showing names of lakes and portage distances.
Current in North and South Kawishiwi rivers is sluggish; rapids are fast.
This route has excellent scenery along the rivers.

Starting point WHITE IRON LAKE, or SILVER RAPIDS (*lodges, meals, housekeeping cabins; boating, swimming, fishing; outfitting*).

First day. East from White Iron Lake, or Silver Rapids, on NORTH KAWISHIWI RIVER (*upstream*) into FARM LAKE; E. across Farm into

North Kawishiwi River (*upstream*); 132-rod portage from south bank North Kawishiwi to CLEAR LAKE (*undeveloped campground*).

Second day. South across Clear to 224-rod portage to SOUTH KAWISHIWI RIVER; S. and W. (*downstream*) on South Kawishiwi to several portages (*swift rapids*) and into BIRCH LAKE (*excellent developed campground; community building; ranger station at east end Birch Lake*).

Third day. Paddle W. across Birch and turn N. to portage into WHITE IRON RIVER; downstream, portaging several times (*swift rapids*) on White Iron to WHITE IRON LAKE; paddle N. to starting point.

CANOE TRIP 9

Fall Lake, or Winton-Basswood Lake; one day.
13 miles of paddling; 4 of portaging.

Good fishing for pike.
Guides available at Ely, Winton, Fall Lake.
There are no public portage signs.
Either of these routes is a quick entry to international waters.

Starting point FALL LAKE (*lodge, meals, housekeeping cabins; boating, swimming, fishing; outfitting*).

Paddle to northeast end Fall Lake; four-mile portage from Fall (*motor transportation*) to BASSWOOD LAKE. Retrace to starting point (*one day*), or paddle N. E. five miles (*see Canoe Trip 1*).

ALTERNATE ROUTE

From Fall Lake to Basswood Lake: via Pipestone Bay; one day.
15 miles of paddling; 0.25 of portaging.

Interesting falls, rapids; topography rugged; not much timber.

Paddle to northwest arm Fall Lake and portage ten rods (*falls*) to NEWTON LAKE; N. on Newton and portage 61 rods (*falls*) to PIPESTONE BAY, a part of Basswood Lake (*see Canoe Trip 1*). Retrace to starting point (*one day*).

CANOE TRIP 10

Burntside Lake—Fenske Lake—Grassy Lake—Murphy Lake; 3 days.
20 miles of paddling; 4.5 of portaging.

Excellent fishing for bass and wall-eyed pike.
Guides available at Ely, Burntside Lake.
Portages are marked by signs showing names of lakes and portage distances.

Ely-Buyck Trail offers other starting points (*see Arrowhead Tour 4*).
Current in rivers is negligible.
This is an interesting route to international waters.

Starting point BURNTSIDE LAKE (*lodges, housekeeping cabins; fishing, swimming; outfitting*).

First day. North from Burntside Lake on DEAD RIVER (*upstream*) and along eastern tip WEST TWIN LAKE into EAST TWIN LAKE; 13-rod portage from north end East Twin to EVERETT LAKE; N. across west end Everett and portage 120 rods, crossing ELY-BUYCK TRAIL, to FENSKE LAKE (*well-developed camp and picnic grounds; bass fishing*).

Second day. East across Fenske and portage ten rods to LITTLE SLETTEN LAKE (*bass*); N. across Little Sletten and portage 70 rods to BIG SLETTEN LAKE (*bass*); N. across Big Sletten and portage 122 rods to T LAKE (*bass*); N. across T and portage 45 rods to GRASSY LAKE (*undeveloped campground; bass fishing*).

Third day. East across Grassy into RANGE RIVER (*downstream*); 26-rod portage (*rapids*) from Range to Range; 141-rod portage (*rapids*) from Range to Range, and into RANGE LAKE; 160-rod portage from north end Range to SANDPIT LAKE; N. across Sandpit to MURPHY LAKE (*undeveloped campground; see Branch Route*). Retrace to starting point (*three days*), or paddle E. across Murphy and portage 1.25 miles to JACKFISH BAY of BASSWOOD LAKE (*see Canoe Trip 1*), or follow either of two branch routes.

BRANCH ROUTE NO. 1

From Murphy Lake to Crooked Lake: via Gun Lake; 2 days; 17 miles of paddling; 1.25 of portaging.

Partly logged-over area but beautiful scenery; excellent bass and pike fishing.

First day. Portage 80 rods from north end Murphy Lake into HORSE LAKE; skirt southwest end Horse and portage 40 rods into a small POND; then 15 rods from small Pond to FOURTOWN LAKE; from west end Fourtown portage 50 rods to BOOT LAKE; W. and N. on Boot and portage 56 rods to FAIRY LAKE; 70-rod portage from north end Fairy into GUN LAKE (*undeveloped campground*).

Second day. Portage 300 rods from northeast end Gun to WAGOSH LAKE (*bass*); 33-rod portage from north end Wagosh to NIKI LAKE (*bass*); from Niki paddle into CHIPPEWA RIVER (*downstream*); after one short portage (*rapids*) on Chippewa paddle to CHIPPEWA LAKE; from west end Chippewa paddle into TURTLE RIVER (*downstream*); after two or three short liftovers (*beaver dam*) follow Turtle River into

PAPPOOSE LAKE; N. on Pappoose into Turtle River (*downstream*) and portage 80 rods from Turtle to FRIDAY BAY of CROOKED LAKE (*undeveloped campground*). Retrace to Murphy Lake (*two days*) or continue as in Canoe Trip 1.

BRANCH ROUTE NO. 2

From Murphy Lake to Crooked Lake: via Horse River; one day; 6 miles of paddling; one of portaging.

Submerged rocks in river; good wall-eyed pike fishing; game plentiful.

First day. Portage 80 rods from north end Murphy Lake into HORSE LAKE (*wall-eyed pike*); paddle from east side Horse into HORSE RIVER (*downstream*); 42-rod portage (*rapids*) from Horse to Horse; 51-rod portage (*rapids*) from Horse to Horse; 234-rod portage (*rapids*) from Horse to Horse; paddle from Horse into BASSWOOD RIVER (*downstream*), then into CROOKED LAKE (*undeveloped campground*). Retrace to Murphy Lake (*one day*) or continue as in Canoe Trip 1.

CANOE TRIP 11

Burntside Lake—Big Lake—Stuart Lake—Boulder River; 3 days. 34 miles of paddling; 6 of portaging.

Average fishing for bass.
Guides available at Ely, Burntside Lake.
Portages are marked by signs showing names of lakes and portage distances; Ely-Buyck Trail offers other starting points (*see Arrowhead Tour 4*).
Current in Stuart, Dahlgren, and Boulder rivers is very slow.
This route passes through an interesting area with numerous beaver dams, moose, deer, and bear.

Starting point BURNTSIDE LAKE (*lodges, housekeeping cabins; boating, fishing, swimming; outfitting*).

First day. North across Burntside Lake into NORTH ARM of lake; 240-rod portage N. W. from North Arm to SLIM LAKE; two-mile portage from Slim to BIG LAKE (*developed campground north end*).

Second day. Portage 77 rods to ELY-BUYCK TRAIL and 1.25 miles from Ely-Buyck to STUART RIVER; N. (*downstream*) on Stuart; 96-rod portage (*rapids*) from Stuart to Stuart; 54-rod portage (*rapids*) from Stuart to Stuart; 64-rod portage (*rapids*) from Stuart to Stuart; 74-rod portage (*rapids*) to STUART LAKE (*developed campground; bass fishing*).

Third day. North and W. across lower half Stuart; 126-rod portage from west end Stuart to DAHLGREN RIVER; N. (*downstream*) on Dahlgren (*submerged rocks, but passable*); 122-rod portage (*rapids*) from

Dahlgren to BOULDER RIVER. Retrace to starting point (*three days*). For alternate return: *see Canoe Trip 12* or paddle N. E. (*downstream*) into LAC LA CROIX (*see Canoe Trip 1*).

CANOE TRIP 12

Burntside Lake—Cummings Lake—Moose Lake—Nina Moose Lake—Lake Agnes; 4 days.
31 miles of paddling; 4.75 of portaging.

Good fishing for bass and wall-eyed pike.
Guides available at Ely, Burntside Lake.
Portages are marked by signs showing names of lakes and portage distances; Ely-Buyck Trail offers other starting points (*see Arrowhead Tour 4*).
Current in river is negligible.
  This route passes through wild, rugged country and affords excellent opportunities to see moose and deer.

Starting point BURNTSIDE LAKE (*lodges, housekeeping cabins; boating, fishing, swimming; outfitting*).

First day. West across Burntside Lake and portage 1.4 miles to CRAB LAKE; N. W. across Crab and portage 16 rods into LITTLE CRAB LAKE (*bass*); paddle N. (*downstream*) from Little Crab into KORB RIVER and portage N. 24 rods to KORB LAKE (*bass*); E. across Korb into Korb River (*downstream*); 60-rod portage (*rapids*) W. from Korb to east shore CUMMINGS LAKE (*partially developed campground; bass fishing*).

Second day. North across Cummings and portage two miles to north shore MOOSE LAKE (*partially developed campground; bass fishing*).

Third day. Northwest across Moose and portage 71 rods (*rapids*) to MOOSE RIVER; 137-rod portage (*rapids*) from Moose to Moose; 130-rod portage (*rapids*) from Moose to Moose; 77-rod portage (*rapids*) from Moose to Moose; 60-rod portage (*rapids*) from Moose to Moose; 117-rod portage (*rapids*) from Moose to Moose; follow Moose to ELY-BUYCK TRAIL (*developed campground*); portage 177 rods across Ely-Buyck and past rapids to Moose River; two short portages (*rapids*) on Moose to NINA MOOSE LAKE (*partially developed campground*).

Fourth day. Cross Nina Moose N. into NINA MOOSE RIVER (*downstream*); two 0.3-mile portages (*rapids*) on Nina Moose to LAKE AGNES (*partially developed campground; wall-eyed pike*). Retrace to starting point (*four days*); or cross Lake Agnes N. E. and portage 116 rods to BOULDER RIVER (*one-half day; see Canoe Trip 11 or Branch Route from Lake Agnes to Lac La Croix*).

BRANCH ROUTE

From Lake Agnes to Lac La Croix: via Oyster Lake; 2 days; 15 miles of paddling; 1.25 of portaging.

Moose and deer; good landlocked salmon and wall-eyed pike fishing; rigorous traveling.

First day. Portage 190 rods from Lake Agnes to OYSTER RIVER; upstream on Oyster with a short portage (*rapids*) from Oyster into OYSTER LAKE (*partially developed campground; landlocked salmon*).

Second day. West across Oyster and portage 64 rods to ROCKY LAKE; N. on Rocky and portage 87 rods to GREEN LAKE; N. on Green and portage 122 rods to GE-BE-ON-E-QUET LAKE; N. on Ge-be-on-e-quet and portage 35 rods (*falls*) to GE-BE-ON-E-QUET CREEK and paddle (*downstream*) into POCKET CREEK; paddle W. (*downstream*) and portage 24 rods (*rapids*) from Pocket to Pocket; paddle from Pocket into POCKET RIVER and W. (*downstream*) into LAC LA CROIX (*see Canoe Trip 1*).

Retrace to Lake Agnes (*two days*), or follow Canoe Trip 1.

CANOE TRIP 13

Moose Lake—Ensign Lake—Thomas Lake—Kekekabic Lake—Knife Lake; 4 days.
35 miles of paddling; 2 of portaging.

Variety of fishing.
Guides available at Ely, Winton, Moose Lake.
Portages are good, some with docks, but are unmarked.
Current in Thomas River is sluggish.
This is a convenient route to international waters.

Starting point MOOSE LAKE (*lodges, housekeeping cabins, meals; boating, swimming, fishing; outfitting*).

First day. North across Moose Lake into NEWFOUND LAKE (*to reach Canoe Trip 1, paddle N. across Newfound to Sucker Lake; N. across Sucker into Carp into Birch Lake*); 36-rod portage (*rapids*) from extreme northeast end Newfound to ENSIGN LAKE and paddle to southeast shore (*partially developed campground*).

Second day. Portage 56 rods S. to BASS LAKE; S. across Bass and portage 177 rods to FLY LAKE; S. across Fly and portage 25 rods to MARSH LAKE; S. across Marsh and portage 45 rods to JORDAN LAKE; ten-rod portage from east end Jordan to IMA LAKE; S. E. across Ima and portage 50 rods to THOMAS RIVER; S. (*upstream*) on Thomas portaging 17 rods (*rapids*) from Thomas to Thomas; 29-rod portage from Thomas to a POND; S. across Pond and portage eight rods to THOMAS LAKE (*partially developed campground*).

Third day. East on Thomas and paddle through channel into FRAZER LAKE; 16-rod portage from north end Frazer to GERUND LAKE; 30-rod portage from north end Gerund to AHMAKOSE LAKE; 96-rod portage from north end Ahmakose to WISINI LAKE; ten-rod portage from north end Wisini to STRUP LAKE; 86-rod portage from northwest end Strup to KEKEKABIC LAKE (*partially developed campground*).

Fourth day. Portage 86 rods from north end Kekekabic to PICKLE LAKE; 28-rod portage from north shore Pickle to SPOON LAKE; N. across Spoon and portage 31 rods to BONNIE LAKE; N. E. across Bonnie and portage 42 rods to KNIFE LAKE; paddle to west shore (*partially developed campground*). Retrace to starting point (*four days*), or follow Canoe Trip 1, then through Sucker, Newfound, Moose lakes (*one day*).

CANOE TRIP 14

Vermilion Lake—Little Trout Lake—Little Indian Sioux River Campground—East Bay of Loon Lake—Lac La Croix; 4 days.
57 miles of paddling; 5.5 of portaging.

Good fishing for wall-eyed pike, bass, and landlocked salmon.
Portages on Little Indian Sioux River from Little Trout Lake to Lac La Croix are marked.
Guides available at Tower, Vermilion Lake.
Current in rivers is sluggish.
This early Indian route takes the canoeist through scenic country where moose are plentiful.

Starting point VERMILION LAKE (*resorts, meals, lodges, campgrounds, housekeeping cabins; excursions; marine mail service; outfitting*).

First day. North across Vermilion Lake around east end PINE ISLAND; W. around north side Pine then N. through NARROWS; 80-rod portage (*motor transportation*) from north end Narrows to TROUT LAKE (*see Branch Route from Trout Lake to Burntside Lake*); paddle from northeast end Trout into LITTLE TROUT LAKE (*undeveloped campground; sand beach*).

Second day. Portage 1.3 miles (*submerged rocks*) from northeast end Little Trout to LITTLE INDIAN SIOUX RIVER (*see Branch Route from Little Indian Sioux River to Burntside Lake*); N. (*downstream*) on Little Indian Sioux to 24-rod portage (*rapids*) from Little Indian Sioux to Little Indian Sioux; 90-rod portage (*rapids*) from Little Indian Sioux to Little Indian Sioux; 15-rod portage (*Sioux Falls*) from Little Indian Sioux to Little Indian Sioux; portage 80 rods (*rapids*) and across ELY-BUYCK TRAIL (*see Arrowhead Tour 4*).

Third day. Portage 125 rods from Little Indian Sioux to Little Indian Sioux and paddle into UPPER PAUNESS LAKE; E. across Upper Pauness and portage 42 rods E. to LOWER PAUNESS LAKE; N. on Lower Pauness and portage 110 rods to LOON LAKE (*forest lookout station; Devil's Cascade Canyon*); paddle to EAST BAY of Loon (*undeveloped campground; sand beach; see Canoe Trip 1*).

Fourth day. Portage 174 rods from northeast arm Loon to SLIM LAKE; 47-rod portage from north end Slim to a CREEK; paddle N. (*downstream*) on Creek into a POND and portage N. 74 rods from Pond to SOUTH LAKE; S. E. on South and portage 125 rods (*very steep portage*) to STEEP LAKE (*bass*); 46-rod portage from north end Steep to EUGENE LAKE; 86-rod portage from north end Eugene to GUN LAKE (*landlocked salmon*); 55-rod portage from north end Gun to LAC LA CROIX (*undeveloped campground; see Canoe Trip 1*). Retrace to starting point (*four days*).

BRANCH ROUTE NO. 1

From Trout Lake to Burntside Lake: via Pine Lake; 2 days; 24 miles of paddling; 6 of portaging.

Good bass fishing; beautiful scenery.

First day. From east shore Trout Lake portage 240 rods to PINE LAKE; 1.8-mile portage from north end Pine to BUCK LAKE (*black bass*); 99-rod portage from southeast end Buck to WESTERN LAKE (*undeveloped campground; black bass fishing*).

Second day. Portage 199 rods from east end Western to GLENMORE LAKE (*bass*); 189-rod portage from southeast end Glenmore to SCHLAMN LAKE (*bass*); 80-rod portage from extreme east end Schlamn to LUNNETTA LAKE (*bass*); 80-rod portage (*rapids*) from northeast end Lunnetta to LUNNETTA RIVER; E. (*downstream*) on Lunnetta into LITTLE CRAB LAKE; S. on Little Crab and portage 16 rods to CRAB LAKE; 1.3-mile portage from southeast end Crab to BURNTSIDE LAKE; E. across Burntside (*lodges; motor transportation*).

BRANCH ROUTE NO. 2

From Little Indian Sioux River to Burntside Lake: via Little Indian Sioux River; 3 days; 24 miles of paddling; 2.5 of portaging.

Route crooked, traveling slow; good bass fishing.

First day. South and E. on Little Indian Sioux River (*upstream*) and portage 21 rods (*rapids*) from Little Indian Sioux to Little Indian Sioux; S. E. and portage 32 rods (*rapids*) from Little Indian Sioux to Little Indian Sioux; ten-rod portage (*rapids*) from Little Indian Sioux to Little Indian Sioux; 74-rod portage (*rapids*) from Little Indian Sioux to Little Indian

Sioux; 27-rod portage (*rapids*) from Little Indian Sioux to Little Indian Sioux; 39-rod portage (*rapids*) from Little Indian Sioux to Little Indian Sioux; 24-rod portage (*rapids*) from Little Indian Sioux to Little Indian Sioux; 99-rod portage (*rapids*) from Little Indian Sioux to OTTER LAKE (*undeveloped campground*).

Second day. East across Otter and portage four rods to CUMMINGS LAKE; E. across Cummings (*undeveloped campground; bass fishing*).

Third day. Portage 80 rods from Cummings to KORB LAKE (*black bass*); paddle W. across Korb and into KORB RIVER (*upstream*); 24-rod portage (*rapids*) from Korb to Korb and paddle into LITTLE CRAB LAKE; S. on Little Crab and portage 16 rods to CRAB LAKE; 1.3-mile portage from southeast end Crab to BURNTSIDE LAKE; E. across Burntside (*lodges; motor transportation*).

CANOE TRIP 15

Vermilion Lake—Vermilion Dam—Vermilion River—Crane Lake; 4 days. 59 miles of paddling; 2 of portaging.

Average fishing for wall-eyed and northern pike.
Guides available at Tower, Vermilion Dam, Crane Lake.
Portages are unmarked.
River current is not rapid.
This route, used by Indians and early explorers, is picturesque, passing by many small farms along the river bank and through several wild rice beds where wild ducks may be seen. Wild rice beds resembling large grain fields in shallow water, usually along lake shores, are feeding places for wild fowl.

Starting point VERMILION LAKE (*resorts, meals, lodges, undeveloped campgrounds, housekeeping cabins; excursions; marine mail service; fishing, swimming, boating; outfitting*).

First day. North and N. W. on Vermilion Lake and N. through NILES BAY to VERMILION DAM (*resorts, meals, lodges, housekeeping cabins; excursions; fishing, boating, swimming; outfitting; undeveloped campground*).

Second day. Portage 100 rods (*falls, dam*) N. E. to VERMILION RIVER; downstream on Vermilion and portage 80 rods (*rapids*) from Vermilion to Vermilion; 60-rod portage (*rapids*) from Vermilion to Vermilion; 40-rod portage (*rapids*) from Vermilion to Vermilion; 50-rod portage (*rapids*) from Vermilion to Vermilion; 30-rod portage (*rapids*) from Vermilion to Vermilion (*undeveloped campground*).

Third day. Portage 40 rods (*rapids*) from Vermilion to Vermilion; 40-rod portage (*rapids*) from Vermilion to Vermilion; 60-rod portage (*rapids*) from Vermilion to Vermilion (*undeveloped campground*).

Fourth day. Portage 40 rods (*rapids*) from Vermilion to Vermilion; 30-rod portage (*rapids*) from Vermilion to Vermilion; o.8-mile portage (*falls, gorge*) from Vermilion to CRANE LAKE (*several campgrounds; meals, lodges, housekeeping cabins; swimming, boating; outfitting; walleyed pike; see Canoe Trip 1*).

PART III

Cities, Towns, and Villages

Aitkin

Arrowhead Tour 3.
Railroad station: Northern Pacific Minnesota Ave. S. (US 169, 2 blocks S.).
Bus station: Northland Greyhound Lines, 117 Minnesota Ave. N.
Taxis: Taxi and livery service within village limits and to surrounding territory.
Accommodations: Four hotels; municipal tourist camp, south foot 3rd Ave. W.
Information service: Aitkin Lions Club Information Bureau, cor. Minnesota Ave. and 2nd St.
Golf: Cuyuna Range Golf Club (open to public), US 210, 8 miles W. (Deerwood); 9 holes.
Tennis: Aitkin Tennis Court south foot 2nd Ave. W.

THE TURKEY CAPITAL

Aitkin (1,230 alt., 2,063 pop.) at the junction of the Mississippi and Ripple rivers, is the administrative seat and largest community of Aitkin County and the focal point of an important farming area.

The site of the village was a Sioux hunting ground until 1750, when the westward-advancing Chippewa definitely established their supremacy. The last Sioux-Chippewa battle, at Kathio, was fought throughout the territory between Mille Lacs and Big Sandy lakes. The 500 dead were buried just north of where the Kathio School stands at Vineland, on the south shore of Mille Lacs; the spot still is an Indian burial ground, where the visitor can see new-turned earth and "spirithouses" over the graves. Radisson and Groseilliers probably passed near Aitkin between 1655 and 1660, and Daniel Greysolon, Sieur du Lhut, camped in the area in 1679 while on his visit to Mille Lacs. To establish posts, fur traders ascended St. Louis River from Fond du Lac, portaged over the Great Savanna (*see Floodwood*), then paddled down the Mississippi. Traces of an overland trail between Fond du Lac and Aitkin, used until 1870, still are visible.

Among the traders was William Aitkin, after whom both the county and village are named. Aitkin operated, independent of any company, among Indians in the northern part of the present county. In 1832, he was made factor of the American Fur Company's post at Big Sandy Lake, but was discharged for incompetence in 1838. Afterwards, he carried on independent operations until his death in 1851. Reverend Edmund F. Ely (*see Duluth, Tour 3*), missionary at the Big Sandy Lake post in 1833-34, de-

71

scribes trips taken up and down the Mississippi, and the site of the present village of Aitkin probably was well known to him, though as yet no permanent settlement had been made.

This region, like the rest of the Minnesota Arrowhead, was covered with pine forests. Local lumbering activities were carried on near the rivers; but big-scale operations were not begun until after 1870, the year in which the Northen Pacific Railroad was extended through the district. The location was chosen as a station of the railroad, and a town immediately founded. The first house was put up in 1870 by Nathaniel Tibbets, who later built Aitkin's first hotel, the Ojibway House, that was torn down before the turn of the century. Immigrants, attracted by rosy tales of the opportunities awaiting them, began to settle in the village and adjacent territory.

Before lumbering activities started in earnest, the only means of travel in the summer between Grand Rapids and Aitkin was by river. Steamboats plied between the two settlements, but the trip was not always comfortable. If conditions were favorable, a one-way journey took 18 or 20 hours. However, sorrowful was the lot of the passenger when conditions were unfavorable. He would have to help shove the boat off shoals, and sometimes a single trip would take the better part of a week. The "pride of the upper Mississippi" at this time was the *Andy Gibson*, owned by Ed Lowell and Leo West of Aitkin and Fred Bonness of Grand Rapids. The boat was 150 feet long, had a 25-foot beam, and carried 150 tons of freight and 200 passengers.

When the forests had been cut, the settlers turned to farming. More immigrants were attracted by the rich soil, among them many from Sweden and Germany in 1884. Agriculture rapidly came to the front, and Aitkin soon developed into a trade center. At present, it is one of the most prosperous farming communities in the Arrowhead. Dotting the surrounding territory are small-fruit, poultry, and dairy farms, and large flocks of turkeys are raised for Eastern markets. Two creameries operate in the town, one of which churns butter and condenses buttermilk into powder; the other makes butter and maintains a milk route. The village has dairy and livestock shipping associations.

The Aitkin County Courthouse (US 210 bet. 2nd and 3rd Aves. N. W.), of white face brick and Bedford stone, was built in 1929 and houses all county offices. Adjoining are the county jail and sheriff's residence. The Aitkin Grade and High schools (2nd St. bet. 3rd and 4th Aves. N. W.) are modern, the former having been remodeled, and the latter built, in 1928; a new gymnasium and auditorium were built during 1939. The Aitkin Armory (adjacent to Northern Pacific Station), with a seating capacity of 2,000, is the headquarters for the 34th M. P. Company of the 34th Division. St. James Catholic Church (2nd St. N. W. opposite High School), whose spire is brilliantly illuminated at night, was erected in 1885.

Aitkin is drawing steadily increasing summer-tourist business, for within easy driving distance are many lakes, of which historic and picturesque Mille Lacs is the largest, and numerous resorts, where good fishing, hunting, water sports, and other recreational facilities are available.

Aurora

Arrowhead Tour 4.
Railroad station: Duluth, Missabe & Iron Range, Railroad Ave. bet. Missabe and Jackson Sts.
Bus station: Northland Greyhound Lines, Jackson St. bet. 2nd and 3rd Aves.
Accommodations: One hotel; tourist homes.
Information service: Aurora Commercial Club, Village Hall, 2nd Ave. bet. Jackson and Vermilion Sts.

DAWN ON THE MESABI

Aurora (1,478 alt., 1,528 pop.), its name from the Latin meaning "morning," is an eastern Mesabi Range mining town that was moved from its original location to improve its railroad facilities.

Although ore had been found in paying quantities at Biwabik in 1891, most of the subsequent exploratory work was done on the western end of the Mesabi. The Meadow Mine (exhausted), the first in the vicinity of the unborn Aurora, was explored in 1898. A settlement grew near the mine and, in 1903, was incorporated as a village. It soon was evident, however, that the location (one mile north of the present site) was too far from the Duluth and Iron Range Railroad, which served the Vermilion Range and the eastern end of the Mesabi. Today's town site was platted by E. J. Longyear, and building was begun in 1905. The village then moved to its new location on the railroad, and a period of rapid development followed.

The mines here have not been operated so extensively as those on other parts of the range, but vast reserves underlie the district. Mining inactivity temporarily has checked the growth of the community. Aurora is, however, the trade center for a growing number of miners who have turned to farming, especially dairying, for a livelihood. It has a municipally owned potato warehouse of 18,000 bushels capacity for certified seed and table stock.

Aurora's three tapestry-brick schools, Aurora High, Hearding High, and Johnson Grade, stand on a 15-acre campus (cor. 4th Ave. and Vermilion St.). Shell-pink Kasota stone and Flemish-gray oak finish the halls of the high school. The agricultural department supervises a complete dairy room, in which milk is pasteurized for distribution to undernourished pupils. The music department has a 30-piece orchestra, which has won State-wide honors, and a 48-piece band. Housed in the high school is a museum containing 225 mounted specimens of birds, 25 mounted animals, 1,694 mounted classified insects, miniatures of a lumber camp, open-pit mine, and farm. There is also a large collection of fossils—fish, reptiles, leaves, and plants. The Village Hall, built in 1910, houses the fire department and library.

The village is within easy driving distance of the Vermilion Lake region, the Superior National Forest, and Esquagama Lake. Colby and White-water lakes, three miles east of Aurora, provide picnic, camping, and recreational facilities.

Barnum

Arrowhead Tour 8.
Railroad station: Northern Pacific, Main St., 3 blocks W.
Bus station: Northland Greyhound Lines, US 61 bet. Oak and Main Sts.
Accommodations: One hotel.
Information service: Barnum Hotel, cor. US 61 and Main St.
Annual event (exact dates vary): Carlton County Fair, August.

AN ARROWHEAD EGG BASKET

Barnum (1,122 alt., 327 pop.), on the Moose Horn River, is the chicken center of the Minnesota Arrowhead country. The cheeping of thousands of chicks has replaced the buzzing of the sawmill to which the town first looked for survival.

The settlement was born in 1870, when the Arrowhead's first railroad, now the Northern Pacific, was constructed from St. Paul to Duluth, and opened a way to the pine lands. The first settlers were loggers. In 1879, there were only four white men, two with families, living here; Bill Oliver, the postmaster, owned the land now included in the village. In that year, seven German families took up homesteads near by. Others soon followed, attracted by jobs in the timber. In 1887, the town site was platted; two years later, it was incorporated as a village and named for George G. Barnum of Duluth, a former paymaster for the railroad.

As the forests were depleted, the life of the small village seemed doomed. In 1904, however, an enterprising citizen, H. C. Hanson, convinced that the region was adapted to dairying, took over an abandoned creamery building and urged farmers to develop purebred herds. Their May Rose Guernsey cattle have won State and national recognition (*see Walker*). With the development of the industry, the creamery became one of the largest in the country. In 1924, it was reorganized and a modern plant was built. Following his success in dairying, Hanson encouraged the development of the poultry industry and recommended the breeding of a pure strain of chicken. The White Leghorn was chosen, and today there are several extensive poultry farms near Barnum. One chicken house has become a Minnesota model. The Maplewood Farm is one of the largest of its kind in the Northwest. Poultry raising, for both egg and chick production, has proved so profitable that producers have installed large electrically controlled incubators. The area is suited to raising potatoes, and crops have won State and district prizes.

Barnum's educational facilities have kept pace with its economic development. The Grade and High School (cor. Main St. and Carlton Ave.) draws pupils from a wide radius. In 1928, Mr. Barnum donated $15,000 for an addition to the school, to be used as a public library. He also was the donor of many of its books. On February 22, 1940, another addition, consisting of an up-to-date auditorium-gymnasium and five classrooms, was dedicated.

Big Hanging Horn Lake (Big Hanging Horn Lake Rd., two miles south), on which is Camp Wanakiwin, Duluth YWCA Camp, is popular with fishermen and vacationists.

The Methodist Assembly Grounds, on Little Hanging Horn Lake, are considered among the most attractive in the United States, and are used throughout the summer season by various denominations.

Beaver Bay

Arrowhead Tour 1.
Bus station: Northland Greyhound Lines, Beaver Bay Trading Post.
Accommodations: One hotel; 2 tourist homes.
Information service: Beaver Bay Trading Post.
Swimming: Three pools in Beaver River, at point of land separating the river from the bay.

A NORTH SHORE HAVEN

Beaver Bay (602 alt., unincorporated), Lake County, about 53 miles northeast of Duluth, nestled around a bay where Beaver River empties into Lake Superior, is the only town site on the north shore between Duluth and Grand Portage boasting of a continuous existence from the boom period of the 1850's to the present time.

The early history of Beaver Bay, largely a "family affair," is the story of the Wieland brothers.

The site of Beaver Bay was occupied from October 20, 1854, by the "subscribers" William H. Newton and Thomas Clark 2nd. The plat of the town was filed on June 24, 1856, with the Register of Deeds of St. Louis County—not Lake County—though both counties had been established simultaneously on March 1, 1856. On May 10, 1866, Lake County was organized and the first county commissioners were appointed by the Governor of Minnesota. Beaver Bay was considered to be the seat of Lake County until 1888, when Two Harbors was made the county seat.

In June, 1856, the first settlers arrived on the chartered steamer *Illinois*. They came from the Maumee Valley in northwestern Ohio. The site had been selected for them by Thomas Clark 2nd and Christian Wieland, both civil engineers and surveyors, who had come to Superior, Wisconsin, in 1854.

The first post office at Beaver Bay was established in 1856, and Robert B. McLean was first postmaster. In June, 1857, the Wieland brothers took possession of all the rights and interests of the "subscribers" at Beaver Bay. The panic of 1857 brought hardships to these pioneers, and several became discouraged and moved to southern Minnesota. In 1859 the Wielands built a sawmill on the Beaver River, which for 25 years was practically the sole industrial support of the village.

During the first two years of the settlement, there were no Indians at Beaver Bay. In the summer of 1858, two Indian families came from Grand Portage and camped on the gravel point at the mouth of Beaver River; the next year, additional families came. They worked in the mill or in the lumber camps and became permanent residents of the settlement, but once a year they returned to Grand Portage to receive their Government annuities.

In 1884, the Wieland brothers sold the sawmill and their timber holdings to Gibbs and Mallett, and some years later these holdings were acquired by the Alger Smith Lumber Company. After the merchantable timber in the surrounding area had been cut, Beaver Bay reverted to its status of the 1850's, with fishing and small-scale farming its only industries.

Today the small settlement is but a part of the town of Beaver Bay, with a Community Hall and a Grade School. In the Indian cemetery, the names of the buried are engraved on a bronze plaque. The first millstone, dating from 1865, is on display at the Beaver Bay Trading Post.

Deep-sea fishing and speed boating are the major attractions at Beaver Bay, which is also noted as a haven for hay fever sufferers. There are many beauty spots in the vicinity.

Bemidji

Arrowhead Tour 3.
Railroad stations: Minneapolis, St. Paul & Sault Ste. Marie, and Minnesota and International, cor. Beltrami Ave. and 1st St. (Union Depot); Great Northern, south foot Minnesota Ave.

Bus stations: Northland Greyhound Lines, Triangle Transportation Co., Northern Transportation Co., Markham Hotel, 200 Beltrami Ave., and New Bemidji Hotel, 102 Minnesota Ave.
Local bus line: Bemidji Local Bus Line, 509 Central Ave., offers service within city limits.
Airport: Municipal, US 2, 2.5 miles N. W.; hangar and service facilities day and night; fuel and oil available.
Taxis: Two cab companies offer service within city limits and to surrounding territory.
Accommodations: Twenty-one hotels and tourist homes; municipal tourist camp, Diamond Point Park, 1700 Doud Ave., on Lake Bemidji; Bemidji State Park Tourist Camp, head of Lake Bemidji.
Information service: Bemidji Civic and Commerce Association, Fireplace of States Bldg., foot 3rd St. on lake shore.
Recreational facilities: Bemidji Sports Arena, 615 America Ave.
Golf: Bemidji Municipal Golf Course, US 71, 1 mile S.; 9 holes. Bemidji Town and Country Club, US 71, 6 miles N., 0.5 mile E.; 18 holes.
Tennis: Municipal court, cor. America Ave. and 6th St.; Public School Courts, High School Athletic Field, cor. 16th St. and Bemidji Ave.
Rifle range: Bemidji Gun Club and Range, US 2, 0.75 mile S. E., on lake shore.
Riding academy: Bemidji Riding Academy, old Trunk Highway 4, 1.5 miles W.; horses also available at Ruttger's Birchmont Lodge, US 71, 5 miles N.
Annual event (exact dates vary): Paul Bunyan Winter Carnival, January or February.

DREAMING OF DIAMONDS, THEY BUILT A CITY

Bemidji (1,351 alt., 9,427 pop.), Beltrami County seat, owes its beginning to a tantalizing glitter, its development to the pine land surrounding it, and its present stability to its wood industries, agricultural processing plants, and tourist trade. The name, that of an Indian chief whose band of 50 had made its home on the south shore of Lake Bemidji, is Chippewa and means "easy crossing" or "place the river flows into and out again," the latter translation referring to the flowing of the Mississippi through the lake.

The old Red Lake Trail, used by fur traders and early settlers, passed through what now is Bemidji, continued north to the southern part of Lower Red Lake, and finally branched off into the War Road and Pembina trails. An Indian path skirted the shores of the lake, passed Chief Bemidji's shack on the east side of the Mississippi, and crossed the river on a sand bar at about the point where the highway bridge (US 2) now stands.

The first white settlement was established in 1866, but the town did not grow rapidly, and it was 30 years before Bemidji was incorporated. A fantastic boom that occurred in 1894 was largely responsible for its ultimate development. One summer afternoon a homesteader was strolling along the west shore of the lake. Suddenly his heavy boot kicked up some pebbles, and at his feet lay one piece of stone that shimmered and sparkled. He dropped to his knees and tremblingly uncovered many with the same glitter. That they were diamonds he had no doubt. The poor settler thought he was standing in the midst of a diamond field that would rival any in Africa! Delirious with joy, he rushed home and then without delay to St. Paul. When he could find no one else to identify the specimen with certainty, he sent it to an expert in New York City. He had no money, so he decided to confide his secret to a few friends. Their response to his enthusiasm was all that could be desired.

Quickly the homesteader was packed off to Bemidji with instructions to secure options in the name of the association on all land in the vicinity. This he did, and then, impatient at the long delay of the New York report, he bought the land outright. Mail was slow in those days, and the "potential Cecil Rhodeses" in St. Paul waited anxiously. At last the report came. It was elaborate and full of confusing detail, but one statement was clear— the stone was simple quartzite. The aspiring diamond kings now had on their hands large tracts of undeveloped land, land at that time remote from civilization and railroads.

The story has a happy ending, however. Before long, aided by a promotion scheme, they were able to recoup their losses, even enjoy substantial profits. A city grew—the city of Bemidji. From then on, development proceeded on a more substantial basis. Not far from the site were excellent stands of pine, and these soon brought loggers and lumber companies. In the winter of 1894-95, the first sawmill, hauled in by team, was set up on the shores of the lake. Then followed a period of wild lawlessness. In its heyday, Bemidji was one of the rowdiest sawmill towns in the Northwest. It grew steadily. In 1900 the population was 2,183; by 1910 it had increased to 5,099, and to 7,086 by 1920.

Today, Bemidji is not only the trade center for a very large territory, but also is becoming an industrial city whose sawmills have been replaced by woodworking plants, notably the rowboat factory of the Northland Boatcraft Company (US 2, one mile east). The David Park Company (Soo Line right-of-way bet. Minnesota and Irvine Aves.), the largest egg-packing plant in the State outside of Minneapolis, handles 250 carloads of eggs annually. Three creameries serve the region. Among the manufacturing establishments are a flour mill, a bottling works, a woolen mill, and a brick plant. Bemidji's mercantile institutions serve the entire northwestern part of Minnesota. The Interstate Power Company (212 3rd St.) owns a hydroelectric plant and supplies power to 60 towns. All the fuel required to generate this electricity is obtained from sawdust, the refuse of the Bemidji Wood Products Company (801 1st St.), a subsidiary of the power company.

In the heart of a recreational wonderland, Bemidji extends along the shores of beautiful Lake Bemidji. A few miles to the south lies Itasca State Park with thousands of acres of virgin forest and scenic Lake Itasca, headwaters of the Mississippi River. To the north is Red Lake on whose shores is the village of Ponemah, immortalized in the poetry of Longfellow. Cass Lake, with its historic, pine-covered Star Island (see Cass Lake), is but a short drive to the east. The entire region is famed nationally for its fishing. Practically all other seasonal sports are carried on.

The Paul Bunyan Carnival (see Brainerd) attracts thousands of visitors each winter, for Bemidji claims to be the birthplace of Minnesota's great legendary logger. On the shore of Lake Bemidji (foot 3rd St.) is an 18-foot steel and concrete statue of Paul, and also a statue of Babe, the Blue Ox, 14 feet high and 18 feet long.

The town owes much of its unusual beauty to its lake shore, and offers to residents and tourists fine beaches, 11 parks, and other points of interest. Three of the parks are State-owned, all sections of Lake Bemidji State Park (205 acres), established in 1923; two of the units (east Birchmont Rd.) are on the north shore, and the third (Lavinia Rd.) on the southeast.

The Fireplace of States, containing stone from every State in the Union, in the building of the same name, and a statue of Chief Bemidji, in Library Park (Bemidji Ave. bet. 3rd and 6th Sts.), invariably arouse comment. As to the origin of the statue, there are several theories; one is that it was carved from a solid log by a lumberman who had been befriended in childhood by the old chief. The State Teachers College (1300 Birchmont Drive), overlooking the lake, was opened in 1919 and is the most recently established in Minnesota.

Bena

Arrowhead Tour 3.
Railroad station: Great Northern, cor. US 2 and 1st Ave. W.
Bus station: Northland Greyhound Lines, Winnibigoshish Tourist Camp, cor. US 2 and 1st Ave. W.
Information service: Great Northern R. R. Station.

HERE THE PARTRIDGE FINDS A REFUGE

Bena (1,311 alt., 319 pop.), on the south shore of Winnibigoshish Lake, is in the heart of the Chippewa National Forest and on an Indian reservation (*see Cass Lake*). Its name is a Chippewa word meaning "partridge."

For centuries, Indians have lived between Leech and Winnibigoshish lakes, a region celebrated for its fishing and hunting. During the era of early fur trading, a number of posts were established in the area. When lumbermen began after 1850 to log off the surrounding pine, there is supposed to have been a settlement of some kind at the site of Bena. In 1890, the foreman of a lumber camp settled here, and the first store was opened in 1898.

Loggers and devastating fires depleted the wooded areas. In 1902, the Minnesota National Forest, now the Chippewa National Forest, was established to protect the remaining stands of virgin timber, and with the reforestation project the small settlement grew. The Bena Townsite Company platted and incorporated the village in 1910. Development has been slow, since there is no basic industry and the population is predominantly Indian. Farming has developed to some extent. The soil is suitable for raising potatoes and other root crops. Logging is carried on only under the supervision of the United States Forest Service.

Bena, an entrance to a vast lake and wilderness region, is an outfitting point for tourists and fishermen. Winnibigoshish, its name Chippewa for "miserable wretched dirty water," is one of the largest lakes in Minnesota and offers excellent fishing. Good roads lead from Bena to the many near-by resorts.

Big Falls

Arrowhead Tour 3.
Railroad station: Minnesota & International, State 6 junction with US 71 bet. 1st and 2nd Sts. S.
Bus station: Northern Transportation Co., Robinson Hotel, cor. 2nd St. N. and Division Ave.
Accommodations: Two hotels; tourist cabins; private rooms in homes.
Information service: Robinson Hotel.
Swimming: Municipal beach, South River Bank Rd., 1 mile N. E.
Rifle range: Big Falls Rifle Club, cor. 2nd St. N. and International Ave.

WHERE AXES STILL RESOUND

Big Falls (1,240 alt., 509 pop.), in the fertile valley and on the falls of the Big Fork River (*see Littlefork*), is the center of an agricultural area, though its main industry is lumbering.

Although Indians did not live in the immediate area, they paddled through it over the Sturgeon and Big Fork rivers to Rainy Lake and Lake of the Woods. Fur traders probably followed this route and, from evidence found, may have built a post for the Hudson's Bay Company on the Sturgeon River, a short distance from the site of Big Falls. At the turn of the century came lumbermen, attracted by pine forests and available water power. A railroad, the Big Fork and Northern, was built from Northome to Big Falls and, in 1905, was leased to the Minnesota and International, the Brainerd to International Falls branch of the Northern Pacific, by which it is still controlled.

Farming developed as the land was cleared. The deep, black, sandy loam is adapted especially to clover, potatoes, and small grains. Blueberries are an important summer crop. Good highways leading in all directions make markets easily accessible. Although farming is becoming more and more important, lumbering still leads. Quantities of pulpwood, cedar ties and poles are shipped each year, and many men are given employment in the logging camps in winter.

A hydroelectric power plant, owned locally by the Croswell Power and Light Company, has been built south of the falls of the Big Fork River, one-fourth of a mile from town.

Also along the Big Fork River is a forestry station and a fire tower, which with several office buildings and living quarters comprise the unit. It operates in conjunction with CCC Camp 4701, one mile east, and Center Camp in the Pine Island Forest, 25 miles west.

In 1939, US Highway 71 received black-top treatment from Big Falls to the Canadian border, and the work is being continued south to Big Falls.

The Byman Museum in Big Falls, with its Indian relics, arrowheads, pictures, oddities, and other interesting features, is open to the public.

East of town and on the Big Fork River is the Mission Covenant Church District Bible Camp, which is open for ten days each summer and offers vacation possibilities for rest, devotion, and instruction.

Game is plentiful and duck hunting is especially popular. There is good fishing in the three near-by streams: the Sturgeon, Big Fork, and Little Fork. This is a potential tourist center, for it is close to wilderness and lake regions, and there are numerous tourist parks and campgrounds.

Biwabik

Arrowhead Tour 4.
Railroad station: Duluth, Missabe & Iron Range, south end Shaw Ave.
Bus station: Northland Greyhound Lines, Main St. bet. Canton and Cincinnati Aves.
Accommodations: Municipal tourist camp, State 35, 0.5 mile E.
Information service: Village Hall, Main St. bet. Chicago and Canton Aves.
Golf: Esquagama Club (open to public), Esquagama Lake Rd., 6.6 miles S.; 18 holes.
Swimming: Municipal beach, municipal tourist camp.
Tennis: Horace Mann High and Washington Grade Schools, 2nd St. bet. Canton and Cincinnati Aves.
Rifle range: Biwabik Rifle Range, Co. Rd. 4, 2 miles S.
Annual event (exact dates very): Potato Show, September.

OLDEST VILLAGE OF THE MESABI

Biwabik (1,448 alt., 1,304 pop.), eclipsing some of the older range settlements and being eclipsed by some of the newer, has a virtual monopoly on Mesabi "firsts." Its name is an Ojibway term meaning "valuable," applied to iron ore by the Indians as mining developed.

In the valley of the historic Embarrass River, traveled by Indians and fur traders (*see Embarrass*), the site of the village evidently was an Indian camping ground, as several mounds near by would indicate. In 1865-66, prospectors rushing to the reputed gold fields of the Lake Vermilion district visited the site, for the famous Vermilion Trail passed through here. The "gold rush" was succeeded by the search for iron ore and the development of mines on the Vermilion Range; explorations, however, did not extend to this section at the eastern end of the Mesabi, and the Biwabik deposits lay dormant for a few years more.

In 1891, one of the Merritt parties (*see Mountain Iron*) was fine-combing the Biwabik district. While Indians were encamped about the location, watching proceedings with interest, a thrill of excitement spread. The miners had turned up high-grade blue ore at what later became the Biwabik Mine (north end Cincinnati Ave.). Samples were sent to Duluth on sleds. Almost simultaneously, ore was discovered at near-by locations, now the Cincinnati (part of the Biwabik), and the Hale and Kanawha mines (both abandoned). A town site was platted on Embarrass Lake, between the Biwabik and Hale mines, and named Merritt for the pioneers.

Mining developed and other town sites were platted, among them one just north of the Biwabik Mine and a mile west of Merritt. This was the embryo Biwabik. Its first supplies were carried from Mesaba Station, the nearest railroad point, about ten miles away. A story is told that a raft was floated down the Embarrass River from Tower to carry Biwabik's first beer. In comparison with Merritt, Biwabik grew slowly; nonetheless, by September, 1892, it was incorporated as a village.

In 1893, two events hastened the decline of Merritt and the rise of Biwabik: the Mesabi Range branch of the Duluth and Iron Range Railroad ran its line to Biwabik, and Merritt practically was destroyed by fire. All the inhabitants moved to Biwabik. As in other range towns, men from many different nations came to earn a living from the mines.

Biwabik was the first of the now existing Mesabi Range towns to be incorporated as a village, the first to be served by two railroads (the Duluth, Missabe and Northern and the Duluth and Iron Range vied in extending their lines to the rich mines); it had the first large mine on the Mesabi (the Biwabik), which was the first to be leased to an outside furnace (*see The Iron Ore Ranges*), and was the first to use a steam shovel in mining operations.

The only mine that has been working steadily in the last few years is the Biwabik, an open pit. With the shut-down of some of the mines, many miners turned to farming. Nationally known certified seed potatoes are grown around Biwabik. Dairying is carried on in the surrounding territory.

The town has two schools, with 24 teachers and 300 pupils. Horace Mann High and Washington Grade schools are equipped with a particularly fine swimming pool. Near-by Esquagama Lake (*see Arrowhead Tour 4*) offers facilities for all water sports and outdoor recreation.

Blackduck

Arrowhead Tour 3.
Railroad station: Minnesota & International, Railroad Ave. bet. 2nd and 3rd Sts. E.
Bus station: Northern Transportation Co., Main St. bet. Summit and Margaret Aves.
Accommodations: One hotel; municipal tourist camp, Pine Tree Park, Blackduck Lake Rd., 2.6 miles S. W., on lake shore.
Information service: Village Hall, cor. Margaret Ave. and Main St.
Swimming: Municipal beach, Pine Tree Park.
Tennis: Blackduck Independent School 60 (municipal), Margaret Ave. bet. 1st and 2nd Sts. E.

A HUNTER'S RENDEZVOUS

Blackduck (1,404 alt., 753 pop.), the most northern point in the Paul Bunyan Playground, Blackduck Lake and Blackduck River took their name from a species of duck common throughout the State.

A prehistoric Indian village once stood on the shores of Blackduck Lake, and some of the early fur traders may have visited this area, portaging over the Continental Divide, then traveling north on the Blackduck River.

The village developed as the center of a lumbering district about 1900. Pine, cedar, and balsam attracted many loggers, and sawmills were built. The Minneapolis Cedar and Lumber Company in 1903 operated a plant that sawed lumber and made ties and cedar posts. The Stoner Lath and Lumber Company was established in 1919; its mill, with a capacity of 100,000 feet in ten hours, specialized in balsam lath.

With the decline of the lumber industry, Blackduck turned to agriculture. The deep black and sandy loam soils proved suitable for diversified farming, and settlers took up land. Dairying and poultry and cattle raising developed. Blackduck's cooperative creamery, the oldest one in Beltrami County, was established in 1915 and ten years later had 200 patrons. In 1927, it constructed at a cost of $12,000 a modern brick and concrete plant, where annually 400,000 pounds of butter are produced. Blackduck is a shipping point for dairy products, livestock, clover seed, flax, and other farm produce.

Tourist trade is becoming important. The village is situated at the northwest corner of the Chippewa National Forest, and adjacent to it is the 75,732-acre Blackduck State Forest, established in 1935. Approximately 5,245 acres of the latter wilderness are covered by water. Game, especially bear, deer, ducks and partridge, being plentiful, hunters come to Blackduck in great numbers during the hunting season.

Blackduck Independent School 60 is a three-story brick building that has facilities for grade and high school pupils. The Village Hall houses the fire department, regarded as the most modern in any town of equal size in the State.

Such rapid strides have been made by the community that it claims to be the "livest small town in the Northwest."

Bovey

Arrowhead Tour 2.
Railroad station: Duluth, Missabe & Iron Range, and Great Northern (freight only), Scenic Highway bet. 4th and 5th Aves.
Bus station: Northland Greyhound Lines, cor. 3rd Ave. and 2nd St.
Accommodations: Two hotels; municipal tourist camp, Scenic Highway bet. 4th and 5th Aves., to Scenic State Park.
Information service: Whitmas Hotel, cor. 2nd Ave. and 2nd St.
Tennis: School Gardens (municipal), cor. 3rd Ave. and 4th St.
Annual event (exact dates vary): Bovey Farmers' Day, September.

FIRST VILLAGE OF THE CANISTEO DISTRICT

Bovey (1,354 alt., 1,355 pop.) was the first village in the Canisteo District, a region of sandy ore on the western Mesabi Range (*see Coleraine; Calumet; Marble*).

By the time it was settled, lumbering activities had denuded a large part of the wilderness. The discovery of the Mesabi was a familiar story, mining operations having been extended as far west as Hibbing. The district's nearest railroad station was Grand Rapids, from which teams could get only as far as the site of the present Bovey, which soon became headquarters and source of supplies for exploration parties.

The town grew and was incorporated as a village in 1904. Businessmen and storekeepers from Grand Rapids, eager for a new and fertile field, moved in, and the settlement further grew in 1907, when the Oliver Iron Mining Company's experiments in ore washing proved successful. The Canisteo Mine (west end 2nd St.), from which the district took its name, was opened, followed shortly by the Orwell (inactive). Then the Duluth, Missabe & Northern Railroad was extended to the village. The population now numbered 1,200.

The Bovey School (cor. 5th Ave. and 3rd St.), a $40,000 brick structure erected in 1906 and remodeled in 1919, and the new $75,000 Village Hall erected in 1934 denote the village's development.

Bovey's principal sources of income are the Canisteo, the Danube, and the Harrison mines, operated by three different companies. Recently it has become the center of a growing agricultural region with a large cooperative creamery.

Bovey is so close to Coleraine that the two have common trade and other interests, including recreational facilities. It is the gateway to the beautiful Scenic State Park.

Brainerd

Arrowhead Tour 3.
Railroad station: Northern Pacific, and Minnesota & International, 102 N. 6th St.
Bus station: Northland Greyhound Lines, 320 S. 6th St.
Local bus line: Brainerd Bus Line, 310 G St. N.E. and 1324 Mill Ave. N.E., offers service bet. northeast and southeast Brainerd.
Airport: Municipal, 13th St. S., 1.25 miles S.; hangar, 2 runways, service available.
Taxis: Two cab companies offer service within city limits and to surrounding territory.
Accommodations: Seven hotels; municipal tourist camp, cor. Chippewa and Laurel Sts.
Information service: Brainerd Civic Association; Junior Chamber Tourist Bureau.
Golf: Brainerd Country Club (open to public), US 371, 2 miles W.; 9 holes.
Swimming: Municipal beach, Lum Lake, junction US 210 and 14th Ave. N.E.
Tennis: Gregory Park, 400 N. 6th St.; Whittier School, 715 Holly St.; Harrison School, 1515 E. Oak St.; Lincoln School, 606 S. 6th St.

PAUL BUNYAN'S CAPITAL

Brainerd (1,213 alt., 12,071 pop.), Crow Wing County seat, is the home of the Northern Pacific's largest shops.

In 1870, the shining ribbon of Northern Pacific tracks crept across the State, connecting Duluth and Staples. Surveyors chose the site of the present Brainerd for the railroad to cross the Mississippi. A town was platted in 1871 by the Lake Superior and Puget Sound Company. When the question of naming the rapidly growing settlement arose, the Indians favored *Ogemagua,* meaning "queen" or "chief woman," in honor of Emma Beaulieu, a beautiful woman of that region. The president of the Northern Pacific, however, wanted his wife's maiden name, Brainerd, memorialized. Brainerd it became, though the Indians referred to it as *Oski-odena,* "new town." The first train, a special, reached the village March 11, 1871, but it was not until September that regular service was established.

Early descriptions tell of stands of virgin pine that bordered the Mississippi River. Nothing was more natural, therefore, than the rise of the lumber industry, and men from the East, especially Maine and New Brunswick, came to work and settle here. Brainerd grew so rapidly that in 1873 it was incorporated as a city. Like other thriving communities throughout the country, it was caught in the financial panic. The population decreased to less than one-half, the Northern Pacific closed its shops, and in 1876 the city charter was revoked and Brainerd was ruled by township government.

For ten years, the pioneers suffered the after-effects of the crash. Even Fate seemed against them. A shipment of food that somehow had been procured was "cast upon the waters" of the Mississippi when a bridge collapsed, and as much as could be salvaged was purloined by the Indians. Returning prosperity brought a boom to the town, and, in 1881, when the population was 14,000—the largest Brainerd ever has known—it was reincorporated as a city. In 1883, the Northern Pacific completed its line to the Pacific Coast. Railroad men went back to work, and lumbering prospered.

During the next few decades, the lumber industry saw its heyday. City and county bonded themselves heavily to induce a lumber company to put up a sawmill. The expansion demanded a branch railroad to haul pulpwood to mills and finished products to market, so in 1892 the Brainerd and Northern was built, extending northwest and terminating so casually no one knew where. In 1894, its tracks were relaid and extended to Hubert, and, in 1898, it was reorganized as the Minnesota and International. As such, a branch of the Northern Pacific, it operates today between Brainerd and the Canadian border. The depletion of the forests was followed by the discovery of iron ore in Crow Wing County, in which the entire active Cuyuna Range lies (*see Crosby*).

None of the hardships and turmoil of its history is reflected in present-day Brainerd. Its well-kept wide streets, modern public buildings, attractive parks, and progressive industries are worthy of a much larger town.

Railroading, which gave Brainerd its birth, still is its leading industry. The Northern Pacific shops (cor. A and 3rd Aves. N.E.), the largest·in the system, consist of a roundhouse and machine, boiler, blacksmith, tin, and car shops. As many as ten freight cars a day have been made in the shops. In West Brainerd is the Northern Pacific Tie Plant (cor. Florence and 10th sts. S.W.) where railroad ties and other timber products are given preservative treatment with creosote.

The Northwest Paper Company's mill on the south side (north and 4th Ave. N.E.) began, in 1935, to make wallpaper and, today, is one of the few such concerns in the State. Brainerd is the major trade center for Crow Wing County, and dairy products are handled by four creameries. A sash and door factory, a garment factory, a foundry, a bottling works, and other smaller industries employ many workers. On the east bank of the river (Emma St. bet. Park and Jenny Sts.) are the $300,000 power distribution plant and the $700,000 municipal water plant with its $62,000 demanganization plant. The latter, designed by Carl Zappfe, manager of iron-ore properties for the Northern Pacific, and built in 1932-33, removes iron and manganese from the water.

Brainerd has fine schools, including the Washington Senior and Junior High (810 Oak St.), built in 1929 at a cost of $450,000, and the Franklin Junior High (302 N. 10th St.), built in 1932 for $225,000. Special courses are offered in the Normal Department of the Franklin School, where a large number of pupils take post-graduate work. With funds provided by the Carnegie Foundation, this school at one time offered classes in pre-parental education—one of the pioneer experiments in this field.

The Crow Wing County Courthouse (326 Laurel St.) houses the Crow Wing County Historical Society Museum, considered one of the most complete of its kind in Minnesota. It contains Indian relics and handicrafts, a complete outfit of logging tools ot 1870, and pioneer farm tools and photographs. The Public Library (206 N. 7th St.), built in 1904 with a $12,000 gift from Andrew Carnegie, is housed in a $25,000 building and possesses 14,000 volumes. Brainerd's Armory (cor. 5th and Laurel Sts.), erected by the Works Progress Administration at a cost of $95,000, has one of the largest assembly halls in this part of the State. The Post Office (403 S. 6th St.), valued at $75,000, and City Hall (509 Laurel St.), with the same valuation, are modern structures.

State Forestry Service District Four, which embraces approximately 2,000,000 acres divided into six patrol districts, maintains headquarters in Brainerd. To the north (on US 371, adjoining the Brainerd Country Club) is the Crow Wing State Forest. This forest and the adjoining Mille Lacs and Bay Lake State forests cover a total of 229,000 acres.

Brainerd is the hub of a region that contains approximately 500 lakes, offering good fishing, canoeing, motorboating, and other types of recreation. There are more than 400 resorts, most of them with facilities for golf, horseback riding, tennis and archery; many remain open in the winter, and seasonal sports are very popular, particularly hunting. Annually in July, the fabulous Paul Bunyan holds sway for one week while citizens frolic. The men in and near Brainerd raise luxuriant beards to add a touch of realism to the occasion, and the program includes athletic contests, log-rolling, chopping, and sawing, canoe tilting, parades, and a sportsmen's show. The festival attracted 80,000 visitors in one year.

Buhl

Arrowhead Tour 2.
Railroad stations: Duluth, Missabe & Iron Range, US 169; Great Northern (freight only), north end Forest St.
Bus station: Northland Greyhound Lines, State St. bet. Jones and Mercer Aves.
Accommodations: Two hotels; municipal tourist camp, US 169, 0.25 mile S.
Information service: Village Hall, cor. Jones Ave. and Forest St.
Tennis: Municipal court, State St. bet. Mercer and Pennsylvania Aves.
Curling: Buhl Curling Club, cor. Jones Ave. and Mine St.

SPRINGS OF HEALTH AND PITS OF WEALTH

Buhl (1,500 alt., 1,600 pop.), one of the progressive smaller mining communities of the western Mesabi, might well have a Town Pump, for it boasts the "best drinking water in the United States," and, from reports of visitors, it is undoubtedly justified.

Although mining operations had begun on the western Mesabi in 1890, the iron-ore fever did not reach the vicinity of Buhl until some time later. Logging operations began in 1898, and in 1900 timber cruisers and loggers still were working in the region's stands of white and Norway pine. As they cleared the way, iron-ore prospectors appeared, and, in March, 1900, the Sharon Ore Company platted the 40-acre town site that was recorded as the "Plat of Buhl," in honor of Frank H. Buhl, a former president of the company. The new town was given encouragement when the Great Northern Railroad extended its line from Swan River. In 1901, Buhl was incorporated as a village.

Mining forged ahead as the chief industry. Men from many countries came to work in the mines, and today ten nationalities are represented. Of the foreign-born, Yugoslavs, Scandinavians, and Italians predominate. There are eight mines, most of them open pits. Only one, the Grant Mine, is operating at present.

The largest mine, the Wabigon (inactive), holds a record of low-cost operation. In three seasons, it was stripped of the overburden and 500,000 tons of ore by electric drag lines, with an average daily crew of five men, each handling approximately 250 tons per day. This was the first open pit on the Mesabi to be electrified, and its shovel, with a dipper capacity of 14 tons, was the largest ever used in an open pit.

In recent years, many of the miners have begun to farm, and much dairying is carried on in the surrounding area.

With the money derived from its mineral wealth, Buhl has erected modern municipal buildings and installed excellent public utilities. The Martin Hughes High School (cor. Jones Ave. and Wanless St.) is an imposing structure. The central part was constructed in 1911, and the two wings in 1918; the total cost was $1,750,000. The Martin Hughes High School is under the jurisdiction of School District 35, which includes Kinney (see Kinney), employs 40 teachers, and has an enrollment of 900.

The Fire Hall (cor. Johns Ave. and Forest St.), of brick and tile, one of the least expensive—it cost only $32,000—but most attractive public buildings in Buhl, also serves as a community center and provides public rest rooms, American Legion club quarters, Boy Scout rooms, and an auditorium.

The Public Library (Jones Ave. bet. Franz and Sharon Sts.) was built in 1917 of tapestry brick with terra cotta trimmings. The interior, finished in silver-gray oak, is decorated with two murals by Charles Rosenkranz. The library owns 14,850 volumes and receives 85 periodicals, and, in a district with a population of but 2,000, it has approximately 1,300 registered borrowers.

The Municipal Power Plant (cor. Jones Ave. and Mine St.) furnishes water and light and heats about 80 per cent of the buildings. Its pure, cold water, pumped from a 700-foot well, is free from the iron taste that is characteristic of most range water. St. Louis County Dispensary No. 2 (Jones Ave. bet. Sharon and Grant Sts.), built by Dr. A. W. Shaw and later bought by the county, distributes medical aid to the needy, but only emergency operations are performed.

Rose Tentoni, a soprano with the Metropolitan Opera Company, is a native of Buhl.

Calumet

Arrowhead Tour 2.
Railroad station: Duluth, Missabe & Iron Range, and Great Northern, 4th Ave. bet. Gary and Morgan Sts.
Bus station: Northland Greyhound Lines, cor. US 169 and Main St.
Accommodations: Three hotels.
Information service: Bliss Hotel, cor. Main St. and 1st Ave.
Golf: Swan Lake Golf Club (open to public), State 65, 5 miles E.; 9 holes.
Swimming: Twin Lakes Beach (municipal), Twin Lakes Rd., 2 miles W.

PIPE OF PEACE

Calumet (1,400 alt., 946 pop.) is the fourth of the villages in the Canisteo District.

The success of the Oliver Iron Mining Company's washing plant at Coleraine brought about the development of ore deposits in this section. In 1908, the Hill Mine (abandoned) was opened, and near it the Powers Improvement Company (Hibbing) platted the town site, cut and graded streets, and constructed a hotel. Lots sold quickly, and buyers, representing all trades, began to erect buildings. Incorporated as a village in 1909, its name is French (from the Latin *calamus,* meaning "reed"), the word used for the Indian peace pipe.

The community's chief source of income is the Hill-Annex Mine, operated on a State lease by the Inter-State Iron Company. It is one of the largest State-owned mines in Minnesota and is the most completely electrified open pit in the Lake Superior District. The ore is dug by electric shovels and loaded into cars pulled by electrically driven locomotives. Sight-seeing facilities have been provided. A two-unit crushing and screening plant is operated adjacent to the mine.

In the business section, which is several blocks long, a modern pendant-type white-way system was installed in 1939. The residential district extends almost to the mining property, and here curbs, gutters, and boulevards were built in 1939. In that same year, four blocks of blacktop streets were added.

Public utilities are modern. The Village Hall (cor. Main St. and 2nd Ave.) is constructed of light-tan brick in a modern design, and the Calumet

School (north end Main St.), up-to-date in every respect, accommodates pupils from the village and near-by mining locations.

Many recreational facilities are available at lakes within easy driving distance.

Carlton

Arrowhead Tour 3.
Railroad station: Great Northern, Northern Pacific, and Chicago, Milwaukee, St. Paul and Pacific, North St. bet. Industrial St. and Grand Ave.
Bus station: Northland Greyhound Lines, cor. Chestnut and N. 2nd Sts.
Accommodations: Two hotels; 2 sets of tourist cabins.
Information service: Village Hall, Chestnut St. bet. N. 3rd and 4th Sts.

BIRTHPLACE OF THE NORTHERN PACIFIC

Carlton (1,084 alt., 700 pop.), Carlton County seat, has one of the most interesting backgrounds of all the villages and towns in the Minnesota Arrowhead. Chippewa Indians inhabited the region at the time the site was visited by fur traders who traveled up the St. Louis River.

When the Military Road was cut from St. Paul to the head of the lakes in 1856, several town sites were platted, some of which had merely a paper existence, while others endured for only a brief time. Among the former was Komoko, a mile west of the present Carlton.

Then came 1870, a momentous year for the entire Arrowhead. A railroad, the Lake Superior and Mississippi, the first in the area, had been constructed from St. Paul to Duluth through the site on which Carlton later was to stand. On February 15, a group of heavily bearded men, including many notables, stood around a blazing bonfire at Komoko. Exultation and satisfaction glowed on their faces. In fervid oratory, one after another depicted the fabulous wealth inevitable now that the head of the lakes was to be linked with the "western empire." In chorus they praised the man among them who promised to make their fondest dreams possible: Jay Cooke, Philadelphia financier, "godfather" to the Northern Pacific. Had not he floated the life-giving bonds? Had not he arranged the purchase of a half-interest in that section of the Lake Superior and Mississippi's line from Duluth to this point? When the oratory had spent itself, officials of the road as well as representatives of Duluth and Superior solemnly dug a shovelful of dirt, placed it in a barrow, and wheeled it to a dumping ground. The Northern Pacific, first northern transcontinental railroad, was born.

These railroads opened up the forests of white pine, and sawmills sprang up throughout the region. One was near the junction of the railroads, where Carlton now stands, and about it a settlement grew. It was first platted as Northern Pacific Junction. It showed a healthy development and, on November 21, 1881, it was incorporated as the village of Carlton.

In the latter year, Northern Pacific Junction won a decisive battle. Thomson (*see Duluth Tour 4*) had been the seat of Carlton County since 1870. In 1886, Northern Pacific Junction started a petition to make itself the county seat. When Cloquet also entered a claim, a three-way fight ensued. In 1889, the county board decided to make a change. Since the signatures of 60 per cent of the voters of the county were necessary, Northern Pacific Junction appointed Sheriff Flynn, one of its citizens, to obtain them. Flynn had two advantages: Northern Pacific Junction already had voted a $10,000 bond issue for the construction of a new courthouse; a Cloquet lumber company opposed Cloquet's becoming a county seat because it feared this would raise the tax rate. The signatures were obtained. Then Thomson sought a writ to restrain action. The Northern Pacific Junctionites, however, were equal to the occasion. While Thomson's attorney was at St. Paul, they hauled the county records and safes from Thomson to their own village hall, after which Flynn lost himself in Duluth so he would not be available to serve the writ when issued. This strategy proved unnecessary, for the writ was denied, and without further excitement the county seat was changed to Northern Pacific Junction. Following this victory, the village changed its name to Carlton in honor of Reuben B. Carlton, pioneer of Fond du Lac, after whom the county also was named.

The village throve, with lumbering and railroading its chief industries. When lumbering began to decline, agriculture superseded it. Railroading still is the most important industry. Both the Northern Pacific and Great Northern maintain extensive yards here, including a Northern Pacific roundhouse.

Carlton County Courthouse (cor. Walnut and N. 3rd Sts.), of cream-colored brick, was built in 1922-23 at a cost of $250,000, and adjoins the county jail. The present Village Hall, also of cream-colored brick, was completed in 1937. The village is the administration center for Carlton County School District No. 2. Carlton Grade and High School (cor. Walnut and N. 4th Sts.) cost $140,000, and serves the educational needs, not only of the village, but also of the high school students of the entire district, as far east as Holyoke and as far south as Atkinson.

A wooden arch (junction US 61 and Chestnut St.) marks the upper entrance to Jay Cooke State Park (*see Duluth Tour 4*), a scenic area of 3,375 acres that offers unusual recreational facilities.

Cass Lake

Arrowhead Tour 3.
Railroad stations: Great Northern, cor. 5th Ave. and 1st St. (US 371); Minneapolis, St. Paul & Sault Ste. Marie, 3rd Ave. bet. 3rd and 4th Sts.
Bus station: Northland Greyhound Lines, Endion Hotel, cor. 2nd Ave. and 2nd St.
Accommodations: Three hotels; public campground—Norway Beach, Pike Bay Loop-Norway Beach Scenic Drive, 3.5 miles E.; Ojibway Beach, Pike Bay Loop-Norway Beach Scenic Drive, 2 miles S.E.
Information service: Cass Lake Commercial Club; Junior Chamber of Commerce.
Golf: Cass Lake Golf Club (open to public), US 371, 2 blocks W.; 9 holes.
Swimming: Norway Beach and Ojibway Beach (municipal).

PERMANENT HOME OF THE PINE

Cass Lake (1,323 alt., 1,904 pop.), on the western shore of Cass Lake and the largest community in Cass County, is the "capital of the Chippewa Nation."

The Indian name for the lake meant "the-place-of-the-red-cedars," and the first whites in the region called it Upper Red Cedar Lake. Fur traders reached it when following the Mississippi River in their search for pelts, and in 1794 Perrault built a post for the Northwest Fur Company at the entrance of the Red Cedar River. Although technically American territory, the region, for many years, was dominated by the English.

The search for the source of the Mississippi brought explorers, and in 1820 the Cass Expedition, headed by Territorial Governor Lewis Cass of Michigan, who was visiting all the Indian tribes under his jurisdiction, reached Upper Red Cedar Lake. Henry R. Schoolcraft, who accompanied Cass, did not agree with the leader's opinion that the head of the great river was Elk Lake. In 1832, Schoolcraft returned with his own expedition and discovered Lake Itasca, the true source; he renamed Upper Red Cedar Lake in honor of Cass.

Until the early 1850's, the area was covered with dense forests of pine, poplar, oak, cedar, maple, birch and spruce. After the organization of Cass County in 1851, lumbermen swarmed in, and logging camps and saw and planing mills sprang up. The Cass Lake Settlement grew, and the arrival of the Great Northern in 1898 hastened the platting of the town site in 1899. The coming of the Minneapolis, St. Paul and Sault Ste. Marie Railroad (Soo Line) in 1900 was also an important factor in the development of the community.

While lumbering was the community's mainstay for decades, with a sawmill and crating factory still operating, farming and dairying have been developed on the cut-over lands. Resorts, recreational facilities, and scenic beauty attract many visitors to Cass Lake.

The town borders the Chippewa National Forest. The U. S. Forest

Service Supervisors' Building (2nd St. bet. 6th and 7th Aves.) is a three-story log structure that adjoins the U. S. Government Nursery, the world's largest pine nursery (1939), supplying 64,000,000 seedlings annually to the Chippewa and other near-by national forests.

Cass Lake village is the headquarters of the Consolidated Chippewa Indian Agency (2nd St. bet. Central and 1st Aves.) that has jurisdiction over seven reservations, five of which are in the Minnesota Arrowhead: Leech Lake (*see Walker*), Fond du Lac, Nett Lake, Vermilion (*see Tower*), and Grand Portage (*see Arrowhead Tour 1*). The General Chippewa Hospital (US 371 and US 2 bet. 3rd and 4th Aves.) offers modern surgical and other medical care to the Indians.

The lake (Cass), six miles long and from three to five wide, is crossed by US 2, as it enters the village from the east. To the south is Pike Bay, an arm of the lake. Star Island, the largest of several islands in the lake proper, is one of the town's most interesting scenic and recreational spots. Shaped like a star, the island was mapped and described by Schoolcraft, who called it "Colcaspi" in honor of its three explorers (Schoolcraft, Cass, and Pike). In the middle of this 1,200-acre island and surrounded by a forest of virgin pine is Lake Windigo, formerly the domain of Chief Yellow Head (Ozawindib), Schoolcraft's guide, whose band of 160 lived on the northeast point, now O'Neil's Point, where the site of the old Indian village is visible.

Chisholm

Arrowhead Tour 2.
Railroad station: Duluth, Missabe & Iron Range, cor. 6th St. S.W. and S. 1st Ave. S.W.
Bus station: Northland Greyhound Lines, Nelson Hotel, 230 W. Lake St.
Taxis: Three cab lines offer services within city limits and to surrounding territory.
Accommodations: Two hotels; municipal tourist camps—Chisholm Memorial Park, Lake St. (US 169), 2 blocks W.; Chisholm City Park, east end Longyear Lake.
Information service: Chisholm Tourist Information Bureau, Chisholm Community Bldg., 316 W. Lake St.
Recreational facilities: Chisholm Community Bldg.
Golf: Chisholm Public Golf Course, 8th Ave. N., 1.25 miles N.W.
Tennis: Chisholm Memorial Park, Independent School District No. 40 Courts, cor. 1st St. S.W. and 3rd Ave. W.
Rifle range: Chisholm Memorial Park.
Annual events (exact dates vary): St. Louis County Rural Winter Frolic, March; Chisholm Homecoming, first week in September; Junior Chamber Trade Exposition, November.

WHERE EVERYBODY GOES TO SCHOOL

Chisholm (1,492 alt., 7,487 pop.), on the shores of Longyear Lake, claims to be the geographical center of the Minnesota Arrowhead, the

Continental Divide being one mile north. Chisholm lays proud claim to having proportionately the highest school enrollment of any community in the State.

Frank Hibbing (*see Hibbing*), while prospecting on the Mesabi Range, came upon a lumber camp here in 1891. With the discovery of rich iron-ore deposits in 1892, the site took on dramatic significance. It changed almost over night into an unorganized mining community and remained such for nearly a decade, during which neighboring sections were bought by explorers and businessmen. Among these was A. M. Chisholm for whom the town was named.

In 1901, this group organized the Chisholm Improvement Company, platted the town site and had it incorporated as a village. In November, the *Chisholm Herald* was established by W. E. Talboys, who also was Chisholm's first postmaster and mayor. The following year, Chisholm established its first school, a frame building, and employed two teachers. During these first two years, the Catholics and the Methodists erected log churches, the Methodist being built in two weeks by men who contributed their labor. In six years, the population had grown to almost 6,000, and the town had an imposing city hall, four blocks of business houses, two banks, an electric-lighting plant, sewers, two weekly newspapers; and it had been necessary to plat two more residential districts.

On September 5, 1908, a brush fire fanned by a shifting wind swept down upon the village. In what seemed but a few minutes, Chisholm was practically destroyed. Fortunately no lives were lost, and rebuilding began immediately. Within nine months, 70 fireproof brick buildings had been constructed as well as a municipal water plant and five miles of mains. Within a year the town again was flourishing, its population growing steadily. Chisholm became a city in 1934.

Forty-five mines, five of them now active, have shipped ore from the district. The largest is the Godfrey (Godfrey Rd., 0.25 mile south), an underground; the Shenango, with a maximum depth of 400 feet, is the deepest open-pit iron mine in the world. Next to mining, the chief source of revenue is dairying, an independently owned creamery providing an outlet for the dairy farms in the vicinity.

As high as 46 per cent of the total population has made use of Chisholm's educational facilities at one time. The Senior High, of iron-spot brick and white Bedford stone, the Junior High, of soft-toned brick in Tudor-Gothic design, and the Washington Grade, of pressed brick and Superior sandstone, all on the main campus (cor. 3rd St. S.W. and 3rd Ave. S.W.), are among the most elaborate school buildings in the Arrowhead.

Chisholm's foreign born, of whom Yugoslavs, Finns, and Italians predominate numerically, have had a profound influence upon the city's development. With the aim of speeding Americanization, the schools have placed much emphasis upon English and reading courses; their work along these lines has attracted educators throughout the country. The schools also are keenly interested in discovering and fostering latent talent. Hundreds of pupils receive instruction in instrumental music, for which special teachers are provided. Forensic and other teams repeatedly have won State and district championships.

The Chisholm Public Library (300 W. Lake St.) has one of the largest collections of foreign-language books in northern Minnesota, with ten tongues represented. The only Serbian Orthodox Church in the Arrowhead outside of Duluth is St. Vasselj (cor. W. 3rd St. S.W. and 3rd Ave.). The Chisholm Community Band gives concerts twice a week in City Park during the summer. Numerous district contests and four State championships have been won by the Chisholm Drum and Bugle Corps.

Chisholm City Park has a bathing beach and a small zoo. Chisholm Memorial Park provides complete recreational facilities.

Cloquet

Arrowhead Tour 4.
Railroad station: Great Northern, and Northern Pacific, north end Arch St. (Union Station).
Bus stations: Northland Greyhound Lines, 218 Arch St.; 1108 Cloquet Ave.
Airport: Municipal, old State Forestry Rd., 2.5 miles S.W.; two 2,500-foot runways, boundary markers, no hangar; no servicing; fuel and oil available by telephoning Cloquet.
Taxis: Two cab lines offer service within city limits and to surrounding territory.
Accommodations: Four hotels.
Information service: Cloquet Commercial Club, 124 C Ave.
Recreational facilities: Civic Recreational Center, 508 Cloquet Ave.
Golf: Cloquet Golf Club (open to public), west end Laurel St.; 9 holes.
Tennis: Court adjacent to Civic Recreational Center.
Rifle range: Cloquet Gun Club, south foot 2nd St.

MODERN PHOENIX

Cloquet (1,189 alt., 7,304 pop.), the largest municipality and only city in Carlton County, was built on the ashes of a sawmill town at the rapids of the St. Louis River and named for a tributary of that stream. Its main industry is the manufacture of wood products (*see International Falls*).

The fur traders' route from the head of Lake Superior to northern and western posts passed through the site of the town (*see Floodwood*). Long before a village was platted, lumbermen had been attracted by the potential water power of the St. Louis River and had established a lumber camp in the coniferous forests. A sawmill was hauled here in 1870, and one was built in 1878, by Charles D. Harwood, above the big falls at Thomson (*see Duluth Tour 4*).

Settlements grew around the mills, and in 1880 one was platted under the name of Knife Falls. When the plats were filed in 1883, the name was changed to Cloquet. At the time of its organization the following year, two lumber companies owned every building in the village. Interested only in white pine, the lumbermen first operated close to the streams beside which they had placed their sawmills, then built roads and railroads farther and farther into the forests.

Gradually uses were found for other varieties of wood, and by 1900 a paper mill was erected. Cloquet was in the path of the great forest fire of October 12, 1918 (*see Moose Lake*), which devastated much of Carlton and St. Louis counties. The fire, whipped by a 70-mile gale, advanced with incredible speed, burning an area of approximately 1,500 square miles. More than 400 persons perished, and the property loss was estimated at $25,000,000. Although Cloquet was destroyed completely, quick action by railroad officials and others saved the lives of all but five persons in the city. Undaunted by the catastrophe, Cloquet began at once to rebuild, and today a modern, attractive city stands on the ashes of the old Cloquet.

The fire changed the course of local industries. Constant cutting had pushed the forests back so far that hauling was expensive, and the holocaust had destroyed great areas of standing timber. By this time, manufacturing interests were developing processes to utilize wood hitherto considered waste, and Cloquet turned to the manufacture of wood products.

In the Wood Conversion Company's plant (cor. Arch St. and A Ave.; *visiting hours: daily 10:30 a. m. and 3:00 p. m., Sat. 10:30 a. m.*) Balsam Wool, Nu-Wood, and other insulating materials are made. The first steps in the manufacture are much the same as in making paper. The fibrous material is fire-proofed, dried, then put through forming, drying, and finishing machines. For Balsam Wool, the fibers are shredded and dried again and blown through cement-laden air onto a moving screen, where they form a mat half an inch thick that finally is covered with water-proofed kraft paper.

The Northwest Paper Company (east end Arch St.; *visiting hours: daily 9:30 to 10:30 a. m., and 2:30 to 3:30 p. m.*) is one of the largest, most complete and progressive mills of its kind in the United States. In 1938, it produced all the paper used in postage stamps up to the 15-cent denomination. In normal times, more than 1,000 persons are employed in the making of book, ledger, drawing, writing, and bond paper. Surplus pulp is sent to other paper mills.

The Berst-Forster-Dixfield Company (cor. Cloquet Ave. and 18th St.; *no visitors*) manufactures clothespins, matches, and toothpicks (*see Deer River*).

Saw and planing mills of the Northwest Company (Information: General Office, cor. Arch St. and C Ave.) finish most of the lumber used in the Cloquet plants.

Dairying is advancing rapidly, and many creameries have been established. The Cloquet Cooperative Society operates one of the largest cooperative retail stores in North America.

The Cloquet Ranger Station, serving District Three, patrols the northern half of Carlton County and the southern half of St. Louis County. Established in 1911 with a single tower, at the present site of the University of

Minnesota Experimental Station (*see Arrowhead Tour 3*), today the district has six strategically located towers that vary in height from 80 to 100 feet. The station, of peeled logs, is a veritable museum and displays on its walls many relics, including logging tools, old firearms, and settlers' equipment.

Cloquet is modern in every respect, with four school buildings, a fine public library, ten churches, a privately owned hospital, and two theaters. It is adjacent to the Fond du Lac Indian Reservation, established by the Treaty of La Pointe (*see Copper and Gold Exploration*).

Coleraine

Arrowhead Tour 2.
Railroad station: Duluth, Missabe & Iron Range, and Great Northern (freight only), cor. Gayley and Corey Aves.
Bus station: Northland Greyhound Lines, cor. Roosevelt and Clemson Aves.
Airport: Municipal, south end Powell Ave., no service.
Accommodations: One hotel; village tourist park, cor. Hartley and Congdon Aves.
Information service: Arcana Hotel, cor. Roosevelt and Morrison Aves.
Swimming: Municipal beach, Elizabeth Ave., 2 blocks S.
Tennis: Village Courts, Powell Ave., 6 blocks S.
Skiing: Slide, cor. Lakeview Blvd. and Hovland Ave.
Annual events (exact dates vary): Ski Tournaments, January and February.

THE MODEL VILLAGE

Coleraine (1,343 alt., 1,325 pop.), the second of the villages in the Canisteo District, was planned and built by the Oliver Iron Mining Company for its employees. Overlooking Trout Lake, it is known as the "Model Village."

Timber cruisers and loggers were the first known white men to visit the site. Lumbering, however, was not responsible for the district's development.

Prospectors located iron-ore deposits, which, because of their sandy admixture, were left untouched until the Oliver Iron Mining Company had successfully experimented in the concentration of ores. Thereupon, the company purchased properties in the district and agreed to a minimum annual output in return for a low royalty rate.

In 1905, John Greenway, district superintendent of the Oliver, visiting the shores of Trout Lake, planned a town and named it Coleraine for Thomas F. Cole, then president of the company.

While the mining company proceeded with its concentration experiments, the richer deposits were worked. The Duluth, Missabe and Northern Railroad was extended into Coleraine in 1906. The Canisteo Mine (*see Bovey*) was opened in 1907, and the first shipment made in 1909. Coleraine was incorporated as a village in 1909.

In 1910, work was begun on a huge iron-ore concentrator, the Trout Lake Washer, in which the sand is separated from the ore by log-washers, and chips, rock, and other foreign materials are removed. Other concentration plants were built, and the region began a rapid development.

The first building erected was the Greenway High School (Kerr Ave. bet. Cole and Roosevelt Aves.), which since 1922 has housed the Itasca Junior College, the only collegiate school in Itasca County. Trout Lake's "Model Village" is very attractive, with well-planned streets and artistically grouped buildings.

The Itasca Ski and Outing Club, among the most active in the Minnesota Arrowhead, has produced several national champion riders. Coleraine is a gateway to Scenic State Park.

Cook

Arrowhead Tour 3; 4.
Railroad station: Duluth, Winnipeg & Pacific, old State 11 bet. Owens Ave. and River St.
Bus station: Northern Transportation Co., cor. River St. and 3rd Ave.
Accommodations: Two hotels.
Information service: Ardin Bros. Hotel and Cafe, cor. River St. and 3rd Ave.
Annual events (exact dates vary): Winter Frolic, February; Cook Community Fair, August.

HOME OF THE CHRISTMAS TREE INDUSTRY

Cook (1,320 alt., 470 pop.), to the north of the iron-ore belt and beyond the Great Laurentian Highland Divide, lies in the fertile valley of the Little Fork River and, at one time, was covered with dense forests.

Lumber companies were responsible for the opening of this vast region north of Virginia. The Virginia Lumber Company, eventually absorbed by the Virginia and Rainy Lake Lumber Company, began to lay a logging road through the district in 1902 and, by 1906-07, offered services to the Canadian border. The first settlers, arriving in February, 1902, were 18 Finnish and Scandinavian homesteaders who came from the iron ranges, where they had worked in mines and woods. Mining had not been to their liking, so they had left for the Little Fork Valley, probably attracted by the similarity of its climate and countryside to their native lands. They settled by squatters' rights, but soon many abandoned their claims because most of the town site was swamp.

The site was accessible only by way of Tower and Lake Vermilion.

In winter, travelers could go direct by stage across the lake and through the timber. In summer, however, though two steamboats operated from Tower to Joyce's Landing, a distance of 30 miles, the rest of the trip to the settlement had to be made either on foot or horseback.

The town site was not surveyed until 1904-05. It first was called Ashawa, Chippewa for "across the river." Since this name was similar to that of a community in southern Minnesota, it was changed in 1910 to Cook, in honor of a partner in an early lumber firm, the Cook and O'Brien Company. As the land was cleared, agriculture developed. The Little Fork Valley has proved to be one of the best clover lands in the country. More farmers came to the community, but it was not until 1926 that Cook was incorporated as a village.

Dairying is the leading industry. The Little Fork Creamery Association, a cooperative, has constructed a $10,000 plant. Diversified farming is carried on in the surrounding region, with hay and small grains the leading crops. The Cook-Marvel Flour Mill grinds home-grown wheat into flour and middlings. The Cook seed cleaning plant is one of the best of its kind in the State.

From Cook, evergreen trees are shipped to all parts of the United States for Christmas use. The Christmas tree industry is carried on in other parts of the Arrowhead, but Cook is its headquarters. The A. J. Thomas Company, employing approximately 75 men during the holiday season, sprays the trees with green or silver paint to prevent the needles from falling. In one year, this concern shipped about 80 carloads. The Northern Evergreen Company ships more wreaths and roping than trees, farmers supplying cedar and balsam boughs and ground pine.

MacDonald's Quarry (US 53, seven miles south) is one of two known deposits of green granite in the world. Anderson's Quarry (Co. Rd. 75, 1.5 miles west) produces a dark, grayish-blue granite (*see Ely; Mountain Iron*).

Cook is an outfitting point for sportsmen, being near Lake Vermilion and several other popular resort lakes, including those on the international boundary.

St. Louis County School 114 (junction State 1 and 3rd Ave.), completed in 1932 and supervised by the St. Louis County Board of Education, is one of the largest and most modern rural schools in the State.

Crosby

Arrowhead Tour 3.
Railroad station: Minneapolis, St. Paul & Sault Ste. Marie (freight only), 101 1st St. N.E.
Bus station: Northland Greyhound Lines, 110 W. Main St.; 427 Mesaba St.

Accommodations: Two hotels; municipal tourist park, 311 3rd Ave., S.W., on Serpent Lake.
Information service: Spaulding Hotel, 1-5 W. Main St.; Information Booth—across street from bank—operated June, July and August.
Golf: Cuyuna Range Golf Club, US 210, 6 miles S.E. (Deerwood); 9 holes.
Swimming: Municipal beach, south end 1st Ave. S.W.
Tennis: Municipal courts, south end 1st Ave. W.; Central High School Courts, cor. 3rd St. S.W. and 7th Ave. W.
Annual event (exact dates vary): Cuyuna Range Fair, August.

THE CUYUNA CAPITAL

Crosby (1,200 alt., 2,954 pop.), on the western end of Serpent Lake, is the largest municipality on the Cuyuna Range, and its chief industry is iron-ore mining.

The name Cuyler Adams is associated even more closely with the Cuyuna Range than are those of Stuntz and Merritt with the Vermilion and the Mesabi respectively. The name Cuyuna is compounded of the first syllable of Cuyler, and the name of his dog, Una.

Crosby was platted October 5, 1905, by George H. Crosby, a mining man of Duluth, whose name it bears. The small community was supported solely by mining activities. As the number of mines increased, the town developed and, in 1910, was incorporated as a village.

Mines, most of them open pit, surround it; the Evergreen is the largest. Observation towers provide extensive views of the colorful chasms and impressive machinery units. Hauled by chugging locomotives over a spiral path of steel tracks, hopper-bottomed cars mount from the iron-ore pits. Strippings accumulate, and ore stock piles await shipment on Great Lakes boats to steel mills in the East. The Minnesota Sintering Company plant, operated by the Evergreen Mines Company, beneficiates the ore by washing, screening, and sintering.

Pulpwood is of some importance, and in the surrounding area are large stands of fine timber. Farming is developing rapidly, and Crosby and other near-by communities furnish a market for farm and dairy products. A cooperative creamery association was established in 1922. Turkey raising and berries have proved profitable enterprises.

The village is well planned, having wide streets, modern public buildings and utilities. The Central High School serves Crow Wing County School District No. 51, which includes Ironton (*see Ironton*) and maintains the Crosby-Ironton Junior College (White Line Rd., 0.15 mile south). The Crosby Armory, of brick and tile, built in 1917 at a cost of $25,000, is the headquarters of the Third Battalion, Two Hundred and Sixth Infantry, Minnesota National Guard.

More than 300 beautiful lakes, offering fine black bass, crappie, sunfish, pike, and pickerel fishing, are within easy driving distance, and these, together with many near-by vacation resorts, attract large numbers of tourists.

Deer River

Arrowhead Tour 2; 3.
Railroad station: Great Northern, 1st St. bet. Herbert and Center Aves.
Bus station: Northland Greyhound Lines, Miller Hotel, cor. Herbert Ave. and North St.
Taxis: Miller Hotel offers service within village limits and to surrounding territory.
Accommodations: One hotel.
Information service: Junior Association of Commerce Information Booth.

PUBLIC SCHOOL DORMITORY

Deer River (1,294 alt., 987 pop.), the largest town in western Itasca County, is noted for its unusual school facilities.

The history of the town begins with logging and lumbering activities that started about 1870 in the surrounding pine forests and reached their peak between 1885 and 1900 (*see Grand Rapids*). During early operations, logs were easily dragged to Deer Lake and floated down Deer River. As the lumbermen penetrated deeper into the timber, getting the logs out became a real problem, and the Itasca Lumber Company constructed a logging railroad. Later this road was rerouted to the present Deer River, first called Itasca City, a point to which the Duluth and Winnipeg (absorbed by the Great Northern) had been extended. In 1897, the logging company lengthened its road, and the Great Northern advanced westward to connect with its line at Grand Forks, North Dakota.

In the same year, Deer River, with a population of 191, petitioned for village incorporation, and in 1898 the privilege was granted. Among the early settlers was Frank L. Vance, the first storekeeper. He was not only Itasca County's Baron Munchausen, but also its "Wild Rice King," as he was among the first to popularize the grain that grows so abundantly in near-by lakes.

A highway between Deer River and Grand Rapids was built in 1907, the first of a wide network. By this time, lumbering was on the decline and agriculture was developing. Two creameries are supported by Deer River and adjacent territory.

Today, Deer River is the trade center for the surrounding farming region. The lumber industry has not disappeared altogether; 8,000 cords of pulpwood are shipped annually to the Berst-Forster-Dixfield Company in Cloquet (*see Cloquet*), and the Armour Company has a box factory in the adjoining village of Zemple.

The tourist trade is developing rapidly. Deer River is the eastern gateway to the Chippewa National Forest and is the base of supplies for sportsmen and vacationists heading for the lakes and the forest. State foresters have headquarters here (Division St., junction US 2 and State 6).

The Deer River Grade and High School (1st St. bet. Laura and Darwin

Aves.), erected in 1920, maintains a dormitory and pays a portion of the students' living expense, being one of the few public schools in the United States that offer such advantages. Accommodations for 100 boys and girls from the rural sections of School District No. 6 are provided.

Duluth

Arrowhead Tours: Starting point for all Arrowhead Tours.
Railroad stations: Great Northern, 506 W. Michigan St. (Union Station), 630 W. Michigan St. (freight only); Northern Pacific, 506 W. Michigan St., 114 S. 5th Ave. W. (freight only), 220 S. 20th Ave. W., cor. 54th Ave. W. and Wadena St., foot Commonwealth Ave. (freight only); Chicago, Milwaukee, St. Paul & Pacific (freight only), all Northern Pacific stations; Duluth, Missabe & Iron Range, 506 W. Michigan St., cor. 27th Ave. W. and Railroad St., 527 E. Gary St. (freight only), 400 S. 15th Ave. E., 47th Ave. E. bet. Superior St. and London Rd., 60th Ave. E. bet. Superior St. and London Rd.; Duluth, South Shore & Atlantic, 602 W. Superior St. (Soo Line Station), foot Ramsey St.; Minneapolis, St. Paul & Sault Ste. Marie, 602 W. Superior St., foot 10th Ave. W. (freight only), foot Ramsey St.; Chicago, St. Paul, Minneapolis & Omaha, 200 S. 5th Ave. W. (Omaha Station), 232 S. 5th Ave. W., foot 8th Ave. W. (both freight only); Duluth, Winnipeg & Pacific (Canadian National), 200 S. 5th Ave. W., 232 S. 5th Ave. W. (freight only), 5431 Grand Ave.
Bus stations: Northland Greyhound Lines, 507 W. Superior St.; Curtis Hotel, 2001 W. Superior St.; 5601 Grand Ave.
Interurban bus line: Duluth-Superior Bus Co., 2631 W. Superior St., offers service between Duluth and Superior, Wis.
Local bus lines: Duluth-Superior Transit Co. and Duluth-Superior Bus Co. offer service within city limits and to Superior.
Sightseeing busses: Northland Greyhound Lines offer trips along Skyline Parkway (*see Duluth Tour 4*); Duluth-Superior Transit Co. charters busses; its busses also meet ship passengers at docks (foot 6th Ave. W.) for specific tours or trips.
Airport: Williamson-Johnson (municipal), Stebner Rd., 5.5 miles N.; *port of entry;* 2 runways, 1 beacon; hangar, service facilities.
Seaplane base: Duluth Boat Club, 1000 Minnesota Ave.; *port of entry.*
Taxis: Six taxicab lines offer service within city limits and to surrounding territory.
Passenger boats: S. S. *Noronic* and S. S. *Hamonic,* operated by the Northern Navigation Division of the Canadian Steamship Lines, 428 W. Superior St., sail between Duluth, Port Arthur and other points on Lake Superior, Sarnia, Ontario, and Detroit, during 2½ summer months; S. S. *Alabama,* Georgian Bay Line, operated by the Chicago, Duluth and Georgian Bay Transit Co., 334 W. Superior St., sails between Duluth and Buffalo, N. Y. during July and August; these ships dock at Northern Pacific Dock No. 4, foot of 6th Ave. W.; S. S. *Winyah,* H. Christiansen & Sons, 20 W. Morse St., sails between Duluth, Grand Marais and Isle Royale.
Excursions: Northland Greyhound Lines; all cab companies; boat trips to Fond du Lac and around harbor and Minnesota Point.
Speed boats: Scenic Boat Service, foot 5th Ave. W., and Duluth Boat Club offer speed rides, Duluth-Superior Harbor tours, and charter trips to points on Lake Superior.
Accommodations: Ninety hotels; lodging houses; tourist homes; municipal tourist camps—Brighton Beach, cor. London Rd. and S. 62nd Ave. E., on Lake Superior; Indian Point, cor. Pulaski St. and 68th Ave. W., on St. Louis Bay.
Information service: Minnesota Arrowhead Association, Hotel Duluth, cor. 3rd Ave. E.

and Superior St. (all-year bureau); Curtis Hotel, 2001 W. Superior St., and Ramsey St. bet. 56th and Grand Aves. (summer bureaus); Duluth Chamber of Commerce, Medical Arts Building, 324 W. Superior St. (all-year bureau); 430 W. Superior St. (summer bureau); Duluth Automobile Club, 600 W. Superior St.

Golf: (Municipal) Enger Park, cor. 19th Ave. W. and Rogers Blvd., 18 holes; Lester Park, 600 Lester Park Rd., 18 holes; (open to public) Northland Country Club, cor. 39th Ave. E. and Superior St., 18 holes; Ridgeview Golf Club, cor. Alden Ave. and Faribault St., 18 holes; Riverside Golf Club, cor. 85th Ave. W. and Grand Ave., 9 holes; Lakewood Golf Club, US 61, 9 miles N.E.; 9 holes.

Swimming: Municipal beaches—Minnesota Point, 10th St. (lake side), 39th St. (bay side), 43rd St. (lake side); St. Louis River, foot 63rd Ave. W., foot Commonwealth Ave.

Tennis: Municipal playgrounds (consult City Recreation Dept.).

Baseball: (Professional) Duluth Athletic Park, cor. 34th Ave. W. and Superior St.; Municipal All-Sports Stadium (also football), 35th Ave. W. and 2nd St.

Curling: Duluth Curling and Skating Club, 1328 London Rd.

Hockey: Duluth Curling and Skating Club.

Skating: Duluth Curling and Skating Club; municipal outdoor rinks.

Boating: Duluth Boat Club; Duluth Yacht Club, 2730 Minnesota Ave.

Skiing, tobogganing: Municipal jump, slide (2 runways), cor. 15th Ave. E. and Rogers Blvd.; Fond du Lac Winter Sports Center—325-foot ski jump hill, with a 62-foot scaffold, and toboggan slide; also cross-country ski runs.

Bowling: Alleys in different parts of the city.

Riding: Lester Park Paddock, 5908 E. Superior St.; Fond du Lac Winter Sports Center; Deer Path Lodge (open to public), Jean Duluth Rd.

Rifle range: Northwestern Gun Club, Rice Lake Rd., 1 block S. junction Blackman Ave., trap- and skeet-shooting (Wednesday evenings, Sunday forenoons during summer), rifle shooting (Sundays).

Annual events (where dates vary only months are given): Winter Sports' Week, Northwestern Annual Curling Bonspiel, Beaux Arts Ball, January; Annual Ski Tournament, February 15; Swedish Midsummer Day, June; Annual Regatta, July; Northwest Annual Trophy Shoot, October; Charity Ball, November.

THE SUMMER CITY

Duluth (alt. 602 at lake level, 1,100 at Skyline Parkway; pop. 101,065) extends 26 miles along the western tip of Lake Superior, the bays of Superior and St. Louis, and the lower St. Louis River. The city mounts rocky bluffs to the north and to the south it takes in a six-mile sand bar, Minnesota Point (*see Duluth-Superior Harbor*).

An aerial lift bridge spans the Duluth Ship Canal and connects Minnesota Point with the mainland. This sand bar is a natural breakwater for the Duluth-Superior Harbor, into which the St. Louis River empties. To the west and south are the iron, steel, and cement plants. Beyond them are the densely wooded islands of the St. Louis River. Along the opposite shore extends the Wisconsin city of Superior.

Duluth, known as "the air-conditioned city," has splendid facilities for year-round outdoor recreation. Lake Superior and St. Louis Bay afford opportunities for swimming, fishing, sailing and yachting, speed boating and ice boating. Natural parks have been developed, and throughout the city there are supervised playgrounds, as well as tennis courts, golf links, skating rinks, and ski and toboggan slides. In fact, there are facilities for almost every outdoor sport.

For beginnings it is necessary to turn back to 1752, the first year that shelters more substantial than tepees are known to have been erected for winter-living at Fond du Lac. These wintering houses, used by the fur traders, probably were located on Minnesota Point. At or near here, Marie Josephe Tellier, daughter of the half-breed fur trader Jean Baptiste Tellier, was born and christened in 1753, so the *Mackinac Register* states. While the fur trade passed through successive hands, a little settlement grew about the stockade at what now is Fond du Lac, though without suggestion of permanence.

In 1832, the Schoolcraft expedition passed here (*see Cass Lake*), and with it was Reverend W. T. Boutwell, who delivered the first sermon in English in the region; 40 persons came to hear him, he tells. Two years later, he returned and married Hester Crooks—the first local wedding. Hester's mother was a half-breed Chippewa, her father, Ramsay Crooks, was a famous trader and director of the American Fur Company. To assist Boutwell in his missionary work came Reverend Edmund F. Ely, a Presbyterian (*see Arrowhead Tour 3*), who built and established a school at Fond du Lac in 1834—Duluth's first—and married one of its teachers, who was part Indian.

In 1852, George R. Stuntz (*see The Iron Ore Ranges*) arrived on a visit, under orders from Surveyor General George B. Sargent, whose headquarters were at Davenport, Iowa. So impressed was he with the possibilities of this wilderness country that he returned the following year to stay. It is he who usually is credited with being Duluth's first settler. In 1854, the north shore of Lake Superior was opened to white settlement, and prospectors poured in. One contemporary observer wrote: "First came the mining men seeking copper, and they were quickly followed by the town site developers, and with these came the lumbermen and the sawmills."

In 1855, the head of the lakes had a little boom all its own. Without title to the land, speculators sold lots and platted towns, most of which never existed except on paper. Oneota, platted in 1855, was one that survived to become part of the modern city. Its post office, the city's first, was opened in 1856, with E. F. Ely, former missionary, in charge, and served from 30 to 40 persons. Another town, the present-day Fond du Lac, had 14 buildings. Still another was Duluth, as yet unplatted and unnamed. Its business was represented chiefly by George Nettleton, whose claim was located near what now is Second Avenue East and Superior Street, where, having taken out a trader's license, he carried on a little barter, and by George Stuntz, who had established a small post near his dock on Minnesota Point. Robert Jefferson built the first frame house, intended as a hotel, about 500 feet north of the present ship canal. Guests, however, were slow in coming, and eventually he left. Nevertheless, in its time the house was the scene of much entertaining, and it was here that the St. Louis County District Court held its first session.

In October, 1855, the first election at the head of the lakes took place in George Nettleton's "claim shanty," its purpose being to choose a delegate to Congress from the Minnesota Territory. Most of the 105 voters lived in Superior, not in Duluth, and were Minnesota residents only by right of claims they had taken for speculation.

The following spring the town site was platted by the Nettletons, Jefferson, Joshua B. Culver, and Orrin W. Rice. To identify it, these gentlemen appealed to Reverend Joseph G. Wilson, a missionary living across the bay, promising two city lots in exchange for a name they would accept. He immediately began a search for old books—a task none too easy in a frontier settlement. At last, in a translated account of early French explorers, he learned of the romantic Daniel Greysolon, Sieur du Lhut, and "Duluth" the town became.

The decision aroused no great excitement. Few there were who thought the place of any importance; all looked to Superior as the future metropolis, and even little Oneota outranked the embryo city. The infant, however, began to grow. Sawmills were springing up, and the surrounding hills were stripped of their pine. In May, 1857, the village was incorporated. The first warehouse was erected on the lake shore, at what now is Third Avenue East, and was used as the county and Federal building, post and land offices, and commercial headquarters. That same year Fond du Lac, Portland, Belville, and Oneota also were incorporated—all, like Duluth, shore settlements, destined to be absorbed.

The first setback was the national panic of 1857. Hard-pressed creditors demanded money, and pioneer builders paid as long as they could. Most of the families left. For those who remained, fish and potatoes were the mainstay. Of meat, sugar, and wheat there was none. Not a store remained open in Duluth, and all supplies, such as there were, came from Superior. To add to the sufferings of the depleted community, an epidemic of scarlet fever affected practically every home.

In 1865, only two houses were occupied, and the post office had been appropriated by Portland. Duluth appeared destined to become a "ghost" town. Notwithstanding, a scattered few maintained an unshakable faith. They seemed vindicated when, before the year had ended, gold-bearing quartz was reported from Lake Vermilion (*see Copper and Gold Exploration*), and prospectors rushed in.

Jay Cooke, the great financier, then decided to make Duluth the terminus of his railroad (*see Carlton*). "The lifeless corpse, touched by the wand of Jay Cooke, sprang full-armed from the tomb," and during 1869 the population jumped to more than 3,000. Lumbermen came from Maine. Sawmills that shot up like mushrooms were unable to meet demands. The construction of the railroad progressed. Soon many ships were passing in and out of the harbor, bringing supplies, taking lumber and wheat.

General George B. Sargent and George C. Stone, as agents for Jay Cooke, opened the first bank. The firebrand Thomas Foster founded the *Duluth Minnesotian*, a weekly, the town's first newspaper, exuberantly proclaiming this "the Zenith City of the Unsalted Seas." Even more important to many was the building of the famous Clark House, under General Sargent's direction. Until it burned in 1881, this rambling hostelry that stood on Superior Street between First and Second Avenues West was the scene for all outstanding banquets, balls, and parties—a community house and social refuge for those who strove to maintain a semblance of dignity and good manners during the rowdy seventies, when Duluth, according to one realistic observer, was a "haphazard, scraggly and repellent settlement— a combination of Indian trading-post, seaport, railroad construction camp, and gambling resort, altogether wild, rough, uncouth, and frontierlike."

In 1870, Duluth obtained a city charter, electing Joshua B. Culver as first mayor. Duluth was opened to the outside world by two railroads: the Lake Superior and Mississippi and the Northern Pacific. About this time the latter built its famous "Immigrant House" for the stream of foreigners who, mostly from Montreal, were compelled to stop over on their way to the Dakotas. The huge frame structure on pilings at what now is the corner of Fifth Avenue West and Michigan Street sheltered as many as 700 at one time.

During the seventies and early eighties, the community experienced its growing pains. Brawls and gang fights accompanied political struggles; a "vigilance committee" was succeeded by police, the first officer of whom absconded. Churches, schools, and utility franchises multiplied. Commercially, Duluth was charging forward at top speed. The Government took over the famous ship canal in 1873, two years after the city had cut it through, and the first of its extensive improvements was under way. Duluthians were confident that their town would become "the leader of the western continents."

The bubble collapsed, and Duluth received a second setback. Jay Cooke, its godfather, went broke. It is doubtful that any other community in the country felt the 1873 panic with more devastating effect. Faith had been boundless; now "it was as though the very heavens had fallen." Thousands were forced to seek work elsewhere, and the population dropped in a few months from 5,000 to 1,300. Interest on bonds issued in the frenzy of expansion no longer could be paid, and, unable to face the appalling debt, the city surrendered its charter, burned canceled bonds, and reverted to village status.

Faith, however, had not died. After all, the panic had not affected natural resources. Forests still were to be cut and railroads to be built. Moreover, western Minnesota and the Dakotas were raising the world's greatest crops of wheat—grain for which this port was the logical outlet. The builders dug in. Elevators and warehouses sprang up along the docks. Ten years after the panic, with mining developing on the Vermilion Range, Duluth, although yet a village, with a population of 14,000, had a Grand Opera House, hospital, telephone exchange, street railway, chamber of commerce, and board of trade, and had become one of the greatest grain ports in the world, able to boast that its 1886 handling of 22,000,000 bushels was "nearly eight million bushels more" than that of Chicago.

By 1887, the greater part of the bankrupt city's debts having been redeemed, it was reincorporated as a city, prepared once again to "take her place among the great cities of the world." The following years were extremely active; real estate and building prospered beyond all expectations, and an extensive public works program got under way.

The first serious labor trouble occurred in 1888. A strike of laborers and sawmill workers was arbitrated by the mayor, and wages were increased to $1.75 per day. The Federated Trade Council of Duluth was organized in November, 1889, and received a charter from the American Federation of Labor.

When iron ore was shipped to Two Harbors from the Vermilion Range in 1884, Duluth was still thinking in terms of lumber and wheat. Not until the Merritts had opened the Mesabi Range, in 1890 (*see Mountain Iron*), and made their first shipment, in 1892, did it become iron-ore conscious. Duluth became the center for mining supplies, every one sharing the excitement of the prospecting expeditions that departed and returned almost every day.

Another panic was on its way, and in 1893 Duluth received its third setback. Small mining ventures failed, and many individual fortunes were lost, but the city as a whole found itself better off than at first had seemed possible, thanks to the uninterrupted operations of lumbering. This time, faith in its destiny hardly wavered.

Iron-ore shipments increased year by year. At the turn of the century, the population had risen from 33,115 to 52,969, despite national depression. Even a confirmed pessimist could not have denied that prospects were rosy. Miles of new steel docks were required for handling iron ore and coal, and large grain elevators gave a dramatic note of modernity to the bustling city. Lumbering, as the dominant economic factor, was gradually replaced by iron-ore mining, and, up to this day, iron ore is the backbone of the region's wealth.

The diversity of raw materials in the region and the unlimited shipping facilities have brought many jobbers and manufacturers.

Large numbers of foreign-born workers were attracted by the rapidly developing industries. The census of 1930 listed 24,929 foreign-born whites in Duluth. The two largest groups were Scandinavian, 10,976, and Finnish, 3,040. Others were: Yugoslavs, 782; French-Canadians, 872; Italians, 787; Poles, 1,280; Germans, 1,070. Before the depression of 1929, there were 1,000 Negroes, but their number has decreased to about 400.

Not long ago, all foreign groups had their respective churches in which services were held in native languages. Today only the following churches conduct regular services in foreign tongues: St. George's Serbian Orthodox Church, St. Elizabeth's for Croats and Slovenians, St. Peter's for Italians, St. Josephat for Poles, and St. John Baptiste for French-Canadians. English services predominate in the Swedish, Norwegian, Danish, and German Lutheran churches.

The children and grandchildren of the foreign born are beginning to take conscious pride in the literature, drama, dancing and handiwork of their forbears, and numerous small groups, notably among Scandinavians and Poles, have been formed to revive and keep alive old country customs and traditions.

Duluth is still looking forward to the fulfillment of an old dream—the completion of the Great Lakes-St. Lawrence seaway. The ambition has become so insistent that opponents say derisively, "It is the old maid city, looking under her bed every night for an ocean."

Duluth takes great pride in its famous chain of boulevards, which make up the 29 miles of scenic drives along the Skyline Parkway; its finely developed park system; its educational facilities, which include a State Teachers College, 35 grade, six junior and three senior high schools, and one junior college, together with the Roman Catholic parochial system of 12 elementary, four high schools, and one college; its Civic Symphony Orchestra, and its many other civic and cultural achievements.

In its brief lifetime Duluth has accomplished much, but knows it is far from having exhausted its possibilities. It possesses ample storage facilities. At the head of the Great Lakes and the hub of eight railroads, it has easy access to far-flung markets. Its adjacent territory is rich in raw materials—iron ore, timber, grain, and dairy products; its St. Louis River provides hydroelectric energy. As the summer city of the continent, it attracts an increasing tourist trade each year.

TOUR 1

LAKE SHORE, 9 miles.

N. from Superior St. on Lake Ave. N.

WASHINGTON JUNIOR HIGH SCHOOL (L), a conspicuous red brick building at 305 Lake Ave. N., has a broadcasting system built by students, with radio, phonograph and public address microphones.

Retrace on Lake Ave. N. to 2nd St.; L. on 2nd st.

Built of Minnesota brownstone, DULUTH CENTRAL HIGH SCHOOL (L) bet. Lake Ave. and 1st Ave. E., is surmounted by a rectangular tower 230 feet high; with 2,700 students it is the city's largest high school. A Foucault pendulum 75 feet long hangs inside the tower, its slow, regular vibrations spanning the face of a graduated circle once every 24 hours.

R. on 2nd Ave. E.; L. on Superior St.

HOTEL DULUTH (L), 227 E. Superior St., 14 stories high, was completed in 1925 of light brick and terra cotta in Italian Renaissance design.

The MINNESOTA ARROWHEAD ASSOCIATION, organized to further the civic, commercial and social interests of the Minnesota Arrowhead country, has its headquarters on the mezzanine floor of the hotel.

L. on 3rd Ave. E.; R. on 2nd St.

At 502 E. 2nd St. is the five-story MILLER MEMORIAL HOSPITAL (R), for needy patients, built of cream-colored face brick and native Minnesota limestone. Endowed by the late Andreas H. Miller with a trust fund set aside in memory of his son, the hospital stands on the former home-site of the late Judge Josiah D. Ensign, prominent pioneer jurist, who came to Duluth in 1870. In his 64-year legal career, Judge Ensign served as both city and county attorney, and mayor of Duluth. He was elected district judge in 1889, a position he held until his retirement in 1921. Judge Ensign was held in high respect; of him William Howard Taft once remarked, "It was worth going all the way across the country to see him." He died in 1924.

R. on 7th Ave. E.; 7th Ave. E. becomes Washington Ave.

A bronze plaque and samples of iron ore, jasper and greenstone at the intersection of Washington Ave. and 1st St. mark the SITE OF THE OLD VERMILION TRAIL, a favorite route of Indians and pioneers. Washington Ave. here follows the original trail as surveyed by George R. Stuntz.

L. on Superior St.

The KITCHI GAMMI CLUB (L), 831 E. Superior St. (*private*), is the oldest club in Duluth.

A STATUE OF JAY COOKE, railroad promoter of post-Civil War years, stands within the triangle (R), cor. 9th Ave. E.; Henry M. Shrady was the sculptor.

L. on 9th Ave. E.; R. on 3rd St.

Aus Franzoesischem Geschuetz—"Made from a French gun" is inscribed on the 900-pound bell that hangs in the belfry of ST. PAUL'S EVANGELICAL CHURCH (R), 932 E. 3rd St. The bell, donated to the church in 1874 by Kaiser William I, was cast from a cannon used by the French in the Franco-Prussian War.

R. on 10th Ave. E.; L. on London Road (US 61).

The *Leif Erikson of Bergen,* a replica of the explorer Leif Erikson's dragon ship, stands as a permanent memorial in LEIF ERIKSON PARK (R), bet. 8th and 14th Aves. E. The little craft was sailed from Bergen, Norway, on May 23, 1926 by Captain Gerhard Folgero of Sannesjoen and a crew of three. The ship was on exhibition at the Sesquicentennial Exposition in Philadelphia, and later at the dedication of Leif Erikson Drive in Chicago. It arrived in Duluth June 23, 1927.

L. on 12th Ave. E.

Established twenty-seven years ago, the LITTLE THEATER (R), 6 S. 12th Ave. E., was one of the first in the country. Its colorful annual Beaux Arts Ball is a leading social event; seven plays are staged each winter, and summer courses are given, covering all phases of dramatic production.

Retrace on 12th Ave. E.; L. on London Rd.

In the red-brick and concrete ARMORY (L), 1305 London Rd., are the permanent headquarters of the One Hundred and Twenty-Fifth Field Artillery (U. S. National Guard), the Minnesota Naval Militia, and the Tenth Battalion U. S. Naval Reserve. In its auditorium, seating 3,500, the 65-piece Duluth Civic Symphony Orchestra offers its annual series of concerts. The orchestra was organized in 1925 on a $15,000 budget, which gave out after three years. In 1933, a new orchestra association was formed, and now many concerts are given jointly with the Civic Symphony Choral Society, organized in 1935, with 250 voices. The orchestra's first radio broadcast was given in 1934.

At 1328 London Rd. (R) is the two-story DULUTH CURLING AND SKATING CLUB BUILDING. Nearly 300 feet in length, the building has a roomy amphitheater, with skating and curling rinks.

L. on 21st Ave. E.; R. on Superior St.

A made-over barn seating 200 is now the CHILDREN'S THEATER (L), 2215½ E. Superior St. Its opening performance, *The Wizard of Oz,* was given in 1928, when the group was still a branch of the Little Theater.

Aladdin and His Lamp was the first production as a separate organization in its own building, then at 114 N. 15th Ave. E.

L. on 23rd Ave. E. to 2nd St.; L. to 19th Ave. E.

THE CHILDREN'S MUSEUM (L), 1832 E. 2nd St., is housed in a rebuilt residence donated by Mrs. Archibald Chisholm. The exhibits were moved there in 1935, after five years in Salter School. With a wide range of exhibits (*open daily except Sun. and holidays 9 a. m. to 5 p. m., Wed. and Sat. 9 a. m. to 12*), the Museum is a valuable visual aid in the education of public school students. Outstanding relics are a paint brush used by Rosa Bonheur and a glass once belonging to George Washington. Children, assisted by the staff, study the displays, draw pictures and make notes.

R. to E. 4th St.; R. on E. 4th St. to Hawthorne Rd.

Tudor-style EAST JUNIOR HIGH SCHOOL (R), cor. 4th St., completed in 1927, offers an inspiring view of Lake Superior from its classroom windows.

R. on Hawthorne Rd. (31st Ave. E.); L. on Superior St.

Picturesque 35-acre CONGDON PARK (R and L), bet. 32nd and 33d Aves. E., is cut by driveways on both sides of Tischer Creek.

A modern, comprehensive playground, ORDEAN FIELD (R), cor. 40th Ave. E., covers 28 acres, has a field house and a brick, 7,000-seat stadium, football and baseball fields, tennis courts, cinder track and jumping and vaulting pits.

R. on 60th Ave. E. (see DULUTH TOUR 4); L. on London Rd.

The only hatchery under Federal control on Lake Superior, the U. S. FISH HATCHERY (R), 6008 London Rd., is the largest in Minnesota. Open daily from 8 a. m. to 5 p. m., the hatchery has young trout which can be seen in outdoor troughs, and pike and whitefish in indoor tanks. Both the Federal Government and the State Conservation Department cooperate in the work, raising fingerlings from eggs taken from State hatcheries or purchased from other States. Most of the species indigenous to the Great Lakes and to the smaller lakes and streams of this locality are distributed from the hatchery.

Cross Lester River Bridge.

(L) BRIGHTON BEACH MUNICIPAL TOURIST CAMP.

KITCHI GAMMI PARK (L and R), bet. E. Lester Blvd. (61st Ave. E.) and Lakewood Rd. (81st Ave. E.) has 153 acres of native trees and several species foreign to Minnesota, with excellent picnic sites along the lake.

(Retrace to 60th Ave. E. and continue on Duluth Tour 4.)

TOUR 2

MINNESOTA POINT, 7 miles.

S. from Superior St. on Lake Ave. S.

At 301 Lake Ave. S. (R) is the MARSHALL-WELLS COMPANY, in the heart of the wholesale district. This company is the largest hardware jobber and distributor in the Northwest.

The U. S. ENGINEERS OFFICE (L), 600 Lake Ave. S. (*open daily except Sun. and holidays 9 a. m. to 4:30 p. m., Sat. 8 a. m. to 12*), has jurisdiction over the Duluth district, from the Lake Superior watershed east to Iroquois Point, just above the Soo Locks. It supervises navigation and power development and oversees all phases of river and harbor improvement. It is a cream brick and gray stone building. On the lawn is a bronze PLAQUE which memorializes Du Lhut's crossing of Minnesota Point in 1679.

Unique among Duluth's structures is the AERIAL LIFT BRIDGE, spanning the Duluth Ship Canal at the base of Minnesota Point. It uses the overhead structure and towers of the original Aerial Bridge, built in 1905 from plans drawn by C. A. P. Turner of Minneapolis. Its electrically operated car, suspended from cables, could carry a load of six vehicles and 350 passengers across the channel. It was replaced by the present structure in 1930, having by that time became inadequate to accommodate the growing traffic to and from the mainland. This new bridge, which operates as a lift span, is 510 feet long, with a vertical clearance of 138 feet to permit lake steamers to pass into the bay. Two 450-ton concrete blocks counterbalance the 900-ton lift. The electrically-operated machinery is extremely rapid in its action, raising the span 120 feet in 55 seconds.

Throughout the shipping season, tourists congregate here to watch boats pass under the bridge. Three hoarse whistle blasts from an approaching ship evoke three answering blasts from the bridge, the entire span rises as the counterweights descend, and the ship slides ponderously through the canal.

MINNESOTA POINT (Park Point) across the bridge, is a community on an island, with a modern school, homes and stores, community building and fire department. This curiously-formed strip of land has small, constantly-moving sand dunes, which often bury vegetation. Legend has it that a storm once blew away an Indian graveyard near the far end of the Point. (*See Folklore and Festivals.*)

R. on 10th St.

With docking accommodations and storage space for boats up to 50 feet in length, the DULUTH BOAT CLUB occupies a large frame building at the west end of 10th St. Julius H. Barnes, nationally-prominent Duluthian, donated the natatorium.

Retrace on 10th St.; R. on Lake Ave. S.

The U. S. COAST GUARD STATION AND WATCHTOWER (R), 1225 Lake Ave. S. (open), fronts on both lake and harbor.

Retrace on Lake Ave. S.; L. on 12th St.

At the west end of 12th St. is the U. S. NAVAL BASE.

R. on Minnesota Ave.

The MINNESOTA POINT DEVELOPMENT PROJECT (R and L), 4300 Minnesota Ave., is a well-equipped recreation center covering 200 acres. It sustains 400 varieties of plant life including Black Hill spruce, Scotch pine and birch trees. Here is Duluth's most popular bathing beach, with a modern bathhouse completed in 1939. Duluthians prefer to swim on cloudy, windy days, and like best to go in during or soon after a northeaster; though the atmosphere may be cool, the wind will have carried the warmer surface water in shore.

Development of the Minnesota Point recreation area on a comprehensive plan already has provided an athletic field, a large amusement center, picnic grounds with tables to accommodate several hundred persons, and parking space for hundreds of cars. A weather-beaten brick ruin, RE-MAINS OF THE FIRST LIGHTHOUSE at the head of the lakes, stands at the southern tip of Minnesota Point. R. H. Barrett, who clerked in George Stuntz's trading post (*see Duluth*), was its first keeper. He blew an old-fashioned warning horn to signal approaching boats in foggy weather. The spot is still the "zero" point for marine surveys.

TOUR 3

WESTERN DULUTH, 19.6 miles.

N. from Superior St. on Lake Ave. N.; L. on 2nd st.

The DULUTH PUBLIC LIBRARY (R), cor. 1st Ave. W. (*open week days 9 a. m. to 9 p. m., Sun. and holidays 2 to 9 p. m.*), occupies a two-story building of Port Wing stone in Grecian design, erected in 1902 through funds donated by Andrew Carnegie. The city's first library consisted of a small collection in a reading room at 106 West Superior Street. This served for 20 years, but was destroyed by fire in 1889. A year later, a library board was appointed and $500 appropriated for books. The library was opened in the old Masonic Temple building, corner Second Avenue West and Superior Street, where it was housed until the present building was erected. In addition to the main library, there are seven branches and numerous stations. Of its more than 150,000 volumes, many are in foreign languages.

R. on 3rd Ave. W.

The FIRST METHODIST EPISCOPAL CHURCH (L), 215 N. 3rd Ave. W., of red sandstone in a Gothic design, had the first chimes in the city. The carillon consists of ten bells that can be played in two keys.

Retrace on 3rd Ave. W.

The WOLVIN BUILDING (L), cor. 1st St., houses the offices of the United States Steel Corporation and its subsidiaries.

The DULUTH BOARD OF TRADE (R), cor. 1st St., is the largest export market of spring wheat in the United States and one of the two largest primary spring wheat markets; it handles grain from Minnesota, the Dakotas and Montana.

R. on Superior St.

The MEDICAL ARTS BUILDING (L), 324 W. Superior St., 14 stories high, of white stone, is Duluth's most modern office building. The main entrance is two stories high with black marble pilasters on each side. Lobby walls are marble, floors black granite, and the ceiling is finished in golf leaf.

The DULUTH CHAMBER OF COMMERCE occupies most of the second floor of the building.

R. on 4th Ave. W.; L. on 1st St.

The DULUTH HERALD AND NEWS-TRIBUNE PLANT (L), 420 W. 1st St., publishes Duluth's two largest daily newspapers.

Three impressive granite buildings make up the CIVIC CENTER (R), bet. 4th and 6th Aves. W.: the FEDERAL BUILDING (built 1930), ST. LOUIS COUNTY COURTHOUSE (1910), and CITY HALL (1927). The center was designed by Daniel H. Burnham of Chicago.

On the fourth floor of the Courthouse is the St. Louis County His-torical Society Museum and Library (*open daily except Sun. and holi-days 8 a. m. to 4 p. m., Sat. 8:30 a. m. to 12*). Here the visitor may examine maps, books, war records, and artifacts of St. Louis County. There is a valuable display of Indian paintings and sketches by Eastman Johnson, who visited the Arrowhead country back in the 1850's.

The SOLDIERS' AND SAILORS' MONUMENT, *Patriotism Guard-ing the Flag,* stands in front of the Courthouse. It was designed by Cass Gilbert.

L. on 5th Ave. W.; R. on Superior St.

The DULUTH AUTOMOBILE CLUB (L) is at 600 W. Superior St.

The NORTHERN BIBLE SOCIETY (R), 715 W. Superior St. (*open daily except Sunday 9 a. m. to 5 p. m.*), has a notable display of Bibles and Testaments, the private collection of the Reverend Henry Ramseyer, secre-tary of the society. The collection includes a first edition of the King James Bible, 1611; a seventeenth-century Hebrew scroll written by hand on 52 sheepskins; an Archbishop Cranmer's Bible, 1541; a Luther's Bible, set in Gothic type, 1560. Represented in the collection are 550 languages, 60 alphabets and phonetic scripts.

Where Mesaba Ave. intersects Superior St. was once an INDIAN VILLAGE.

Duluth gabbro with glacial markings outcrops at POINT OF ROCKS (R), bet. 8th and 14th Aves. W. At 10th Ave. W. and Michigan St. is a tunnel driven 375 feet through solid rock. It was opened many years ago by a group of men who hoped to find silver in paying quantities. The project finally was abandoned, but not until after an estimated $30,000 in silver and copper had been taken out.

L. on Garfield Ave. (16th Ave. W.).

The PEAVEY-DULUTH GRAIN ELEVATOR (L), 900 Garfield Ave. (*not open to visitors*) is the largest in Duluth, its 310 tanks having a capacity of 7,500,000 bushels. It is equipped to unload 180 cars a day. Most of Duluth's elevators are in this district.

The INTERSTATE BRIDGE (*toll: cars, 10¢; passengers, 5¢*), leading to Superior, Wisconsin, was completed in 1898. Both highway and railway traffic are carried over the 2,142-foot structure.

Retrace on Garfield Ave., which becomes Piedmont Ave. at Superior St.; L. on 1st St.

The CENTRAL BAPTIST CHURCH (R), 2001 W. 1st St., has a removable suspension roof, anchored by cables to concrete piers in the ground, and a sanctuary floor that can be tilted forward or backward on a central axle.

R. on 25th Ave. W.; L. on 3rd St.

LINCOLN PARK (R), bet. 25th and 26th Aves. W., is a favorite picnic ground with fireplaces, benches, tables and shelters. Its 38 acres, overlooked by timbered slopes, follow the banks of Miller's Creek. At the Scandinavian Midsummer Festival, held here each year in June, picturesque folk songs and dances in native costume are performed.

Steel and concrete IRON ORE DOCKS (L) (*open by permission from offices in the Wolvin Building*) invade St. Louis Bay from the Duluth, Misabe and Iron Range Railroad trestle, cor. 33rd Ave. W. During one 24-hour period in 1926, these docks loaded 225,258 gross tons of iron ore into 26 vessels. Newest of the docks is 2,304 feet long, with 384 loading pockets.

R. on 44th Ave. W.

DENFELD HIGH SCHOOL (L), bet. 4th and 6th sts., an H-shaped red-brick and gray stone building in English Gothic style, is the most modern high school in Duluth. DULUTH JUNIOR COLLEGE, in the same building, offers a three-year academic course. Many of the city's athletic events are held in the adjacent PUBLIC SCHOOLS STADIUM.

Retrace on 44th Ave. W.; R. on Grand Ave. (3rd St.); L. on 46th Ave. W.

The SITE OF THE MERRITT MEMORIAL METHODIST CHURCH, cor. Superior St. (R), pioneer place of worship in Oneota, is marked by a bronze plaque. Erected in 1892, the old church was under the pastorate of the Reverend Lucian F. Merritt, one of the seven Merritt brothers who discovered iron on the Mesabi (*see Mountain Iron*). The building was razed in 1921, when the congregation joined another to form a new church.

Retrace on 46th Ave. W.; L. on Grand Ave.

The combination BRIDGE AND STATION of the Duluth, Winnipeg and Pacific Railroad (Canadian National) (R), 5431 Grand Ave., is an elevated frame building. The waiting room and loading platform are on the railway level, three stories above the ground.

L. on 55th Ave. W. (Central Ave.); L. on Raleigh St.; R. on Lesure St.

The INLAND COAL DOCK (R), capacity 750,000 tons, is one of several lining St. Louis Bay and River.

The ARROWHEAD BRIDGE (*toll: cars, 10¢; passengers, 5¢*), end of Lesure St., is a long jackknife span leading to Superior, Wisconsin. It is 2,200 feet long, was completed in 1926.

Retrace on Lesure St., Raleigh St.; L. on 59th Ave. W.

The ZENITH FURNACE PLANT of the Interlake Iron Corporation (L), south foot 59th Ave. W., supplies gas to the city.

Retrace on 59th Ave. W.; L. on Raleigh St.; R. on 63rd Ave. W.

The KLEARFLAX LINEN LOOMS, INC. (L), cor. Grand Ave. (*open daily except Sat. and Sun. 10 a. m. to 2 p. m.*), the only plant of its kind in the country, manufactures carpets and other floor coverings from linen, wool and cotton yarns.

L. on Grand Ave.

FAIRMOUNT PARK, 56 acres, cor. 72nd Ave. W. affords a fine natural setting for the DULUTH ZOO (R) (*open daily 8 a. m. to 8 p. m.*). Larger animals are kept in the round Big House, while the Little House, crescent in shape, is for smaller animals. Included in the collection are monkeys, zebus (sacred cattle of India), elephants, guanacos, giraffes, polar, grizzly, and brown and black bears, in addition to native Minnesota animals. Oddly enough, jungle animals such as the lion and tiger appear to have become acclimated to the cold northern winters; most of them spend some time outdoors the year around.

The suburb RIVERSIDE (L), bet. Calais and Gogebic Sts., developed around a ship-building plant which operated there during the first World War.

Grand Ave. becomes 93rd Ave. W.; 93rd Ave. W. becomes Arbor St.; R. on 88th Ave. W.

MORGAN PARK was built by the Minnesota Steel Company as a model city for its employees.

One of Minnesota's largest factories, the AMERICAN STEEL AND WIRE COMPANY PLANT (L), 1434 88th Ave. W. (*guides on application at office or gatehouse*), is a subsidiary of the U. S. Steel Corporation. The plant is open to visitors, who may watch the transformation of Minnesota iron ore into steel, steel into wire. From the East comes the coking coal, from Michigan comes the limestone, and manganese, so essential to manufacture of high-grade steel, is imported from abroad.

Before crude iron ore can be turned into a finished product, it has to go through many refining and shaping processes. The first step is to purify the ore; the preliminary action is to remove the oxides at a temperature of 3,000 degrees F., the melted ore being drawn from the bottom of the furnace. The purification process continues in open-hearth furnaces, and the iron is drawn off to cool into ingots. These ingots are heated again and forced by enormous pressure into blooms, heavy sections which are later lengthened and made thinner in the billet mill. By this time, the product is beginning to assume its final shape—flat, round or square bars, small angles, T-bars, reinforcing bars or fence posts—depending upon the process it goes through in the merchant mill. Wire is made in the rod mill. After passing through various solutions, it is tempered in ovens, and then drawn through dies of different sizes. The finished product may be any one of 900 different sizes of nails, or more than 100 kinds of woven or barbed wire.

An interesting Indian legend is associated with SPIRIT ISLAND (L), which lies in Spirit Lake, a widening of the St. Louis River east of Morgan Park. While the Sioux and the Chippewa were at war, long before the coming of the whites to the territory, the son of a Sioux chieftain eloped to the island with a Chippewa princess. A pursuit party, landing there next morning, could find no trace of the lovers. The savages, attributing their disappearance to supernatural causes, named the place Spirit Island.

R. on Idaho St., L. on Hilton St.; Hilton St. becomes Commonwealth Ave.

The UNIVERSAL ATLAS CEMENT COMPANY PLANT (L), 2402

Commonwealth Ave. (*visitors by appointment*), another subsidiary of the U. S. Steel Corporation, started operation in 1916.

R. on Gary St.; L. on 104th Ave. W.

A red brick Byzantine-style building, ST. GEORGE'S SERBIAN ORTHODOX CHURCH (L), 1218 104th Ave. W., is unique in that the liturgies are recited in old Slavonic and the sermons are delivered in Serbian.

Retrace on 104th Ave. W., and Gary St.; R. on Commonwealth Ave.; L. on McCuen St.

The only double-decked bridge at the head of the lakes, the DULUTH-OLIVER BRIDGE (*no toll charge*) is owned by the Duluth, Missabe and Iron Range Railroad. It leads to South Superior.

Retrace on McCuen St.; L. on Commonwealth Ave.; Commonwealth Ave. becomes State 23.

FOND DU LAC, dating back to 1793, is one of the historic spots of Minnesota. This neat modern suburb adjoining the St. Louis River was once an important fur trading post of the Astor Company. To this place in 1834 came the Reverend Edmund F. Ely, to conduct a school and mission; two years later his wife gave birth to the first white child born in the Arrowhead. In that year, too, the spot was visited by General James Dickson, one of the half-legendary characters of the American frontier, then engaged in forming his "Liberating Army of the Indian Nations." Calling himself Montezuma II, Dickson was on his way to Pembina on the Red River, to recruit an army of half-breeds to free Texas from Mexican Sovereignty; after that, he planned to set up an Indian Empire in California, wresting that territory also from Mexico.

Now under development at Fond du Lac is a winter-sports area which, when completed, should rival the Nation's best. Topographical conditions are ideal. There is a 325-foot ski-jump hill for experts, topped by a scaffold 62 feet high, and a number of gentler slopes for novices; there is also a toboggan slide half a mile long, and a hill for slalom racing, one of the best in the country. Most of Fond du Lac's 577 acres are under development, including facilities for ice skating, dancing, sleigh riding and picnic grounds.

BALM O'GILEAD (R), cor. 123rd Ave. W. (open), is a bird haven on a small private estate.

L. on 133rd Ave. W.

An Astor Trading Post was established in 1817 at the SITE OF CHIP-PEWA VILLAGE, foot 133rd Ave. W., now marked by a bronze plaque. It was here that Du Lhut stopped in 1679, and here in 1826 the first Minnesota Chippewa treaty was signed.

Retrace on 133rd Ave. W.; L. on State 23.

A REPRODUCTION OF A TYPICAL ASTOR TRADING POST is in Chambers Grove (R). The composite log stockade is a replica of one found at the Leech Lake Post (*see Arrowhead Tour 3*); some of the old logs in the structure bear the Astor stamp. In the grove is an APPLE TREE (*marked*), one of the oldest in the Arrowhead. It was brought as a seedling from Montreal by Francis Roussain, factor of the post.

TOUR 4

THE SKYLINE PARKWAY, 35 miles.

N. from London Road (US 61) on 60th Ave. E.; R. on Superior St.;
L. on Snively Blvd.

This route for the greater part follows the Skyline Parkway, which traverses sections of several well-known boulevards and is marked by a uniform sign (*evergreen tree on aluminum background*).

Starting point of the Skyline Parkway is 47-acre LESTER PARK (R), bet. London Rd. and Graves St.

The city of Duluth has planted 50,000 evergreens in AMITY PARK (R and L) in a reforestation project covering most of the park's 152 acres. Here the parkway circles a high cliff, affording a magnificent view of the lake and lake shore.

L. on Woodland Ave.; L. on 5th St.

Founded in 1902, DULUTH STATE TEACHERS COLLEGE (L), 2205 E. 5th St., has an average enrollment of 400 students. It trains teachers for elementary and secondary schools, with a full four-year course for Bachelor of Education degree. A natural ravine is one of many attractive features of the wooded campus, which rests near the brow of a hill overlooking the lake.

R. on 24th Ave. E.; R. on 4th St.

THE PILGRIM CONGREGATIONAL CHURCH (L), 2310 E. 4th St., is of red-brick and sandstone, built in English Gothic style. An amplifier installed in the belfry enables residents for blocks around to hear the organ melodies.

R. on Woodland Ave.; L. on Skyline Parkway.

CHESTER PARK (R and L), 108 acres bet. Chester Park Drive and Chester Parkway, appeals primarily to the devotees of sport. At the upper end is the Park Bowl with skating rink, tennis courts, toboggan slide, athletic field, artificial ski jump and clubhouse.

R. on Kenwood Ave.

Staffed by the Sisters of St. Benedict, VILLA SANCTA SCHOLASTICA (L), cor. College Ave., has 500 girls registered in its college and high school courses. In the attractive campus setting are four English Gothic buildings of blue-trap granite.

Retrace on Kenwood Ave.; R. on Skyline Parkway.

The A. P. COOK HOUSE (R), cor. 5th Ave. W. (*open*), is built on solid rock, its walls of Duluth gabbro. This picturesque estate, with its stone walks, steps and fireplace, resembles a terraced mountainside manor.

Weather reports and storm warnings are sent out from the U. S. WEATHER BUREAU STATION (R), cor. 7th Ave. W. (*open daily except Sun. and holidays 9 a. m. to 4 p. m.*).

L on 8th Ave. W.; R. on 3rd St.

With their own hands, in 1927, the congregation of ST. PETER'S ITALIAN CHURCH (Roman Catholic) (L), at the cor. 8th Ave. W., laid the blue, gray and yellow granite walls of the church building.

At 910 W. 3rd St. (L) is DARLING OBSERVATORY (*open by appointment*). A former Government engineer, John H. Darling became interested in astronomy, and built the observatory after he retired in 1913. To insure public access to its facilities, he enlisted the aid of the University of Minnesota Extension Division. Maintenance is provided through an endowment fund.

R. on 10th Ave. W.; L. on Skyline Parkway.

Scenic ENGER PARK (R and L), 330 acres bet. 10th and 24th Aves. W., includes the Enger Park Municipal Golf Course and Enger Club House. Among its attractions for sightseers are the TWIN LAKES.

R. on branch road that circles bluff; L. on steep road.

On ENGER PEAK is a 60-foot observation tower of blue granite, octagonal in shape, from whose balconies the visitor has an excellent panoramic view of lake and city. A ten-foot beacon with visibility of 25 miles tops the tower. The green light, emanating from 32 vertical tubes, was first switched on at the time the tower was dedicated by Crown Prince Olav of Norway, June 15, 1939. There is a shelter house and picnic ground.

Retrace on steep road; L. on branch road that becomes Skyline Parkway.

ONEOTA CEMETERY (L), bet. 65th and 69th Aves. W., is the burial place of the seven Merritt brothers, who discovered iron on the Mesabi Range, of George R. Stuntz, discoverer of the Vermilion Range, and many other prominent figures in the history of the Arrowhead. It is one of the oldest burial grounds in Duluth.

R. 1 mile on US 61 (see Arrowhead Tour 3); L. on Skyline Parkway.

SNIVELY PARK, named for Samuel F. Snively, a former mayor of Duluth, is 50 acres of woodland through which the parkway winds for 1.2 miles.

BARDON'S PEAK (L), 680 feet above lake level and bearing the name of a pioneer family at the head of the lakes, offers a fine view of the western outskirts of the city (*see Duluth Tour 3*).

MAGNEY PARK (R and L), 300 acres of rocky woodland, was named in honor of District Judge C. R. Magney, at one time mayor of Duluth. Here the first sign of spring is the white-flowered bloodroot, as it pushes its way up through the dry leaf bed. In the fall, the hardwood trees of the park are riotous in their color combinations. Benches, tables and fireplaces intersperse the area.

ELY'S PARK (L), approximately the same height as Bardon's Peak, bears the name of an early missionary. This is a favorite lookout point, with its view of the bay and the Wisconsin shoreline opposite. Below, the tracks of the Duluth, Winnipeg and Pacific (Canadian National) enter a tunnel in the rock. Within a half mile, the parkway crosses five stone bridges over MISSION CREEK, a tributary of the St. Louis River. In season, the road is bordered with snowy masses of trillium. For a time threatened with extinction through heedless picking, trillium is now protected by law and is once more abundant.

The road forks; L. Branch leads to Fond du Lac.

R. to Oldenburg Parkway; R. on Oldenburg Parkway.

Henry Oldenburg, after whom this section of Skyline Parkway is named, was a pioneer Carlton attorney who was largely responsible for establishment of Jay Cooke State Park.

The TRADING POST CEMETERY (*no longer in use*), within a white picket fence, was the first in Duluth. Established as the Roussain (*see Duluth Tour 3*) family burying ground, it also has a number of Indian graves.

JAY COOKE STATE PARK (R and L), is 3,375 acres of rugged, creek-veined woodland. The parkway here follows the roadbed of the old St. Paul and Duluth Railroad along the ST. LOUIS RIVER GORGE. Created a quarter of a century ago by a grant of 2,000 acres from the estate of the railroad financier, Jay Cooke, the park was expanded to its present size through subsequent acquisitions of land by the State.

LOOKOUT POINT (L) is a favored resort of sightseers seeking a comprehensive view of the surrounding country. From here, ridges that mark the successive shorelines of receding Lake Duluth (*see Geology*) are clearly visible. Nearby are vestiges of two portage trails used by early *voyageurs* in making their way up the St. Louis River (*see Floodwood*).

Beyond Lookout Point is a PLAQUE memorializing the work of Henry Oldenburg in the acquisition and development of this area. Overnight camping in tent or trailer is permitted at a TOURIST CAMPSITE. Many excellent springs along the road are indicated by signs.

Widely known is the SWINGING BRIDGE (L), a boardwalk suspended by steel cables from stone towers. Near it is a shelter house for picnickers, while swimmers enjoy the deep, cool pools underneath the bridge.

R. on three-mile fork.

Near the village of Thomson (*see Carlton*) is THOMSON DAM (L. across bridge), by which the Minnesota Power and Light Company provides power for Duluth. When the water is not too high, fishermen take splendid catches below the dam. Interesting color effects are formed by the quartz and slate rock formations in the vicinity.

CARLTON (*see Arrowhead Tour 3*).

Ely

Arrowhead Tour 4.
Railroad station: Duluth, Missabe & Iron Range, cor. Camp St. and 1st Ave. E.
Bus station: Northland Greyhound Lines, 23 E. Chapman St.
Airport: Auxiliary, State 1, 1.5 miles E.; two 2,600-foot runways; no hangar or servicing; fuel available by telephoning Ely.
Accommodations: Four hotels; municipal tourist camp, cor. Lawrence St. and Central Ave.

Information service: Ely Commercial Club, Community Center Bldg., 30 S. 1st Ave. E.
Golf: Shagawa Country Çlub (open to public), 700 S. Central Ave.; 9 holes.
Swimming: Municipal beach, cor. Lawrence St. and Central Ave.
Annual events (exact dates vary): Ski Tournament, January, February; Winter Carnival, February; Yugoslav Convention and Picnic, July; Community Fair, August.

GATE TO THE SPORTSMAN'S EDEN

Ely (1,417 alt., 5,970 pop.) is the "capital" of the Vermilion Range. Its personality is reflected by the towering black headframes of underground mines and the surrounding lakes of the Superior National Forest. The town was named in honor of Samuel P. Ely, who was prominent in the development of local mining properties.

In 1886, iron ore was discovered at the South Chandler Mine (inactive), which was started as an open pit. A town site was platted the following spring, only accessible from Tower (*see Tower*) over lakes, then through forests on an Indian foot trail that wound deviously for 25 miles to avoid bogs and marshes. That winter the effort was made to bring supplies necessary for the entire summer in one trip on sleds over the lakes, but the little community grew fast and a wagon road had to be cut.

In 1888, the Duluth and Iron Range Railroad (*see Two Harbors*), already linking the other mining settlements, was extended to the new village, which numbered only 177 persons, and the town began a steady growth. Ore was shipped from the Pioneer Mine in 1889; from the Zenith in 1892, and from the Sibley in 1899. In 1891, the village had been designated a city, and by 1910 its population was 3,572.

Iron-ore mining is still the main industry. Since its famous mines are of the underground type, permitting operation in all seasons, the city is a year-round mining town. In underground mining, a shaft, reinforced by permanent wooden or concrete sides, is sunk outside the ore body at various points, and, from it, drifts (tunnels) are driven horizontally to the deposit. Raises (openings) are bored upward and sub-drifts made, until the ore body is honeycombed; then the ore between the sub-drifts is blasted out and dragged to the main shaft by scrapers or pulled by air-driven electric hoists. The ore is dumped into steel skips (boxes), hoisted to the surface and emptied into cars for distribution to the stock piles.

Thirteen miles southeast of the city's boundaries, on State 1, a native black granite is quarried. This is one of the few important quarries in the Minnesota Arrowhead country (*see Mountain Iron; Cook*).

Farming is growing in importance in the Ely area, especially in the White Iron Lake district.

Ely's first school was opened in 1889 with Miss Wilson from Duluth as its first teacher. Today the school campus (500 E. Harvey St.) covers four blocks and contains the attractively grouped buildings of the Washington, Industrial, Memorial High, and Junior College. Three State champion divers received their training in the Memorial High swimming pool, and several widely known athletes trained in its gymnasium.

Ely's City Hall (205 E. Chapman St.), of Indiana limestone in a modernistic design, erected in 1930, houses all city departments and serves as St. Louis County's part-time auxiliary courthouse. The motorized volunteer fire department is the largest of its kind in the State. A municipally owned water and light plant supplies electricity and water to city consumers. The Community Center Building, maintained for community activities, houses the Public Library, Ely Commercial Club, and Tourist Bureau.

The South Slavonic Catholic Union, organized as a local venture in 1898, maintains national headquarters here (cor. 4th Ave. E. and Harvey St.). The building, erected in 1934, is of pink Kasota stone in a modern American design.

At Sandy Point (Sandy Point Rd., 1.5 miles), on Shagawa Lake, is the Oliver Iron Mining Company's recreational park with playground apparatus, a pavilion, and a bathing beach. Whiteside Park (Harvey St. bet. 7th and 8th Aves. E.), a ten-acre square, is another recreational area.

Ely in recent years has developed an extensive tourist trade. Fishermen, hunters, and canoeists, starting into the Superior National Forest, use Ely as a base of supplies. Its many resorts offer accommodations at a wide range of prices. Many tourists visiting the territory now travel by plane; hydroplane fishing trips are becoming popular. Three planes, equipped with pontoons, take fishing parties from Shagawa Lake to remote lakes (*see Superior National Forest: Information for Canoeists*).

Ely is reached by good hard-surfaced highways.

Embarrass

Arrowhead Tour 4.
Railroad station: Duluth, Missabe & Iron Range, junction Pike-Embarrass Rd. and Co. Rd. 21.
Information service: Cooperative Store, junction Co. Rds. 21 and 301 (part time only).
Tennis: St. Louis County School 70, junction Co. Rds. 21 and 104.
Annual events (exact dates vary): Winter Frolic, February; Embarrass-Pike Community Fair, September.

THE ARROWHEAD'S FINLAND

Embarrass (1,427 alt., unincorporated), a railway station and post office in the fertile valley of the Embarrass River (named by French fur traders because of the difficulties it presented to canoeists), is in Embarrass Township, whose population of 652 includes only two persons who are not Finns.

The first white visitors were fur traders who paddled along the Embarrass River to and from their posts. For many years the valley lay uncultivated and unoccupied, and even in 1895 there were only two men living on the site of the future Embarrass.

Among the foreign born who migrated to the mining regions for work were many Finns. Some did not like mining, and others were eager to farm; so, attracted by the similarity between the valley and their homeland, a group left the mining communities and settled along the Embarrass River. Here they homesteaded, cutting the dense forests of pine and draining the cedar swamps. Embarrass Township was organized in 1905, but there is still no incorporated village.

The chief industries are farming and logging. Certified seed potatoes raised here are among the best in the Minnesota Arrowhead. Dairying and chicken and turkey raising are carried on extensively. A considerable amount of pulpwood is shipped from this section.

With the coming of so many Finns, Embarrass naturally took on many of the characteristics of Finland. The buildings of the small farms that dot the valley are roofed with birch bark weighted down by slender poles. To build a haystack, a pole three or four inches thick and from 15 to 20 feet long is driven into the ground, and around it a log "flooring" is laid. When the hay stacked on this floor reaches a height of from 12 to 14 feet, mountain ash or alder twigs, attached to the pole, are pulled over the stack to hold it in place. These "gumdrop" haystacks give the valley a foreign appearance.

An essential part of each Finnish farm is the *sauna,* or bathhouse (*see Arrowhead Tour 3*). Usually a log structure, 8 x 10 feet, it is considered of such importance that often it is built before the house itself. Steam for the bath is generated by dousing hot stones with water. Soap and brushes are used vigorously, and in many cases the bather swishes himself with cedar boughs to stimulate perspiration. The bath is completed with a pail of cold water or, for the more hardy, a plunge into a snowbank.

Some of the older Finns still practice native handicrafts. Wool-felt boots for wear inside rubbers are made. They are pressed and pasted on a foot-shaped mold, and are black, white, or gray because no dye or substitutes are used. These are sold at the Embarrass Cooperative Store (junction Co. Rds. 21 and 301).

Eveleth

Arrowhead Tour 2.
Railroad station: Duluth, Missabe & Iron Range, Fayal Rd. bet. Lincoln and Grant Aves.
Bus station: Northland Greyhound Lines, 402 Grant Ave.
Taxis: Two cab lines offer service within city limits and to surrounding territory.
Accommodations: One hotel; municipal tourist camp, Eveleth Lake Park, US 53, 2.5 miles S., on lake shore; numerous tourist homes.
Information service: Eveleth Chamber of Commerce (all-year bureau), 225½ Grant Ave.; (summer bureau), Eveleth Lake Park.

Recreation facilities: Recreational Bldg., cor. Adams Ave. and Garfield St.; Hippo-
drome, Douglas Ave.; municipal and school playgrounds.
Hockey: Hippodrome.
Golf: Municipal, US 53, 2.5 miles S., on St. Mary's Lake; 9 holes.
Swimming: Municipal beach, Eveleth Lake Park.
Tennis: Eveleth Junior College Courts, Jones St. bet. Elba and Fayal Aves.
Rifle range: Franklin School basement.
Annual events: Winter Sports Carnival, February (exact dates vary); Curling Bonspiel;
Arrowhead Hockey Tournament; Northern Minnesota Tennis Tournament; Municipal
Kittenball Tournament; Range Bocce Ball Tournament; Range Archery Tournament;
Water Sports Carnival; Farmers' Day Fair, September (exact dates vary).

UNDERGROUND AND OPEN PITS

Eveleth (1,574 alt., 6,887 pop.), the "Hill Top City," was named for
Erwin Eveleth, a lumberman from Michigan who had been sent to purchase pine lands in the region.

In 1893, with the discovery of iron ore in the region, a town site was
platted and incorporated about a mile southwest of the present location,
on land now included in the Adams-Spruce Mine (Douglas Ave. bet. Jones
and Monroe Sts.). Unfortunately, the disastrous financial panic of that
year almost coincided with the founding, and the tiny settlement was hard
pressed to survive. No new buildings were added to the four or five that
formed the nucleus, and at times food was so scarce residents are reported
to have existed solely on moose meat. Mail service was practically discontinued; the only letters to arrive came by way of Virginia on dog sleds.

The first council meeting was held in the back room of a store October 25, 1894; the village hall, built a year later, was a two-story frame
building that cost $659.69. The first school, a frame shack, was opened in
1895, and Florence Kent was the first teacher.

In 1895, ore was discovered beneath the town site, and five years later
the village was moved to its present location. Men of all nationalities
worked side by side in the mines. From 1900 to 1910, the population increased from 2,752 to 7,036.

The community was incorporated as a city in 1902. When a new cemetery became a necessity, the problem was where to locate it, for valuable
ore might turn up almost anywhere. While the city fathers had no com-
punction in moving houses of the living, they did object to disturbing the
resting places of the dead. Finally, after exhaustive experiments proved
that a certain section had no potential mineral wealth, it was designated as
a graveyard, and thus far no other annoying conflict between sentiment and
riches has arisen (*see Hibbing*).

Mining still is Eveleth's chief industry. The open-pit method is the
favored process here, and visitors can view the colorful, man-made excavations, from whose depths millions of tons of iron ore have been taken and
hauled by rail to Duluth. The Adams-Spruce Mine, a combination of
seven properties, is operated by both underground and open-pit methods.
The Leonidas (Co. Rd. 20, two miles northwest), the deepest underground
mine on the Mesabi Range, has reached a depth of over 650 feet.

Agriculture and dairying are becoming increasingly important, and

Eveleth is the center of a prosperous farming district from which large quantities of dairy and other farm products are shipped daily.

Among the city's outstanding public buildings is the City Hall, erected in 1906 and remodeled in 1921 at a cost of $60,000. Eveleth's nine schools include a junior college and high school and a manual training school erected in 1914 (Roosevelt Ave. bet. Jones and Jackson Sts.), the first in the State devoted entirely to boys' shop work. The Public Library, in Memorial Park (McKinley Ave. bet. Fayal Rd. and Pierce St.), with more than 22,500 volumes, is one of the most modern and complete in the Arrowhead. The Recreational Building was the first of its kind on the Mesabi Range. The Hippodrome, recently remodeled at a cost of approximately $160,000, is probably the only one of its kind in Minnesota. This building is used as a hockey arena and equipped with an ice plant. It is convertible into a dance hall and is also used for basketball tournaments.

Eveleth is the "hockey capital of the nation" and has produced such hockey greats as Ching Johnson, Frank Brimsek, and Mike Karakas. The Eveleth teams are members of the International American League and Northern Amateur League. The Eveleth High School and Junior College teams have been taking State and national honors annually in hockey.

Eveleth has three beautiful parks: Memorial, six acres, with a $6,000 band shell; Northside (junction US 53 and Adams Ave.), 65 acres, where the Hearding log cabin, Eveleth's first structure, stands; and Eveleth Lake Park, 200 acres.

Floodwood

Arrowhead Tour 2.
Railroad station: Great Northern, junction US 2 and 7th Ave.
Bus station: Northland Greyhound Lines, 7th Ave. bet. Pine and Elm Sts.
Accommodations: One hotel.
Information service: Congress Hotel, cor. Pine St. and 7th Ave.
Rifle range: Floodwood Gun Club, cor. Fir St. and 8th Ave.
Annual events (exact dates vary): Water Carnival, August; Community Fair, September.

AT THE BEND OF THE RIVER

Floodwood (1,257 alt., 571 pop.), at the junction of the St. Louis, Floodwood, and Savanna rivers, once a typical logging town, is now an agricultural center.

This was one of the strategic points in the earliest days of the Minnesota Arrowhead, for it is near the westernmost bend of the St. Louis River, one of the main waterways traveled by fur traders. They paddled from Fond du Lac (*see Duluth Tour 3*) on the St. Louis River, then into the

East Savanna; from there they portaged, over the once famous Savanna Portage, about six miles across swamps to the West Savanna, and thence to Big Sandy Lake (*see Arrowhead Tour 3; McGregor*) and the Mississippi River. Daniel Greysolon, Sieur du Lhut, may have traveled this route in 1679. Others were Perrault, who made many trips over it between 1784 and 1794, the Cass Expedition in 1820, and Schoolcraft in 1832.

Ancient mounds, almost obliterated by sawmill operations, have been found in the vicinity, indicating predecessors to the Sioux and Chippewa, who were living within the region when the first white man came.

As soon as it was known that a railroad was to pass through the area, homesteads were acquired (1889), and Floodwood came into existence. There is some doubt whether the first settler was Bob Sutherland, cook for the construction crew laying the Duluth and Winnipeg Railroad, or Jean W. New, who was engaged by the crew to hunt deer and moose for their camps.

Although it is probable there had been early logging operations in the area, large-scale activities did not begin until after the building of the railroad in 1890, when J. C. Campbell started to operate here. In that year, too, the C. N. Nelson Lumber Company of Cloquet built the first logging railroad in the district, but it operated only in winter. The Nelson Company continued until 1894, when the Weyerhauser interests purchased its holdings.

Floodwood grew and in 1899 was incorporated as a village. For many years only the white pine, then plentiful, was considered marketable. Later, there was a demand for tamarack and cedar ties for railroad construction, and paper mills began to use more spruce. In 1923, the last timber was hoisted from the rivers, and by 1926 most of the big companies had completed logging operations in the vicinity. Much pulpwood, however, is still shipped.

With the passing of large-scale timber operations, fertile farm lands were developed. Dairying has now become the main industry, Floodwood having a cooperative creamery, the largest rural plant of its kind in St. Louis County.

Floodwood Independent School District No. 19, with four schools under its jurisdiction, now operates only one, Lincoln Grade and High (Elm St. bet. 3rd and 4th Aves.), in the village limits.

Gilbert

Arrowhead Tour 4.
Railroad station: Duluth, Missabe & Iron Range, Nevada St. bet. Broadway and 1st Court Sts.
Bus station: Northland Greyhound Lines, 105 N. Broadway St.

Accommodations: One hotel; municipal tourist camp, Hopkins Park, State 37, 4 blocks W.
Information service: Village Hall, 15-17 S. Broadway St.
Swimming: Municipal beaches, Cedar Island Lake, Beach Rd., 1 mile S.; Hopkins Park.
Tennis: Gilbert High School, Summit St. bet. Ohio and Iowa Aves.

VILLAGE OF DESTINY

Gilbert (1,593 alt., 2,504 pop.), hailed at birth as the prospective "principal city of the range," has been incorporated twice and involved in many controversies.

It was inevitable after iron ore had been found at Biwabik (*see Biwabik*) and points farther west on the Mesabi that the section between Biwabik and Mountain Iron (*see Mountain Iron*) would be explored. Ore in the Gilbert district was discovered as early as 1891 at the McKinley Mine (inactive), but none was shipped until 1896, when the Genoa (inactive) was opened. Development was slow because of the hard taconite formation, quicksand, and large amount of water beneath the deposits. One of the early companies reported pumping as much as 4,000 gallons per minute from one mine.

Settlements soon grew near the mines, but it was not until 1907 that the Gilbert Townsite Company, organized by W. J. Smith, J. A. Robb, C. E. Bailey, and D. W. Freeman, of Eveleth, platted an 80-acre town site at the logical center of activity. They named it in honor of Giles Gilbert, a fee-owner of a mine also bearing his name.

Gilbert was incorporated as a village in 1908, despite a protest filed by the Pitt Iron Company, which insisted that part of the area was mining land, not "conditioned . . . to be subjected to village government." The State Supreme Court upheld the company, and the newly elected village officials were ousted. During this period, Gilbert's population was increased by an influx from the town site of Sparta, one-half mile south, on Cedar Island Lake, which had been purchased by the Oliver Iron Mining Company when a deposit of high grade ore was found beneath it. The village of Sparta, organized in 1897, was dissolved in 1911.

A year after its defeat by the mining company, Gilbert petitioned successfully for village status. More trouble was brewing, however, for animosity between the Gilbert and Sparta factions kept the town involved in disagreements for some time. Gilbert wished to annex more property, increasing its valuation from less than $1,000,000 to more than $5,000,000. The Oliver Iron Mining Company objected. This suit the village won.

Gilbert has been built substantially. The old road that became Broadway Street (State 37) was hewn from the stand of pine that covered the town site, and at one time was part of a 28-mile boardwalk connecting the Mesabi Range towns. The Bailey Block (202-214 N. Broadway St.), a concrete structure, was the first permanent building to be erected. The Village Hall, of stone and brick, was built in 1915 at a cost of $30,000. Modern public utilities have been installed, and water is piped from Cedar Island Lake (Sparta and Ely Lake Rd., 1.5 miles south).

Four of the eight schools in School District No. 18 form the Gilbert campus: the High (built in 1911), the Junior High, the Primary, and the Technical (built in 1916). The Technical School has a swimming pool, two gymnasiums, and excellent shop-work facilities as well as an agricultural department. The district employs 60 teachers and has an enrollment of approximately 1,000. The Public Library (1-5 S. Broadway St.) is a modern structure of cream-colored brick.

Grand Marais

Arrowhead Tour 1.
Bus station: Northland Greyhound Lines, Wisconsin St. bet. Broadway St. and 1st Ave. W.
Airport: Landing field, old US 61, 5 blocks N.; 2 runways; no hangars; service available.
Accommodations: Two hotels; municipal tourist park, US 61, 7 blocks W.
Information service: Grand Marais Commercial Club, US 61 bet. 2nd and 3rd Aves. W.
Golf: Maple Hill Golf Course (open to public), Gunflint Trail, 3.5 miles N.; 18 holes.

WHERE LAKE MEETS FOREST

Grand Marais (616 alt., 855 pop.), Cook County capital, is a French name, meaning "big marsh." Nestling along the shores of a crescent-shaped harbor—in early days a haven for Indians and fur traders—this picturesque village has at times been overrun by the waters of Lake Superior.

The history of Grand Marais is rich in the lore of the fur traders, whose headquarters were only a few miles away, at Grand Portage, the metropolis of the fur-trading days (*see Grand Portage*). There was no settlement at Grand Marais, as no independent trader dared to build a post there until after Congress excluded all foreign companies.

In 1834, the American Fur Company established a fishing station but was forced to abandon it in 1842. Nothing more was heard of Grand Marais until after the Treaty of La Pointe (*see Copper and Gold Exploration*); then H. Godfrey, an independent trader from Detroit, opened a post that he operated for only a few years. He was in charge of the first Grand Marais post office, established in 1856; but in 1858 he resigned, closed his post, and moved back to Detroit.

Henry Mayhew and Sam Howenstine, who reached the site in 1871, were the actual founders of the village. At that time, the Grand Marais country was still inaccessible except by boat or trail. In 1879, a wagon road between Duluth and Pigeon River was begun, and by 1887 it was ready for use. Water transportation was more feasible, however, and so in 1882 the community constructed a breakwater. Later, the United States Government took charge of the harbor and built a lighthouse.

Travel to and from Grand Marais was mainly by way of Lake Superior. Even now Grand Marais, as well as Cook County, has no railroads other than those used for logging.

Lumbering and fishing and the tourist trade are the town's main industries. Most of the pulpwood is shipped by boat to the Hammermill Paper Company at Erie, Pennsylvania. The bulk of the fish goes by truck to Duluth for dressing, packing, and distribution.

Strangely enough Grand Marais does not secure its water supply from Lake Superior. Huge pipes carry it from spring-fed lakes beyond the hills to two reservoirs that store a total of 500,000 gallons.

The Federal Government maintains the North Superior Coast Guard Station (foot Broadway St.), and Forestry Office and Warehouse (US 61 bet. 4th and 5th Aves. W.). The offices of the Minnesota State Forestry Department and the State Game and Fish Department occupy one building (old State 1 bet. 4th and 5th Aves. W.). The Grand Marais School (cor. Broadway and 3rd Sts.), the Public Library (cor. 1st Ave. W. and 2nd St.), and the Cook County Courthouse (cor. 4th Ave. W. and 2nd St.) are modern buildings.

Grand Marais is the eastern "gateway" to the Superior National Forest and the outfitting point for many canoe trips (*see Superior National Forest: Canoe Trips*). The Gunflint Trail, which ascends into the heart of the Superior National Forest and to the famous chain of border lakes, begins here.

Grand Rapids

Arrowhead Tour 2.

Railroad station: Great Northern, cor. Pokegama Ave. N. and 3rd St.

Bus station: Northland Greyhound Lines, 4th St. bet. Pokegama Ave. and 1st Ave. E.

Airports: Auxiliary, Lily Lake Rd., 1.5 miles S.E.; one 2,500-foot and two 2,000-foot landing strips; entire field available; no service; Otis Airfield, 6 air miles S.W., on Sugar Lake; one 3,000-foot, one 2,600-foot, and one 1,600-foot runway; 4-plane hangar; gas and oil service.

Taxis: One cab line offers service within village limits and to surrounding territory.

Accommodations: Three hotels; municipal tourist camp, cor. 3rd Ave. E. and 13th St. N.; tourist homes and cabins.

Information service: Commercial Club Information Booth, cor. 4th St. and Pokegama Ave.

Golf: Pokegama Country Club (open to public), Pokegama Rd. (Pokegama Ave. S.), 3 miles S., on Pokegama Lake; 9 holes.

Swimming: Municipal beach, McKinney Lake, cor. 3rd Ave. W. and 15th St.

Tennis: Grand Rapids Senior High School, cor. Pokegama Ave. N. and 10th St.

Annual events: Ski Tournament, January, February (exact dates vary); Old Settlers' Dance, February 12; Itasca County Fair, latter part of August; Potato Day, latter part of September.

FROM LUMBER TO PAPER

Grand Rapids (1,290 alt., 4,875 pop.), Itasca County seat, the radial point of several important highways, is the home of one of the largest paper mills in the Northwest.

Not much lumbering was carried on in the vicinity until 1860. The heavy stands of Norway and white pine finally proved too great a temptation, and, between 1870 and 1890, logs on their way to sawmills farther south fairly choked the Mississippi and its tributaries. Shortly after 1870, Warren Potter, the "Father of Grand Rapids," built a log store building at the spot, thus founding the permanent settlement.

In 1890, the Duluth and Winnipeg Railroad reached Grand Rapids, and so many settlers came in its wake that the village was incorporated in 1891. (A "Golden Jubilee Celebration" of the event drew crowds of visitors on July 18, 19, and 20, 1941.) With the discovery of iron ore on the western Mesabi Range (*see Mountain Iron*), prospectors hastened to the region, but lumbering continued to be the leading industry. In 1894, the first railroad station was destroyed by fire. That same year, a waterworks system was constructed, and, on Thanksgiving Eve, the Pokegama Hotel was illuminated by the first electric lights in the town. A dam was built at the rapids of the Mississippi in 1899 to supply water power, and a year later lath and shingle mills commenced operations that continued until 1918, the date of the last log drive down the river from the Itasca County region.

In 1902, a paper mill was erected that subsequently was taken over by the Blandin Paper Company (32 W. 1st St.; *visitors not permitted*). Remodeled, of cream-colored brick and trimmed with white terra cotta, it is modern in every respect. Its windowless design insures adequate space and standard control of air-conditioning and lighting facilities—important factors in paper making. One of the most modern paper mills in the Northwest, the Blandin Paper Company employs 225 persons; in the last 20 years it has increased its daily output from 25 to 150 tons.

Grand Rapids, still retaining the village form of government, is a thriving, active community, the trade center for an extensive area, and the outfitting point for sportsmen en route to beautiful lake and wilderness regions that surround it. The near-by Chippewa National Forest (*see Chippewa National Forest*) and the Scenic State Park attract great numbers of visitors each summer. Grand Rapids is also the supply depot for the Minnesota State Forestry Service (US 2, one mile east) and headquarters for the district game warden.

The Itasca County Fairground (cor. 3rd Ave. E. and 13th St. N.), 45 acres in extent, on the shore of Crystal Lake, is one of the most beautiful fairgrounds in Minnesota. The Village Hall (cor. Pokegama Ave. N. and 5th St.), of brick, concrete, and steel, trimmed with terra cotta, was erected in 1929 at a cost of $70,000. The Great Northern Station, built the same year, is a copy of the one at Glacier National Park. Opposite the station is a 15,000-foot load of pine, commemorative of "The Last Load."

Grand Rapids is the administration center for School District No. 1, in area the largest organized school district in the United States. Within boundaries 85 miles apart, are 65 graded, consolidated, and high schools. Its school bus system extends 30 miles and carries 2,000 pupils. The North Central School of Agriculture (US 169, 1.5 miles northeast), operated by the Univerity of Minnesota on a 300-acre farm, instructs about 80 farm boys each year.

Hibbing

Arrowhead Tour 2.

Railroad stations: Duluth, Missabe & Iron Range (North Hibbing), south foot 2nd Ave., (South Hibbing), cor. Park St. and 4th Ave.; Great Northern, cor. Wilson St. and 4th Ave.

Bus station: Northland Greyhound Lines, 1927 4th Ave.

Local bus lines: Mesaba Transportation Co., 630 E. Howard St., offers service between North and South Hibbing, and Shubat Transportation Co., 704 E. Howard St., to mining locations.

Airport: Municipal, Co. Rd. 61, 5 miles E.; 4 runways, graveled, oiled, and rolled, all 200 feet wide; well-marked hangar, landing area flood-lighted; facilities for servicing aircraft during day only.

Taxis: Two cab lines offer service within village limits and to surrounding territory.

Accommodations: Fifteen hotels and lodging houses; municipal tourist camp, cor. Howard St. and 12th Ave.

Information service: Hibbing Village Information Bureau, Androy Hotel.

Recreational facilities: Memorial Bldg., cor. Adeline St. and 4th Ave.

Golf: Municipal, east end Park St.; 9 holes; Mesaba Club, 1st Ave., 3 miles S.

Tennis: Municipal courts, Memorial Bldg.

Rifle range: Hibbing Gun Club, Dupont Rd., 1 mile E.

Annual events (exact dates vary): Ski Tournament, January; Winter Sports Frolic, February; St. Louis County Fair, August, September.

IRON ORE CAPITAL

Hibbing (1,537 alt., 16,385 pop.), the "iron ore capital of the world," has the world's largest and richest iron-ore mine, the Hull-Rust-Mahoning open pit.

Timber cruisers were the first white men known to have visited the Hibbing region, and they brought back reports of ore outcroppings. It has been told that a cruiser, John Day, and a companion, lost in the woods, stopped at dusk to get their bearings. To Day's consternation, his compass whirled dizzily wherever he moved. He remarked uneasily that either it had gone crazy or iron must be near by, adding that, if the latter were true, the iron never would be used in their day. That night they camped on a spot almost within a stone's throw of the present Mahoning Mine. Lumber companies noted the cruiser's findings but gave them little attention, and when lots were sold, timber—not iron—was the attraction.

After the Vermilion Range had demonstrated its wealth, the search for iron ore spread westward. Frank Hibbing entered the region, and in 1892 men in his employ discovered valuable deposits where now is located the Burt-Pool Mine (old Sturgeon Lake Rd., three miles north). The following year he platted a town site that was incorporated as a village on August 15. At first the streets were practically impassable because of large pine stumps and mud, and the hauling of food supplies and equipment needed by mining, logging, and railroad operations was impeded. Drinking water was another problem, the nearest being three miles away, at Carson Lake. An epidemic of typhoid broke out in the village.

During this period, all eyes were turned on Virginia (*see Virginia*), and few purchasers could be found for Hibbing property. During the nationwide panic of 1893, the struggling village seemed doomed. Work of any kind was scarce; even the monthly wages of lumberjacks ($6-$12) were paid in "due bills" not collectible until the following January. There was little inducement to go into the timber, and exploration for ore was reduced to a minimum. The men still employed in the Mahoning Mine and those who found jobs with the newly organized Hibbing Water and Light Company were objects of envy. The rest lived in hope of a better future.

By the end of 1894, signs of increasing activity were evident. Frank Hibbing advanced $3,000 for a railroad to run from town to the Mahoning pit, and in 1895 several mines were opened. Miners and lumberjacks swarmed in from Eastern States and European countries. Soon saloons outnumbered stores, streets were dangerous places for the unwary, drunks slept on the floor in the rear of barrooms. Here, foremen would come to look over the snoring men, select huskies, and herd them into mines and lumber camps.

The village school, started in a store in 1893, was moved into a building of its own. Teachers probably never found themselves in a more difficult position, for many of the children knew no English, and the languages and dialects they spoke were extremely varied. Preachers, too, had great need of tolerance and patience; generally they were met by an indifference harder to overcome than active resistance. However, if there was little enthusiasm for religion, there was plenty of kindness. One Lutheran pastor, unable to find shelter in a home, was glad to accept a portion of an already crowded saloon floor proffered by a bartender. The early rector of Christ Memorial Church, of Hibbing's edifices then the proudest, had a particularly troublesome problem. This church, built in 1895 from plans by Cass Gilbert, designer of the State Capitol at St. Paul and the Soldiers and Sailors Monument at Duluth (*see Duluth Tour 3*), was presented to the town as a memorial. Greeks and Montenegrins, numerous among the miners, apparently saw in its ritual the nearest approach to their own, and they chose it for most of their funerals. Again and again, the distracted minister was confronted by a colorful procession that marched down the aisle with bands playing and banners flying, while over their heads he could see an overflow of miners gathered at the doors, lustily relieving aching hearts and thirsty throats with beer.

In the busy period between 1898 and 1900, the Swan River Lumber

Company, whose large camp with 1,500 men was located one mile east of town, built a permanent sawmill. Logs were transported to Hibbing, and the lumber was shipped by rail to Swan River for the first lap of the journey down the Mississippi.

By the turn of the century, Hibbing had a population of more than 2,000, with a constantly shifting and uncounted army of transients. However, the village soon found itself in a dilemma. When platted, a site thought to be south of the ore deposits had been selected, but now, beneath its very streets, valuable ore was found. The Oliver Iron Mining Company, a subsidiary of the United States Steel Corporation, already in control of mineral rights, began to acquire all surface rights. By the end of 1910, there was not an available building lot. Mining operations had been expanded. The company decided the town must be moved. It chose a location a mile south, then known as Alice, and there laid out and built a modern community, with lights, water, sewers, and paved streets. In 1919, the move started. Some of the old buildings were cut into sections, transported piecemeal, and put together again. Churches were towed intact, arriving with spires, pews, and decorations undisturbed.

The shifting of the village necessitated a means of transportation between the old and new towns, and a motor bus service was started, the nucleus of the Mesaba Transportation Company, later the Northland Greyhound Lines and part of the nation-wide Greyhound System.

Many differences over the question of property compensation were fought out in the courts and legislature, and at last they were settled by a compromise, the "North Hibbing Purchase Plan," which provides that the company by 1944 will have acquired the surface rights of all that part of the township known as "North 40," the original Hibbing, and this part of the town will be razed to permit ore excavation.

Hibbing, in Stuntz Township, has retained its village status, because Minnesota's tax policy is more lenient toward communities of that class (*see The Iron Ore Ranges*).

More than 73 mines have shipped ore from the district. The Hull-Rust-Mahoning (north end 3rd Ave.; observation towers; north end 2nd Ave.; east end Superior St.; Town Rd., 3.5 miles northwest), the largest open-pit iron-ore mine in the world, lies almost wholly within the village limits. It is three miles long, one mile wide, 375 feet deep at its deepest point, covers 1,100 acres, and has more than 70 miles of railroad tracks. More than 250,000,000 tons of ore have been shipped, the excavation approximating 231,000,000 cubic yards—stupendous when it is realized that 232,000,000 is the figure for the Panama Canal.

The Hibbing Technical and Vocational High School (Mesaba St. bet. 7th and 9th Aves.), the second largest of its kind in the United States, is nationally famous. This "Monument to Education," completed in 1923, is an E-shaped structure with a 596-foot frontage. The main section, or north wing, contains classrooms, laboratories, and offices; the south wing has a library and auditorium, two gymnasiums, and an indoor track, swimming pools, and a study hall. Its complete industrial equipment makes possible a wide range of shop work. The auditorium, whose seating

capacity is 1,805, has a modern pipe organ and a stage (40 feet x 60 feet)
with electrically controlled settings and unusual lighting effects. The
school, housing all grades from kindergarten through junior college, is
decorated by murals. One by David Workman, in the library, depicts
various phases of the mining and steel industry; six panels by David Ericson, to the left and right of the main entrance, illustrate the history of
the region.

Park School (cor. Park St. and 7th Ave.), in Bennett Park, is called the
"Glass School" because of large wall areas of structural glass. An electric
eye controls the lighting system. Streamlined desks and chairs are movable
so that they may be grouped informally.

The War-Service Memorial Building (*open*), of modern design, covering an entire block, contains an auditorium, Memorial Hall; also, a large
curling rink, a service club and labor temple quarters, a Little Theater, and
an arena with a terrazzo floor that can be converted in ten hours into a
hockey rink with a spectator capacity of 2,500, or into a basketball court
seating 5,000.

The Hibbing Public Library (cor. Mahoning St. and 3rd Ave.) was constructed in 1916 to replace one built in 1908. It is of pink Kettle River
sandstone and is decorated with many murals and paintings, among the
latter an original by Tait, *The Halt on the Carry*. A branch library is maintained in the Village Hall (cor. Mesaba St. and 5th Ave.), and a bookmobile
carries books to all outlying districts of Stuntz Township. The main
library is still in North Hibbing, as are the district headquarters of the
Oliver Iron Mining Company (1st Ave. bet. Sellers and Lincoln Sts.); one
of St. Louis County's two full-time auxiliary court-houses (cor. McKinley
St. and 2nd Ave.); and Christ Memorial Church (cor. Mahoning St. and
4th Ave.). All these buildings may have to be moved. Christ Memorial
Church already has been moved once (1912) to make way for mining operations. Transported stone by stone, it was rebuilt after the original Cass
Gilbert design, except for minor details.

The Village Hall is in striking contrast to the modern architecture of
the other buildings. Modeled after historic Faneuil Hall in Boston, it is of
red finishing brick. Four murals illustrate the history of Minnesota and the
mining industry, and two symbolize Law and Justice. The municipal
power plant (cor. Wilson St. and 7th Ave.) supplies water and electricity
and provides heat for a large number of dwellings and buildings.

A tablet (junction US 169 and Co. Rd. 61) memorializes George R.
Stuntz for his part in the discovery of iron ore on the Vermilion Range.
The township also was named in his honor.

Recreational facilities are excellent in Hibbing and the surrounding
district. The village maintains six parks, of which Bennett, 47 acres (Park
St. bet. 1st and 7th Aves.), is the most developed. On the east side of
Third Avenue Boulevard, which traverses this park, is the park department's administration building, adjacent to which are five greenhouses
where 370 varieties of flowers and 140 other kinds of plants are grown
and exhibited. There is also a zoo with a variety of animals. On the

west side of the boulevard are two wading pools, a shelter house, a bandstand, and a refectory.

Within driving distance of the border lakes, the Mississippi basin lakes, and the Lake Vermilion region, Hibbing offers opportunities for fishing and hunting, camping, and other vacation sports.

International Falls

Arrowhead Tour 3.
Railroad stations: Big Fork & International Falls, cor. 2nd Ave. and 4th St.; Minnesota, Dakota & Western, cor. 1st Ave. and 4th St.
Bus station: Northern Transportation Co., Rex Hotel, 245 3rd St.
Airport: Landing field, State 11, 1.25 miles S.W.
Taxis: Two cab lines offer service within city limits and to surrounding territory.
Accommodations: Four hotels; municipal tourist camp, State 11, 3 miles E., on Rainy Lake.
Information service: Tourist Information Bureau, Daily Journal, 237 3rd St.
Golf: Rainy Lake Golf and Country Club (open to public), State 11, 3.5 miles W.; 9 holes.
Swimming: Municipal beach, municipal tourist camp.

TRAIL'S END

International Falls (1,124 alt., 5,626 pop.), Koochiching County seat, its pulsing wood industry mills producing a steady stream of products, is the northernmost point in the Minnesota Arrowhead country. On the falls of the Rainy River, part of the international border, it is on the fringe of a magnificent wilderness area (*see Superior National Forest*), romantic with the lore of fur traders who traveled the interior waterways in their canoes.

The first white man to visit the site was Jacques de Noyon, a French *voyageur* from Canada, who traveled over the Kaministiquia Route to Rainy Lake and wintered at the falls in 1687 or 1688. He was followed by Zacherie Robutel, Sieur de la Noue, and by Pierre Gaultier de Varennes, Sieur de la Vérendrye. Although fur-trading posts were built in the region at an early date, they were located on the Canadian side of Rainy River. The date of the first post established on the American side is not known, but it probably was between 1816 and 1822.

As the fur trade dwindled, lumbering came into importance. Extensive stands of conifers covered the area. Logs were floated down the Big and Little Fork Rivers to sawmills farther north (*see Big Falls; Littlefork*). Lumbermen early realized the value of the falls, at the head of an 18,000-square mile watershed, as a source of water power.

Some settlers came to the region when steamboats began plying the Rainy River as part of the Dawson Route, which had been laid out between

Port Arthur (*see Arrowhead Tour 1*) and Fort Garry (Winnipeg) in 1870 and followed in part the international boundary (*see Superior National Forest: Canoe Trip 1*). After railroad facilities were established on the Canadian side, steamboat service on Rainy River was abandoned, and once more the only mode of water travel was by canoe. In 1881, the first homesteader, Alexander Baker, a Hudson's Bay Company factor, filed a claim on the site of International Falls. The village was incorporated in 1901.

In 1904, a paper company brought about joint control of American and Canadian riparian rights and contracted for both development of water power and establishment of manufacturing industries. The falls, known as Chaudiere (cauldron) to the French, had a natural 24-foot drop and made available 25,000 horsepower from a 27-foot head.

In 1910, International Falls, with a population of 1,487, was incorporated as a city.

The International Lumber Company, a subsidiary of the Minnesota and Ontario Paper Company, erected a sawmill in 1910. The mill, its capacity 300,000 feet in a ten-hour day, cut as much as 75,000,000 feet in one year. Then the largest in the State, it ceased operations in 1937.

The Minnesota and Ontario Paper Company (cor. 4th Ave. and 2nd St.) manufactures newsprint, sulphite, and kraft ground-wood paper, all of which have nation-wide markets. In 1911, it began the construction of a railroad that today has 11 locomotives, 400 cars, 35 miles of tracks, and provides employment for 120 men. In 1916, it built the world's first Insulite mill. Insulite, a wood-fiber board used for insulation, was in such demand that in 1925 a larger mill had to be built, which has a capacity of 750,000 board feet in 24 hours. Since 1931, it has been complemented by a second mill at Karhula, Finland.

The warehouse of the International Falls plant has a storage capacity of 25,000,000 board feet. Aspen is utilized in the manufacture. Mando (the trade name of the Minnesota and Ontario Paper Company) maintains mills at other points and owns the world's largest cedar telegraph pole yards and treating plant at St. Paul (Minnesota Transfer).

These wood industries are the main source of income for International Falls, and the city's industrial development is assured by its water power and the wood supply held by the Minnesota and Ontario Paper Company.

International Falls is headquarters for the three branches of the U. S. International Border Patrol (Post Office Bldg., 400 4th St.). They can be distinguished readily by the color of their uniforms: Immigration, forest green; Customs, dark gray; and Customs Inspection, dark blue (*see General Information: Border Regulations*). The Border Patrol supervises the 350-mile stretch from Pigeon River to Roseau.

A curio collection in the Log Cabin Inn (434 3rd St.) displays interesting mounted specimens of birds and native animals in natural poses; a moose that must have weighed 1,000 pounds, a black bear, a buck deer, and the hides and heads of bears, foxes, and wolves.

International Falls, a port of entry, is rich in primeval beauty, historic lore, and natural resources. It is an outfitting center for vacationists and sportsmen.

Ironton

Arrowhead Tour 8.
Railroad station: Minneapolis, St. Paul & Sault Ste. Marie, and Northern Pacific, cor. Winona Ave. and 3rd St.
Bus station: Northland Greyhound Lines, cor. Ironton Ave. and 5th St.
Taxis: One cab line offers service within village limits and to surrounding territory.
Accommodations: Two hotels.
Information service: Spena Hotel, cor. Ironton Ave. and 4th St.
Golf: Cuyuna Range Golf Club, US 210, 7 miles S.E. (Deerwood); 9 holes.
Tennis: Ironton Park, 6th St. bet. Irene and Viola Aves.

CUYUNA TWIN

Ironton (1,260 alt., 827 pop.), on Serpent Lake, at first spurned by Crosby and now acknowledged its twin (*see Crosby*), is a mining town and one of the leading municipalities of the Cuyuna Range.

In 1864, the United States Government granted the Northern Pacific Railroad the land that was to become the town site of Ironton. Thirty years later, the railroad sold its holdings to G. E. Premo, who subsequently transferred his equity to his cousin, David Sutton. The sale price was five dollars an acre. Sutton did not own the mineral rights and traded the land for some stock in a company which almost immediately went into bankruptcy.

Ironton (a contraction of Iron Town) was platted by Carrie P. and John Hill and Agnes I. Lamb on September 6, 1910. Crosby, organized in the same year, attempted to include Ironton within its limits, but county commissioners, deeming the site of little value, would not allow the annexation.

Ironton named its main street Pennington Avenue in honor of the president of the Minneapolis, St. Paul and Sault Ste. Marie (Soo Line); then, fearing so important a personage might not feel complimented, quietly substituted Ironton Avenue. The summer of 1910 was marked by building activity—stores, houses, and a hotel being built.

Ironton again was spurned in 1911, when the Soo Line skirted it in running tracks out to the Pennington Mine (inactive). The following summer, however, the Northern Pacific extended a branch from Deerwood, and Ironton was given transportation facilities, though the station was only a box car. Later, the Soo Line recognized the existence of the village by entering an agreement with the Northern Pacific to use the latter's station and tracks.

Mining is Ironton's main industry. The Sagamore Mine (Riverton Rd., 3.5 miles northwest), an open pit, was discovered beneath a deposit of peat, and, as it was stripped, skeletons of buffalo and extinct animals were found.

Its drying and crushing plant removes excess moisture from the ore by means of revolving ovens. Other active mines are the Alstead (Evergreen Mine Rd., 0.5 mile north) and the Mahnomen (Mahnomen Lake Rd., 0.75 mile northwest), both open pits; the Armour No. 1 (north end Irene Ave.), underground; and the Louise (Mahnomen Lake Rd., 1.5 miles northwest), open pit and underground. The Manganiferous Iron Company operates the Louise Mine crushing and screening plant (Trommald Rd., four miles northwest), built in 1936 at a cost of $200,000.

Ironton is only one mile from Crosby, and this nearness, together with their common industry and school district, has caused them to be referred to generally as "Crosby-Ironton, the Cuyuna Twins."

Keewatin

Arrowhead Tour 2.
Railroad station: Great Northern (freight only), cor. 2nd St. and Hibbing Ave.
Bus station: Northland Greyhound lines, 1st St. bet. 2nd and 3rd Aves.
Accommodations: One hotel.
Information service: Theodore Hotel, cor. 1st St. and 3rd Ave.

NAMED FOR A WIND

Keewatin (1,505 alt., 1,942 pop.), with large mines operating and larger reserves available, is a mining community near the eastern Itasca County line.

Iron-ore explorations had been carried on extensively throughout the western Mesabi Iron Range by 1904, when large deposits were found at the site of the present Keewatin. A settlement sprang up and took its nam from the Ojibway *giwedin,* meaning "north" or "north wind."

Keewatin grew slowly in its first years. In 1905, the St. Paul Mine (St. Paul Rd., one mile northwest) started operations, followed three years later by the Bray (inactive). Development became more rapid when the Great Northern Railroad reached here in 1909, and two mines, Mississippi (inactive) and Bennett (Bennett Mine Rd., three miles north), were opened in 1910 and 1912.

Although some of the first pits have been exhausted, others have replaced them, and mining remains Keewatin's only industry. In 1927, work was started at the Mesabi Chief Mine. By the end of 1939, it had shipped 6,638,581 tons; today, it is the largest mine in Keewatin. The Mesabi Chief and the Mississippi No. 2 (St. Paul Rd., 1.5 miles northwest), another open pit, are operated by the Hanna Ore Company under State leases. The St. Paul has a belt system that carries ore from the open pit to the surface and a washing plant (Washing Plant Rd., one mile northwest), where the iron ore is beneficiated. Other active mines are the Sargent (Sargent Mine Rd., one mile west), an underground, and the Bennett, which is operated by both underground and open-pit methods.

Keewatin is in Itasca County School District No. 9, of which Nashwauk is the administration center. The village has two schools: the Robert L. Downing High (cor. 3rd St. and 3rd Ave.) and the Keewatin Grade (cor. 3rd St. and 4th Ave.), both of red brick.

The Village Hall (cor. 2nd St. and 3rd Ave.), a two-story building, also of red brick, was erected in 1909. In its basement is a municipally owned and operated bowling alley. The Public Library (cor. 3rd St. and 3rd Ave.) has several thousand volumes. A Boy Scout Cabin on the edge of town, for the exclusive use of Boy Scouts, was completed in 1940.

One of Keewatin's summer show spots is the School Garden, on US 169 just west of the Village Hall. Many prizes have been won at the Itasca County Fair on vegetables raised in this garden.

Kinney

Arrowhead Tour 2.
Accommodations: One hotel.
Information service: Kinney Hotel, cor. Main St. and Pine Ave.
Tennis: Wilson School, 1st St. N. bet. Pine and Birch Aves.

TALE TOLD BY A MINE

Kinney (1,500 alt., 462 pop.), its history beginning with the opening of the Kinney Mine (inactive), is surrounded by the open pits on which its very life depends.

After the Buhl group of mines was opened (*see Buhl*), explorations were carried on more extensively in the region. Just north of Buhl, O. D. Kinney, E. B. Hawkins, and George H. Crosby (*see Crosby*) discovered the ore deposit that was to bear Kinney's name. The property was leased to the Republic Iron and Steel Company. A shaft was sunk, as underground methods of mining were to be used, and the first ore was shipped in 1902. Later, the mine became an open pit.

A community grew up near the mine, but it remained unorganized for some time. Other mines were opened in the adjacent territory, and men, predominately Finns and Slovenians, who came to work in them settled at the site.

In 1909, when a census was taken prior to petitioning for incorporation, the population numbered 367. The first attempt at organization failed, but in 1910 the town was incorporated as a village. Kinney, unlike Buhl, never has voted itself out of Great Scott Township, which owes its name to the favorite ejaculation of one of the county commissioners, uttered at the time the township was formed.

From time to time, Kinney has annexed valuable sections of land, despite objections from the mining companies upon whom the burden of both municipal and State taxes falls. The taxable valuation of Kinney increased from $40,680 in 1911 to $1,753,491 in 1919. The population was 1,200 in 1920, but during the next ten years decreased to 737.

Kinney is in School District No. 35, organized in 1901, of which Buhl is the administration center. In 1921, the district built the Wilson School at Kinney, at a cost of $350,000. The earlier frame structure has since been razed. The village has both grade and junior high school facilities, and secondary school students are transported to the Martin Hughes High School at Buhl. It also has a Public Library, and a Municipal Band of 35 members.

Kinney has a modern water system, including a new purification plant, a modern sewage plant, electric light and power, and paved streets throughout the entire village.

Mining is still the main industry, although in recent years the Kinney mines within the village have been inactive. A farming region has developed to the north, many unemployed miners having turned to agriculture.

Kinney is near the southern border of the Superior National Forest.

Littlefork

Arrowhead Tour 3.
Railroad station: Big Fork & International Falls, junction US 71 and State 65, 1 mile W.
Bus station: Northern Transportation Co., Dusmar Hotel, cor. Main and 3rd Sts.
Accommodations: One hotel; Littlefork State Public Campgrounds, US 71, 1.25 miles W.
Information service: Dusmar Hotel.
Tennis: Littlefork Post 490 Tennis Court, Main St. bet. 3rd and 4th (State 65) Sts.
Annual event (exact dates vary): District Fair, August.

IN THE CLOVER

Littlefork (1,153 alt., 608 pop.), on the great horseshoe bend of the river of the same name, a tributary of Rainy River, is the principal community in one of the best agricultural regions in the Minnesota Arrowhead country.

Some of the early *voyageurs* and explorers, no doubt, traveled over the inland waterways that now form the northern boundary of Minnesota, paddled along the Little Fork, and visited this site. The first white men known to enter the region were lumbermen who worked along the Little Fork and Big Fork rivers, floating logs down to Rainy River.

Settlers arrived about 1905 and found the region covered with fine stands of cedar, spruce, balsam, tamarack, and some white pine. Logging was the chief industry for many years, and even today a large amount of timber is hauled to the mills at International Falls (*see International Falls*).

As the land was cleared, agriculture developed in the fertile valley of the Little Fork River. The chief money crops, clover seed and alfalfa, yield from six to ten bushels per acre on cut-over land, and cash returns of $100 to $150 per acre are not unusual.

For many years, a lack of good roads retarded the development of Little-fork, but today it is the second largest community in Koochiching County, and the market and trade center for the district. A potato wholesale associa-tion, organized for cooperative shipping, maintains a warehouse. Littlefork has two schools, a high (north end Main St.) and an elementary (Main St. bet. 6th and 7th Sts.).

There is good hunting for bear and deer, and for pintail and ruffed grouse. The 100-foot tower of the State Ranger Station (3rd St. bet. State 65 and Main St.) affords a fine view of the surrounding territory.

A 19-mile graveled shortcut connects Littlefork with Ray on US 53.

McGregor

Arrowhead Tour 3.
Railroad station: Northern Pacific, and Minneapolis, St. Paul & Sault Ste. Marie, Union Station, 3 blocks west of Maddy St.
Bus station: Northland Greyhound Lines, Maddy St.
Accommodations: Two boarding houses; municipal tourist park, High School grounds, 1 block S. US 210.
Information service: McGregor Chamber of Commerce; McGregor Lakes Region Association.

NEAR HISTORIC SITES

McGregor (1,254 alt., 311 pop.), Aitkin County, gateway to the Savanna State Forest and to an extensive resort region, is an important junction point of two railroads and two highways, US 210 and State 65.

When white men first advanced to the head of the lakes in the second half of the seventeenth century, the area southwest of the St. Louis River, and including the Big Sandy Lake region, was Sioux country. It was not until the middle of the eighteenth century that the Chippewa gained the upper hand in northern Minnesota. One of the most important portage routes of the Northwest (*see Floodwood*), connecting the Mississippi and the St. Louis River systems, thus came into possession of the Chippewa.

The relocation of this historic six-mile portage between the West Savanna and the East Savanna rivers—about 18 miles north-northeast of McGregor—was accomplished in 1926 by Professor Irving H. Hart and William P. Ingersoll, and permanent markers were placed along its course in July, 1940, by 50 Eagle Boy Scouts.

By the end of the eighteenth century, the Big Sandy Lake region had developed into one of the main fur-trading centers. The Northwest Company established a post on Brown's Point at Big Sandy Lake in 1794. It was taken over by the American Fur Company in 1816 and abandoned six years later, at which time a new post was established by William and Allan Morrison at the confluence of the Sandy and Mississippi rivers, just west of the present Government Dam. William A. Aitkin, for whom Aitkin County was named, was for many years a leading trader in this area.

Through this region in 1798 came David Thompson, explorer and geographer, Lieutenant Zebulon M. Pike in 1805, Territorial Governor Lewis Cass and Henry R. Schoolcraft in 1820 (*see Chippewa National Forest*), Giacomo Costantino Beltrami in 1823, and Joseph N. Nicollet in 1836.

In the autumn of 1832, Frederick Ayer started a missionary school at Big Sandy Lake, and completed while there an Ojibway spelling book. When William T. Boutwell visited the fur-trading post in that year, he found "stables for 30 head of cattle, three or four horses, and 15 swine." Aitkin told him he had raised 600 or 700 bushels of potatoes the year before, and also cultivated barley and peas.

Lumbering on a commercial scale began about 1873, reached a peak around the turn of the century, and then declined until the big trees had practically vanished from the region in 1916.

The central location of the present village between several good-sized lakes suggested itself for a railroad station, for which, in 1880, a siding was constructed by the Northern Pacific. An old box car served as a depot, and it was named McGregor.

Henry Lozway, a Frenchman from New York State, came to McGregor about 1890, and for a short time operated a small store, serving the lumber workers in the region. Following him came Pasquale Memmola, Frank Spicola, and C. A. Maddy, who are considered the actual founders of the village. McGregor was incorporated in 1903.

Extensive drainage operations have transformed the area into a farming district, with McGregor as its marketing center.

Well-equipped resorts abound in the surrounding lake region. Among the larger lakes are Big Sandy, Minnewawa, Rice, and Gun. The region is known for its good fishing and hunting, and it is upon these that McGregor bases its claim to the title, "Hub of a Sportsman's Paradise."

Marble

FROM THE MIDST OF THE FOREST

Marble (1,382 alt., 792 pop.) is one of the mining villages in the Canisteo District on the western Mesabi Range.

Marble came into existence with the discovery of iron-ore deposits beneath dense forests covering the area. The town site embraced 80 acres, with 20 acres adjoining reserved for a public park, when the Oliver Iron Mining Company began the building of the village following the completion of Coleraine.

The station of the Duluth, Missabe and Northern Railroad, now the Duluth, Missabe and Iron Range, though only a frame building, was for some time the most imposing structure.

In 1909, Marble was incorporated as a village, and in 1911 had a population of 900.

Mining is the only industry. The Oliver Iron Mining Company has given up its lease on the Hill Mine and today operates no mines within the village. Since the abandonment of the Hill, the largest local mine is the Hill-Annex, to which Calumet also owes its being and support. Opened in 1914, it has shipped 22,879,647 tons of iron ore. The Hill-Trumbull Mine (White City Rd., 0.5 mile north), an open pit started in 1919, includes the former Hill Mine. Operated by the Mesaba-Cliffs Mining Company, it has produced 12,900,700 tons of ore. It has a washing plant (Sand Lake Rd., 1.5 miles southeast). The Oliver Iron Mining Company controls vast reserves in Marble.

The Olcott School, a $45,000 structure (Alice Ave. bet. Bawden and Kate Sts.), was built in 1911. The streets, once only mud trails, are now paved or surfaced, and the main one is as wide as a boulevard. The village has modern public utilities.

Marble is within easy driving distance of Scenic State Park.

Moose Lake

Arrowhead Tour 3.
Railroad stations: Northern Pacific, cor. East Ave. (US 61) and .5th St.; Minneapolis,
St. Paul & Sault Ste. Marie, West Rd. (State 27), 0.5 mile W.
Bus station: Northland Greyhound Lines, cor. East Ave. and 4th St.
Taxis: One cab line offers service within village limits and to surrounding territory.
Accommodations: Three hotels; municipal tourist camp, east end 3rd St., on lake shore.
Information service: Hotel Moose Lake.
Golf: Moose Lake Municipal Golf Club, Sand Lake Rd., 3.5 miles S.E., on lake
shore; 9 holes.
Swimming: Municipal beach, municipal tourist camp.

SOUTHERN GATEWAY

Moose Lake (1,085 alt., 1,432 pop.), skirting the shores of the lake of
the same name, is the center of a large agricultural district.

It came into existence in the early 1860's, shortly after the Military Road
had been cut from St. Paul to Superior and a stagecoach line established
(*see Carlton*). This was a stop-over point, located on the shore of Little
Moose Lake, about three miles east of the present site, where a hotel, some
barns, a few homes, and an Indian village made up a settlement.

In 1870, the Lake Superior and Mississippi Railroad, now the Northern
Pacific, the first in the Minnesota Arrowhead, was constructed about three
miles west of the stage line. The settlers lost no time in moving to the
railroad, and here the town developed.

The entire region was covered with beautiful stands of virgin white
pine. Logging activities started in the early 1870's, and for many years
this was the only means of livelihood. The first timber, cut on the east
side of the lake, was hauled to the lake shore, then floated across to a sawmill that started operations in 1874. Other mills appeared, but today the
sawmills are gone from Moose Lake, although some pulpwood is shipped.

As land was cleared, settlers turned to the soil, and during the early
1880's there was a heavy influx of immigrants, principally Scandinavians
and Finns. The town was platted in 1888 and incorporated in 1899.
Farming replaced lumbering, and in 1910 a second railroad, the Minneapolis, St. Paul and Sault Ste. Marie (Soo Line), was constructed.

The thriving village received a jolting setback in 1918, when, together
with Cloquet (*see Cloquet*) and several other towns in northern Minnesota,
it was destroyed by a forest fire that swept over approximately 1,500 square
miles. In Riverside Cemetery (US 61, 0.5 mile north) is a 27-foot granite
shaft erected by the State in memory of the victims. The town was rebuilt
with modern buildings and beautiful homes overlooking the lake.

Dairying is the main industry, one creamery annually producing 1,000,-
000 pounds of butter and handling 5,000 cases of eggs. There is a co-

operative produce association, which wholesales and retails farm products, and also a farm marketing association. Power is supplied by a municipal plant that was built in 1933.

The Nemadji Tile and Pottery Company (Soo Line right-of-way, 0.6 mile west), organized in 1923, manufactures Indian pottery and unglazed tile for walls, fireplaces, and general construction, in various colors produced by mixtures of local clays. The products are marketed throughout the United States.

On a slope overlooking the southeast shore of the lake is a State hospital for the insane (Island Lake Rd., two miles southeast). The construction of the $2,500,000 institution on a 1,700-acre site was begun in 1936. All structures are fireproof and are connected by tunnels, so that it is not necessary to take patients out-of-doors in inclement weather. Special windows, opening only five inches, have been installed.

The modern Moose Lake Grade and High School (cor. G Ave. and 5th St.) was erected in 1936, after a fire had destroyed the former building.

Among the many recreational facilities are several fine lakes that offer good fishing and water sports, and, although there are few resorts in the vicinity, a large summer population is attracted to the cabins built along the shores.

Mountain Iron

Arrowhead Tour 2.
Railroad station: Duluth, Missabe & Iron Range, 2nd St. (US 169) bet. 1st and Missabe Aves.
Bus station: Northland Greyhound Lines, Post Office, 2nd St. bet. Mountain and Biwabik Aves.
Accommodations: Village tourist camp, US 169, 5 blocks W.
Information service: Village Hall, cor. Mountain Ave. and 2nd St.
Tennis: Village and School District No. 21 Court, cor. Biwabik Ave. and 2nd St.

OPENING A NEW ERA

Mountain Iron (1,510 alt., 1,492 pop.) may be called the "birthplace of the Mesabi"; for it was here that the first iron ore of the Mesabi Range was discovered, and here that the first railroad to ship that ore was run.

The history of the town is linked indissolubly with the Merritt family of Duluth. Timber cruisers and prospectors, they estimated the wealth above their heads and searched for that below their feet. They made a dip needle survey of the entire range and sank test pits. No rich ore turned up, but they did not lose faith. Had not Leonidas Merritt found surface ore while exploring areas being logged? Had not his brother

Cassius brought back a rich chunk from a railroad right-of-way he was surveying? The work went on, with crews test-pitting in different parts of the range.

In 1890, the crew working under Captain J. A. Nichols discovered blue ore at the site of the present Mountain Iron Mine (inactive). He carried a bushel of it to Duluth, where it was assayed and found to have a high iron content. The Merritts had no way of shipping the ore, but at last they came to an agreement with the Duluth and Winnipeg Railroad (*see Proctor*), and the first shipment from the Mesabi was made in 1892. The mining camp grew. In April, an 80-acre town site was platted, named Grant in honor of the Duluth, Missabe and Northern Railroad contractor, and in November it was incorporated as the village of Mountain Iron.

The panic of 1893 dealt harshly with the new community. A sawmill built that year operated just long enough to supply the immediate lumber needs of the town. With the working of the near-by iron-ore deposits and the influx of new settlers, the village gradually became stabilized.

By 1900, the Mountain Iron Mine alone had produced 3,792,629 tons. Mining is still the town's main industry, though only one of the four mines in the vicinity, the Wacootah, is operating.

A granite quarry (Co. Rd. 63, two miles north), owned by the Mesabe Granite Company, commenced operations in 1935 and yields Mountain Iron pink granite (*see Ely; Cook*). A fire lookout tower, on the edge of the quarry, provides a good view of the surrounding country.

Mountain Iron's public buildings are of yellow brick. The High School (cor. Biwabik Ave. and 2nd St.) was built in 1911 at a cost of $95,000. Adjacent to it and connected by a tunnel is the Grade and Athletic Building (Biwabik Ave. bet. 2nd and 3rd Sts.), constructed in 1919 at a cost of $305,000.

The Village Hall (cor. Mountain Ave. and 2nd St.) and the Public Library (Mountain Ave. bet. 1st and 2nd Sts.) were erected in 1915. The library contains 13,000 volumes, many of which are in foreign languages, and receives 82 periodicals and 12 newspapers.

A bronze plaque mounted on a nine and one-half ton granite boulder on the High School lawn commemorates the fortieth anniversary of the first shipment of ore from the Mesabi. The fiftieth anniversary of the discovery of iron ore on the Mesabi Range was celebrated in Mountain Iron on August 9, 10, and 11, 1940, as the "Mountain Iron Golden Jubilee." A ten and one-half foot granite and cement statue of Leonidas Merritt, leader of the famous "Seven Iron Men," was unveiled by one of his sons, Harry Merritt, on the grounds of the Public Library. Lucien Merritt, another son of Leonidas, Glen Merritt, Alva Merritt, and Mrs. Robbins, daughter of Cassius Merritt, also participated.

Mountain Iron has several good trout streams in its vicinity, and the West Two River flows through the village.

Nashwauk

Arrowhead Tour 2.
Railroad station: Great Northern (freight only), south foot 1st St.
Bus station: Northland Greyhound Lines, Main St. bet. 2nd and 3rd Sts.
Accommodations: One hotel.
Information service: Ollila Hotel, cor. 3rd St. and Central Ave.

MINES AND ORE WASHING PLANTS

Nashwauk (1,500 alt., 2,228 pop.) is the largest mining community and second largest town in Itasca County.

Pine forests first attracted men to the western Mesabi Range. The region had no streams or rivers down which to float logs, so in 1890 the Wright-Davis Lumber Company laid tracks from the present site of Jacobson, where the Swan River flows into the Mississippi, to the heart of their timber land, near what is now Hibbing. James J. Hill of the Great Northern bought out their interests in 1899 and incorporated the road into his system.

In 1900, the Itasca Mining Company explored property that later was developed into the Hawkins Mine (west end Central Ave.). When iron ore was discovered, the deposit was leased to the Deering Harvester Company, and the mine was opened in 1902.

The Nashwauk Townsite Company platted the village on what was once the site of a lumber camp. Its name, from Nashwaak, a river and village near Fredericton, New Brunswick, is of Algonquian origin, probably meaning "land between," as does Nashau, the name of a city and river in New Hampshire.

In 1908-09, the Great Northern was extended from Nashwauk to connect with its main line at Grand Rapids, and tiny Nashwauk's growth really began. Mining operations expanded. In 1901, stripping had begun on an extensive scale at the Hawkins Mine; by the end of 1936, 12,164,000 tons of ore had been shipped from this open pit, the village's chief source of income. In connection with the mine is a washing and jigging plant (Washing Plant Rd., two miles south), in which the ore is separated on sieves or screens after impurities have been carried off by a water process. The La Rue Mine (La Rue Mine Rd., 1.5 miles east), opened at approximately the same time as the Hawkins, is operated by both open-pit and underground methods, as was the Headley (abandoned), formerly known as the Crosby, opened in 1903. The La Rue has a washing plant. Five other open-pit mines in the vicinity are active; two operate washing plants.

Nashwauk, with all this wealth at her door, has made steady progress. Among its public buildings are the Village Hall (cor. Central Ave. and 3rd St.), built of gray brick in 1916; the Nashwauk High School (2nd St.

bet. Platt and Roberts Aves.), constructed in 1922 of red brick, and the Soldiers Memorial Building (Central and 3rd St.), of red brick, built in 1928.

Northome

Arrowhead Tours 2, 3.
Railroad station: Minnesota & International, west end Main St. (Park Ave.).
Bus station: Northern Transportation Co., Scenic Hotel, cor. State 1 (Park Ave.) and State 46 (2nd St.).
Accommodations: One hotel.
Information service: Scenic Hotel.
Annual event (exact dates vary): Koochiching County Fair, August.

FROM FOREST TO FARM

Northome (1,451 alt., 343 pop.), its name contracted from North Home at the request of the United States Postal Service, is one of the Koochiching County communities that are turning from lumbering to farming.

With white pine, cedar, elm, balsam, maple, birch, and basswood covering the area, the village, settled about 1897, grew as a typical lumbering center. Sawmills were built, and the Big Fork and Northern Railroad was constructed between Northome and Big Falls (*see Big Falls*). In 1912, Chris P. Ellingson bought 200 acres of timber land on the north shore of Island Lake, put up a sawmill that had a ten-hour capacity of 40,000 feet, and organized the Island Lake Lumber Company, which gave the community new life. Sawmills are still operating in Northome, and pulpwood is shipped to the mills at International Falls.

The rich, black loam prevalent in this vicinity attracted settlers, who have developed cut-over lands for farming. Many of the lumber workers have also turned to agriculture. The soil is adapted to the growing of alfalfa and clover, and a principal source of income in the Northome region is the sale of clover and alfalfa seed. Northome has a cooperative creamery that handles most of the dairy products of the district.

The Northome Consolidated School (cor. State 46 and Lake St.) is a grade and high school for Koochiching County pupils in the unorganized school district. In 1922, a fireproof, shale-brick addition to the original four-room frame structure was built at a cost of $50,000.

Northome is popular as a vacation town. Several lakes offering good fishing are within easy driving distance, and there are many scenic attractions for tourists, among them Island Lake, three miles south of Northome, which has 12 resorts and lodges. Game is plentiful, and the hunting season brings an influx of sportsmen.

Orr

Arrowhead Tours 3, 4.
Railroad station: Duluth, Winnipeg & Pacific (Canadian National), junction US 53 and Orr-Buyck Rd. (Co. Rd. 23).
Bus Station: Northern Transportation Co., US 53, 0.1 mile N.
Taxis: One cab line offers service within village limits and to surrounding territory.
Accommodations: One hotel; municipal camp grounds, US 53, 0.25 mile N.
Information service: Orr-Arrowhead Club, Post Office, junction US 53 and Orr-Buyck Rd.
Swimming: Pelican Beach (municipal), US 53, 0.25 mile N.
Tennis: St. Louis County School 142, Orr-Buyck Rd., 0.3 mile S.E.
Rifle range: Orr-Pelican Lake Rifle Club, Pelican Rd., 2 miles W.
Annual event (exact dates vary): Water Carnival, July.

LAST OUTFITTING POINT

Orr (1,305 alt., 234 pop.), on the east shore of Pelican Lake, is a village on the road to the wilderness. The region was the hunting grounds of Indians, who roamed the forests and paddled the waters. They have had a settlement on Nett Lake since about 1600. Nett Lake is one of the reservations under the jurisdiction of the Consolidated Chippewa Indian Agency (*see Cass Lake*).

Into this area replete with wild life came fur traders. In 1889, Henry Connors, from Superior, Wisconsin, built a trading post on the Pelican River, about one mile south of the site of the present Orr. After passing through different hands, the post was bought in 1895 or 1896 by William Orr, who held undisputed sway over both Indians and whites for many years, and after whom the village was named.

Lumbering helped to open up the country. Fine stands of pine covered the area, and records show that a man named Saunders was logging on the south shore of Pelican Lake as early as 1891. The logs were hauled to the Willow River, floated on the Little Fork to Rainy River, and thence across Lake of the Woods to Rat Portage (Kenora), a drive of nearly 400 miles. Stephen Gheen built a sawmill at Elbow Falls on Elbow River, a short distance from the village site, in 1900, and sawed lumber for the first buildings in Orr. Several logging companies were operating in the territory; later they joined to form the Virginia and Rainy Lake Lumber Company.

By 1905, the right-of-way for a logging railroad had been cut beyond Orr, which now had a hotel, store, and other buildings. In 1906-07, train service to the Canadian border was begun.

As lumbering waned, Orr became a virtual "ghost" town. Although agriculture has been developed to some extent in the area, today the town relies largely on the tourist trade. It is the last outfitting point for sportsmen bound for the border lakes and is the railroad station for freight going to that region.

Orr was incorporated as a village in 1935. Its new brick school, St. Louis County School 142, was constructed in 1936; the first school was built in 1907. The Senior High Department is the farthest north of all rural high schools in St. Louis County.

Orr is headquarters for forest rangers (junction Orr-Buyck Rd. and US 53) supervising the 918,560-acre Kabetogama State Forest, now largely incorporated in the Superior National Forest.

Proctor

Arrowhead Tour 2.
Railroad station: Duluth, Missabe & Iron Range, W. 2nd St. bet. 2nd Ave. E. and Short St.
Bus station: Northland Greyhound Lines, 223 West Side Ave.
Information service: Village Hall, 100 E. 2nd St.
Golf: Duluth, Missabe & Iron Range Employees' Association Golf Course (open to public), cor. Forest St. and 2nd Ave. E.; 4 holes.
Tennis: Proctor High School, cor. Central Ave. and E. 3rd St.
Annual event (exact dates vary): Southern St. Louis County Fair, August or September.

THE HUB

Proctor (1,236 alt., 2,468 pop.), a village whose history parallels that of the Duluth, Missabe and Iron Range Railroad, is the greatest iron ore transportation center in the world.

In 1892, the Merritts built the Duluth, Missabe and Northern Railroad from Mountain Iron to Stony Brook, a distance of 45 miles, to transport ore from the Mountain Iron Mine to the Duluth and Winnipeg Railroad, which had agreed to carry the output from Stony Brook to the lake. A year later, because the Duluth and Winnipeg failed to supply sufficient cars, and, moreover, was shipping the ore to docks in Superior, the Duluth, Missabe and Northern was extended into Duluth.

The site of the present Proctor, then regarded as part of Oneota (*see Duluth*), was selected for the shops and classification yards. In 1894, the village was incorporated.

Now officially rechristened as Proctor, it was originally named Proctor-knott for the Honorable J. Proctor Knott, former Governor of Kentucky and United States Congressman, who in 1871 delivered a satirical Congressional speech ridiculing Duluth. It was on January 27, 1871, that one group in Congress tried to secure the extension of a land grant for "the construction of a railroad from the St. Croix River or lake to the west end of Lake Superior and to Bayfield," while the other group was anxious to secure the passage of a bill designed "to appropriate $500,000 to improve the harbor at Duluth." The latter group was influenced by the Lake Superior and Mississippi Railroad, which had just been completed in July, 1870. Mr. Knott evidently supposed that the proposed appropriation for the Duluth harbor was a part of the scheme of those interested in getting a land grant for the railroad. As a matter of fact it had no relation to the railroad land grant. The Duluth people as well as the Lake Superior and Mississippi Railroad were very much opposed to the land grant, mainly on account of the intense rivalry between Duluth and Superior in those days. The St. Croix and Bayfield Railroad was to have its terminus at Superior, and there is little doubt that the building of that railroad would have promoted the growth of Duluth's rival.

Mr. Knott, who had no connection with either of the opposing groups, tried in his speech, as a matter of principle, to fight the extension of the land grant. His words were so packed with sarcastic humor that the House repeatedly rocked in laughter. The land grant bill was killed, but his humorous speech caught the public fancy. Attention was focused on Duluth, which he had termed "the center of the universe," and within 20 years many of the predictions that Proctor Knott had made in mocking jest became a reality.

Railroading is Proctor's only industry. The shops and ore classification yards of the Duluth, Missabe and Iron Range Railroad cover approximately 240 acres and ordinarily employ about 1,000 men. These classification yards, the largest in the world, with 57 miles of track and a capacity of 6,479 hopper-bottomed cars, make up trainloads of ore according to quality specifications, to be hauled by mallet engines down the heavy six-mile grade to the Duluth ore docks (*see Duluth Tour 3*). The roundhouse has 30 stalls, with equipment for repairs, and is a modern engine terminal. When cold weather sets in, the ore-steaming plant thaws ore that has been frozen, thus facilitating loading and lengthening the shipping season.

Proctor's public school system consists of three schools: Proctor High; Proctor East Side Grade (cor. Central Ave. and E. 2nd St.); and Summit Grade and Junior High (cor. 8th Ave. and W. 2nd St.). There is one parochial school, St. Rose of Lima (116 E. 3rd St.), conducted by the Sisters of St. Benedict.

The $102,000 two-story brick Village Hall was completed in 1940, replacing the frame structure that had been in use for 30 years.

Tower

Arrowhead Tour 4.
Canoe Trips: 14, 15.
Railroad station: Duluth, Missabe & Iron Range, cor. Pine and 2nd Sts.
Bus station: Northland Greyhound Lines, Main St. bet. Birch and Spruce Sts.

Information service: Tower Commercial Club, 609 Main St.
Swimming: McKinley Park Beach (open to public), McKinley Park, McKinley Park
Rd., 3 miles N. (via Soudan).
Tennis: Tower Public School, cor. Spruce and N. 3rd Sts.
Annual event (exact dates vary): Winter Frolic, January.

FIRST CITY OF THE RANGES

Tower (1,367 alt., 820 pop.), guarded by Jasper Peak and Lake Vermilion, and in the shadow of the historic Soudan Mine (State 1, 1.5 miles east), to which it owes its existence, is the Arrowhead's oldest incorporated municipality north of Duluth.

Over inland waterways, in the early days of the Northwest, paddled adventurous fur traders, one of their well-traveled routes being through Lake Vermilion.

During 1865-66, rumors of gold were rampant, and so many prospectors rushed into the district, accessible only by complicated and difficult water and land routes, that the Vermilion Trail (*see Duluth Tour 1*) was cut from Duluth to the site of Tower.

Among the gold prospectors was George R. Stuntz of Duluth. When he found outcroppings of iron ore at the site of the present Soudan Mine, he was not surprised, because he knew of the existence of iron ore in the region and had seen samples of it. Stuntz surveyed a town site at the wilderness end of the Vermilion Trail in 1882, after a sawmill and a planing mill had been set up to saw the pine logs floated down the East Two River. Stuntz's town site was selected for a business section to serve the location (Soudan) where the Minnesota Iron Mining Company already had put up homes. In 1883, it was organized as a village and named in honor of the Philadelphia financier, Charlemagne Tower.

The early settlers suffered many hardships. Transportation facilities were poor—it took two nights and three days to travel by wagon over the Vermilion Trail from Duluth. The weekly mail service was, of course, uncertain. (The mining company's payroll was sent nailed in a wooden box.) During a severe cold spell, the clerk at the store is said to have requisitioned a six-foot thermometer guaranteed not to freeze at 40 below zero.

In 1884, the Duluth and Iron Range Railroad, running between Two Harbors and Soudan, was extended to Tower. Lumbering then became a thriving industry. The population of the village was increasing, and Tower was incorporated as a city in 1889.

Tower is on the south shore of Lake Vermilion, one of the largest and most popular summer resort lakes in the region, and one to which fishermen from all parts of the United States are attracted. Wall-eyed and northern pike, perch, and rock bass are plentiful. Lake Vermilion, 35 miles long, with 365 islands, has a 1,000-mile shoreline backed by coniferous trees and lofty hills of granite. It was called *Sah-Ga-Ee-Gum-Wah-Ma-Mah-Nee,* "lake-of-the-sunset-glow," by the Chippewa. Swimming, boating, fishing, and canoeing facilities are available at numerous resorts.

The remnant of a large band of Chippewa still lives on the shores of

Pike Bay (Co. Rd. 413, 10.5 miles northeast). Their handiwork is exhibited in the stores at Tower. A few years ago the Government (*see Cass Lake*) transferred the majority of the Lake Vermilion band to the Bois Fort Reservation on Nett Lake (*see Arrowhead Tour 3*), but many preferred to stay where they were.

The McKinley Monument (cor. Main and Alder Sts.) was erected shortly after the assassination of the President in 1901, and Tower gained distinction as the first city in the United States to unveil a memorial in his honor.

Agriculture is being developed in the surrounding area, while lumbering, though a declining industry, is still of some importance.

Two Harbors

Arrowhead Tour 1.
Railroad station: Duluth, Missabe & Iron Range, cor. South Ave. and 6th St.
Bus station: Northland Greyhound Lines, 530 1st Ave.
Taxis: Three cab lines offer service within city limits and to surrounding territory.
Accommodations: Eight hotels and lodging houses; municipal tourist camp, foot 3rd Ave., fronting Burlington Bay.
Golf: Lakeview Golf Course (municipal), US 61, 4 blocks E.; 9 holes.
Tennis: D. M. & I. R. Courts, 710 1st Ave.; municipal court, cor. 10th Ave. and 6th St.
Badminton: Municipal court, cor. 10th Ave. and 6th St.
Annual events (exact dates vary): Winter Frolic, January; Lake County Fair, August.

MINNESOTA'S FIRST ORE PORT

Two Harbors (635 alt., 4,046 pop.), Lake County seat and linked historically with the Vermilion Range, placidly overlooks Burlington and Agate Bays, from whose harbors it received its name. The Chippewa, ever poetic, called the spot *Wass-we-win-ing*, "place-to-spear-by-moonlight."

All the north shore of Lake Superior, including the site of Two Harbors, was Indian territory until 1855. The first white settler on Agate Bay was Thomas Saxton, who arrived in 1856. A village was platted and named for him. In 1857, J. J. Hibbard, with his brother and brother-in-law, built a sawmill at Burlington Bay, which had been platted in 1856. These little villages succumbed during the financial panic of 1857.

When iron ore was discovered on the Vermilion Range, Two Harbors—then called Agate Bay—was made the Lake Superior terminus of the Duluth and Iron Range Railroad. It was not until 1887 that the railroad was extended from Two Harbors to Duluth. The dock that received the first ore shipped was 552 feet long and 44 feet high, and each of the 46 pockets had a capacity of 300 tons.

The building of the railroad brought an influx of Americans, Swedes, Norwegians, Danes, and Canadians. "Whiskey Row," popular name for the main street, extended from where the lighthouse now stands (foot Lighthouse Rd.) to the site of the present coal dock (beyond foot 5th St.; *visitors not permitted*). The town spread to the north and west. In 1887, the first church, Presbyterian, was organized, with Reverend J. L. Johnstone its pastor.

In 1888, the seat of Lake County was moved from Beaver Bay to Two Harbors. Following the incorporation of the village in that year, many civic improvements were undertaken. In 1906, a new courthouse (cor. 3rd Ave. and 6th St.) was completed at a cost of $80,000. The village became a city in 1907. As shipping and railroad facilities improved, Two Harbors continued to thrive and today it is a busy lakeside community, a port for iron ore, the trade center of a developing agricultural region, and a favorite stopover for tourists.

The original iron-ore dock, made of wood, the first to be built at the head of the lakes, has been replaced by three of concrete and steel (3, 4, 6 blocks, respectively, southwest foot 6th St.; *visitors not permitted*). At one time, Dock No. 1, 1,368 feet long and 59½ feet high, with 202 loading pockets, was the largest iron-ore dock in the world. Ten million tons of ore have been shipped in one season, and nearly 40,000,000 tons over a six-year period. A record was made when a ship at Two Harbors was loaded with more than 12,000 tons in 16 minutes. These three docks, together with one lumber or merchandise and one coal dock, all owned by the Duluth, Missabe and Iron Range Railroad, give the harbor a combined frontage of 6,000 feet. Coal received here is distributed to the Vermilion and Mesabi ranges.

The Duluth, Missabe and Iron Range Railroad, originally the Duluth and Iron Range, hauls both Vermilion and eastern Mesabi iron ore to the docks. Lumber is still shipped from Two Harbors, though in far smaller quantities than formerly.

The city has three cooperatives, retailing hardware, groceries, meats, general merchandise, and farm products.

The United States Coast Guard Service (bay front bet. 6th and 7th Sts.) maintains a year-round base here.

Adjoining the Duluth, Missabe and Iron Range Railroad station are relics of the early railroad days. *The Three Spot,* the first locomotive used on the Duluth and Iron Range, brought from Duluth on a scow towed by the tug *Ella Stone* during a severe storm, was in use for many years. The old sleigh and wagon, also on display here, were the means of land transportation between Duluth and Two Harbors for officials of the company during the construction of the railroad.

A globular monument in Owen's Park (6th St. bet. 2nd and 3rd Aves.) commemorates the first shipment of iron ore from Minnesota (1884), and, on the lawn of the Public Library (cor. 4th Ave. and 6th St.), are 700-pound samples of the ore. Owen's Park also contains a 25-millimeter German Minenwerfer Howitzer, taken by the Americans at St. Mihiel in 1918, and a bell once used as the town's fire signal. In Courthouse Square

are a Soldiers' Monument and a 15,945-pound cannon made in South Boston in 1884 and used in coast defense at Fort Monroe, Virginia.

Educational facilities in Two Harbors are excellent. The city lies within a school district unique in the State—all Lake County, including Two Harbors, is embraced in one consolidated school district governed by a board made up of one member from each of the five commissioner districts.

Two Harbors is the most important point along the north shore of Lake Superior between Duluth and the twin Canadian cities of Fort William and Port Arthur on Thunder Bay.

Virginia

Arrowhead Tours 2, 3, 4.
Railroad stations: Duluth, Winnipeg & Pacific (Canadian National), 537 Chestnut St.; Duluth, Missabe & Iron Range, cor. Chestnut St. and 1st Ave. S.
Bus station: Northland Greyhound Lines, and Northern Transportation Co., 3rd Ave. bet. Chestnut St. and 1st St. N.
Local bus line: Lambert Motor Coach Co., 3rd Ave. bet. Chestnut St. and 1st St. N., offers service within city limits.
Airport: Municipal, cor. Hollywood Ave. and Wilson St., 2 miles S.W.; 4 sod runways, all 300 feet wide; the name VIRGINIA imbedded in field; facilities for servicing aircraft during day only.
Taxis: Three cab lines offer service within city limits and to surrounding territory.
Accommodations: Three hotels; municipal tourist camp, west end Chestnut St., on Silver Lake; tourist homes.
Information service: Virginia Chamber of Commerce, City Hall, cor. 4th Ave. and 1st St. S.; Tourist Bureau, 6th Ave. and 3rd St. N.
Recreational facilities: Memorial Bldg., cor. 3rd Ave. and 1st St. S.
Golf: Municipal, cor. 9th Ave. and 9th St. N.; 18 holes.
Tennis: Municipal courts.
Annual event (exact dates vary): Civic Exposition, October.

QUEEN CITY OF THE RANGE

Virginia (1,438 alt., 12,264 pop.), the second largest municipality of the iron ranges, sits enthroned near the crest of the Great Laurentian Highland Divide. Its history is written in the story of lumbering and mining.

With the iron-ore fever spreading as the result of the discovery of iron ore on the Mesabi (*see Mountain Iron*), prospectors and timber cruisers swarmed over the region. In 1892, the Missabe Mountain Mine (east end Chestnut St.) was discovered by Captain Cohoe, an employee of the Merritts. In the same year, at the height of the boom, the Virginia Improvement Company platted the town site, naming it in honor of Alfred E. Humphrey, president of the company, whose home was in the State of

Virginia. That this was virgin country covered with stands of virgin pine gave the name further significance.

The original plat of 80 acres was recorded in September, 1892, and the first lots were sold at public auction in Duluth, where eager buyers, excited by the news of ore deposits, paid from $300 to $400 for small business sites in the timber they never had seen. Pine was slashed to make the main thoroughfare, now Chestnut Street. Rough buildings were thrown together, and businessmen, lumbermen, investors, lumberjacks, and cruisers flooded into the settlement. A small portable mill on the east side of Silver Lake marked the beginning of industry.

On November 12, 1892, Virginia became a village after its initial election, at which 66 ballots were cast by the resident population of 181. Development was slow until 1893, when the Duluth, Missabe and Northern Railroad built a spur track from Wolf Junction, to handle heavy mining machinery.

The Virginia Enterprise was founded by A. E. Bickford, who also was its sole staff member; it was printed at Hurley, Wisconsin, whence it was brought to Virginia, often with the mail, in a trunk.

Reverend E. N. Raymond spent his first Sunday watching a poker game, which he finally broke up by announcing that, since he had watched their play all day, it was only fair the players should watch his. About 80 men attended; thus church activities (Presbyterian) were inaugurated.

By the middle of the year, with 15 developed mines in the district, the population of the town had grown to 5,000.

Then came two serious setbacks. On June 18, 1893, a forest fire destroyed practically the entire village. Close on its heels spread a financial panic. Many who had invested in the mines were unable to hold their interests. Work was almost at a standstill, and wages, when paid at all, were very low.

Iron from the near-by rich deposits must have seeped into their very blood, for the Virginians refused to accept defeat, and set about rebuilding their town.

In 1894, another period of rapid development began, and on April 1, 1895, the village was incorporated as a city. Although many families left during the hard years that followed, Virginia continued to grow.

As railroad facilities were extended into the pine lands to the north, lumbering became a major source of income, second only to mining. The Bailey sawmill was erected in 1895, and two more were in operation to 1900; Virginia had become one of the leading lumber centers of northern Minnesota.

On June 7, 1900, another fire, starting in the Finlayson Mill, destroyed the town. Again the Virginians had to rebuild, but this time all construction on the main business street was restricted to brick, stone, or concrete. Following the second fire, the population dropped to 2,692, but five years later it had increased to 6,056.

Virginia had found its stride, and the period between 1904 and 1913 was one of rapid expansion; 13 contracts for schools were let; more sawmills opened, notably the Virginia and Rainy Lake Lumber Company's white pine mill in 1909; railroad facilities were expanded, and the district headquarters of the Oliver Iron Mining Company moved here from Mountain Iron in 1910.

With the depletion of the forests, the lumber industry declined, though the W. T. Bailey Lumber Company (708 6th Ave. N.) still produces 35,000 feet of pine lumber daily. Mining has grown steadily, and Virginia's 20 iron mines, both underground and open pit, have made it one of the most important communities of the three Arrowhead ranges.

The Missabe Mountain is the largest single iron-ore producing mine in the world, shipping about 7,000 tons per day. The Wheeling Steel Corporation, the Republic Iron and Steel Corporation, the Oliver Iron Mining Company, the Interstate Iron Company, and the Evergreen Mining Company all operate in the vicinity.

Virginia is a large trade center, having 264 retail establishments, several small factories, and one cooperative and two independent creameries. There are three cooperative stores, clearing through the Range Cooperative Federation.

Varied activities have brought an influx of many nationalities. The Finnish influence is evident in the place names of surrounding communities: Palo, Makinen, and Toivola.

The city is rightly proud of its public buildings. In 1904, all school buildings were frame structures except Roosevelt High School, the first brick school building on the range. The new Roosevelt High (cor. 5th Ave. S. and 3rd St.), completed in 1929, is of Gothic design and elaborately equipped. The Technical Building, opposite and equally imposing, houses the Junior High and Junior College. Its auditorium, with a seating capacity of 1,500, has complete sound-movie apparatus.

Memorial Building (*open*), erected in 1919 at a cost of $500,000, commemorates the city's World War dead. It has 50,000 feet of floor space; the main floor is used for dancing during summer and in winter for hockey and skating. In the basement are clubrooms, a large dining room with adjoining kitchens, and a seven-lane curling rink.

The City Hall (cor. 4th Ave. S. and 1st St.) is a four-story reinforced concrete and brick structure. The Courthouse (cor. 5th Ave. S. and 2nd St.), of cream-colored brick, is one of St. Louis County's two fulltime auxiliary courthouses. The Public Library (cor. 5th Ave. S. and 2nd St.) contains over 41,300 volumes, of which 5,315 are at the North Branch (cor. 7th Ave. N. and 11th St.).

Virginia was one of the first cities in the State to adopt a commission form of government. Gas, water, light, and heat are furnished by municipal plants. These utilities are administered by the City Water and Light Commission, with headquarters in its own building (620 2nd St. S.).

Interest in music is fostered by four organizations: Municipal Band, Municipal Symphony Orchestra, High School Band, and High School Orchestra. Weekly concerts are held in the Technical School during winter; during the summer, on Wednesday evenings at South Side Park (cor. 5th Ave. S. and 11th St.), and on Sunday evenings in Olcott Park (cor. 9th Ave. N. and 9th St.).

Olcott Park, 40 landscaped acres, contains a zoo and also boasts an intricate floral display of special design, a monkey island, and an electric, multi-colored fountain. Baseball, hockey, fishing, and other sport facilities are available.

The Superior National Forest, Lake Vermilion, and the border lakes are within easy driving distance and attract a large tourist trade.

Walker

Arrowhead Tour 3.
Railroad stations: Great Northern, 12th St. bet. Birch and Maple Aves.; Minnesota & International, cor. Railroad and 5th Sts.
Bus station: Northland Greyhound Lines, Minnesota Ave. bet. 5th and 6th Sts.
Airport: Tianna Golf Club Field, State 34, 2 miles S.W.; no hangar or service.
Taxis: One cab line offers service within village limits and to surrounding territory.
Accommodations: Two hotels; municipal tourist camp, 2nd St. bet. Minnesota Ave. and Prospect Place.
Information service: Information Bureau, Conservation Bldg., Minnesota Ave. bet. 2nd and 3rd Sts.
Golf: Tianna Country Club, State 34, 1 mile S.; 10 holes.
Tennis: Conservation Bldg.
Swimming: Municipal beach, cor. Cleveland Blvd. and 3rd St.
Riding academy: Danworthy Camp for Girls, State 34, 3 miles S.W.
Annual event (exact dates vary): Flower Show, August.

VACATIONER'S PARADISE

Walker (1,336 alt., 939 pop.), Cass County seat, is located in the southwest corner of Chippewa National Forest, on an Indian reservation (*see Cass Lake*), and along the shores of historic Leech Lake.

Indians have lived along the pine-covered shores of this lake for centuries. The first white men to penetrate the area bought pelts from them, and soon fur-trading posts were established. One of these posts stood a few miles from the site of the present Walker, on a point jutting into Leech Lake.

When Cass County was established in 1851, the influx of lumbermen already had begun. Thomas Barlow Walker in 1868 purchased a large stand of pine in the vicinity. A few years later, he sold the ground on which the village was built to the Leech Lake Land Company, reserving rights to the timber. After the village was established and named in his honor (incorporated 1896), he sent in his timber cutters. The settlers protested, and their attempt to drive the cutters out was the cause of bitter resentment for many years.

In 1897, the Park Rapids and Leech Lake Railroad was constructed between Park Rapids, Walker, and Cass Lake and, in 1899, was leased to the

Great Northern; in 1900, the Minnesota and International was extended to Walker, and took over the Brainerd and Northern in 1901 (*see Brainerd*).

The soil, a mixed black, brown, and sandy clay, is adapted to the raising of small grains, potatoes, and grasses. Dairying has become the leading industry; an independent creamery began operations in 1923.

The county offices, jail, and sheriff's residence are in the modern Cass County Courthouse (Minnesota Ave. bet. 3rd and 4th Sts.), and the municipal offices are in the Village Hall (6th St. bet. Minnesota Ave. and Front St.), erected in 1937. Pupils from the rural areas are brought by bus to the Walker Public School (cor. Highland Ave. and 4th St.), a brick structure. The Walker Museum (Minnesota Ave. bet. 2nd and 3rd Sts.), started in 1894, contains a collection of native animals and birds. In the Conservation Building, Indian bead work and articles of handicraft are made and displayed.

Herds on the 1,000-acre Tianna Farms (State 34, 5 miles south) include 100 purebred Guernsey and 50 Aberdeen Angus cattle that have set State and national records. Approximately 75 per cent of the Guernseys have the blood of La Noce of Riverside Farm, first Guernsey-bred cow to make a world's production record (*see Barnum*).

Walker is in the center of the region known as the Paul Bunyan Playground (*see Brainerd; Bemidji*), which each year attracts vacationists, fishermen, and hunters to its lakes. Summer resorts, built to accommodate a steadily increasing tourist trade, furnish launch service and provide both Indian and white guides.

PART IV
Tours

Arrowhead Tour 1

(*To See North Shore*)

Duluth—Two Harbors—Beaver Bay—Grand Marais—Mineral Center—
International Border—Fort William—Port Arthur; 199 *m.*, US 61.

US 61 is paved from Duluth to Two Harbors, hard-surfaced to Arrowhead (Brule)
River, and graveled to border; Scott Highway is hard-surfaced from border to Port
Arthur.

This north shore tour runs northeast on US 61, from its junction with
US 53, along the shore of Lake Superior to Pigeon River on the international border, through country notable in the history of the Minnesota
Arrowhead; it continues on Scott Highway 1 from Pigeon River to Port
Arthur. Good tourist facilities are available; there are many summer
resorts; and trout fishing is excellent in the numerous streams. Deep-sea
fishing is growing in popularity. Boats and equipment may be rented;
professional fishermen are available as guides (*see General Information:
Fishing and Hunting*).

DULUTH, 0 *m.* (cor. Superior St. and Piedmont Ave.) (602 alt.,
101,065 pop.). The waters of Lake Superior and Superior and St. Louis
Bays offer a fascinating playground (*see Duluth*).

The country adjoining US 61 along LAKE SUPERIOR is, to a large
extent, typical of the entire north shore. Norway pine, mountain ash, and
white birch grow along the shore. Strawberries, raspberries, blueberries,
and huckleberries are abundant in season. Blossoming chokecherry and
pin cherry trees, violets, cowslips, fireweed, and buttercups add color to
woods and rocks. Back of the lake is a line of hills marking the escarpment—a geologic fault or dislocation of the earth's crust (*see Geology*)—
that extends far into Canada. At intervals along the shore, on bays and
inlets, are fishermen's cottages, and nets stretched out on frames to dry.
The cascades and high falls of streams draining the north shore enhance
the beauty of the drive.

The Duluth WATER PUMPING STATION (R) is in a red-brick
building at LAKEWOOD, 9.4 *m.* Duluthians boast of their unlimited
supply of pure water, but older citizens recall the city's long fight to obtain
it. In 1883, the Duluth Gas and Water Company, a private corporation,
was granted a franchise; a pumping station was built at 14th Avenue East.
The city acquired the plants of the Duluth Gas and Water Company in

1898, and the pumping station at Lakewood was then constructed. All the water delivered by the main water works system is pumped from Lake Superior at the Lakewood Pumping Station. It is drawn into the station through a five-foot intake pipe, about 1,560 feet in length, which terminates in water about 75 feet deep. This end of the intake is an elbow, so the water actually is drawn from a depth of about 60 feet below the surface of the lake. Pumping is ordinarily done by one of the three electrically driven centrifugal pumps, which together have a total daily capacity of some 57,000,000 gallons. In 1939, the daily average of water pumped was 11,139,781 gallons. The total available capacity of reservoirs, tanks, and cisterns is almost 51,000,000 gallons. There are 262.54 miles of water mains.

The STATE FISH HATCHERY (L), 12.7 m., at FRENCH RIVER, a small settlement, supplies a greater variety of freshwater fish than any other State hatchery. Several millions each of lake trout, pike, and white-fish are reared annually, in addition to hundreds of thousands of rainbow and brook trout and other varieties in lesser quantities.

At 16.2 m. is the historic SITE OF BUCHANAN (Marker R.), where the Arrowhead's first Federal Land Office was established during the boom in 1856.

KNIFE RIVER, 19.4 m. (627 alt., 125 pop.), was so named because of the sharp-edged stones in the river that divides the town. It was settled by copper prospectors, the first of whom came in 1854 in anticipation of the opening of the north shore to white settlement by the Treaty of La Pointe; others followed in the 1860's and 1870's. No paying lode was found, however, but lumbering operations were started on a small scale. In 1898, the Alger-Smith Lumber Company made Knife River the terminus of its railroad, which ran northeast into Lake and Cook counties. The settlement continued to thrive as a lumbering center until 1919, when the Alger-Smith Company sold its interests. In 1929, it received impetus from a short-lived attempt to mine copper.

TWO HARBORS, 27 m. (635 alt., 4,046 pop.) (see Two Harbors): Ore Docks, Old Three Spot, Old Sleigh and Wagon, 700-pound Samples of First Ore Taken from a Minnesota Mine, Commemorative Globular Monument, U. S. Coast Guard Station, Soldiers' Monument, Fort Monroe Cannon, German Minenwerfer Howitzer.

At SILVER CREEK CLIFF, 32.7 m., the road passes under a birch arch and winds upward to the face of a precipice overhanging the lake. The highway was cut with great difficulty, because loose rock, shaken by the blasting, broke off the top and side of the cliff, and repeatedly blocked the road.

A BRONZE PLAQUE (R) mounted on granite in the retaining wall along the road gives data pertaining to Lake Superior—known to the Indians as Kitchi Gummi.

At ENCAMPMENT RIVER, 34.3 m., a narrow section of virgin timber has been saved by owners of summer homes in the neighborhood.

CROW CREEK, 38.2 m., is called also Prohibition Creek because it usually is dry.

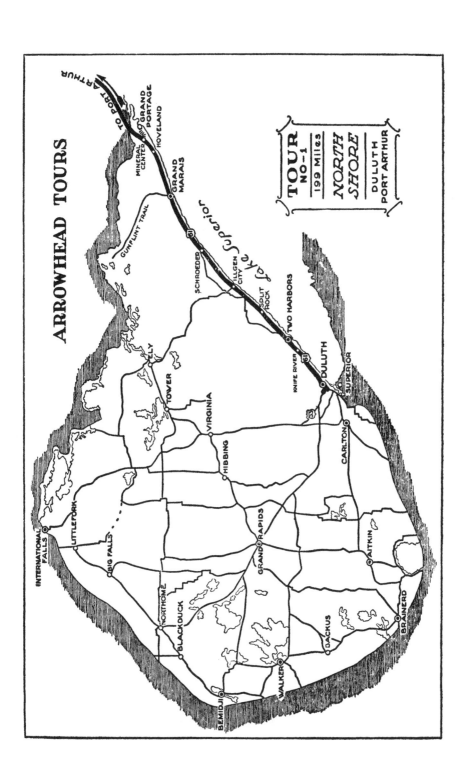

ARROWHEAD TOURS

TOUR
NO-1
199 Miles
NORTH SHORE
DULUTH
PORT ARTHUR

GOOSEBERRY STATE PARK, 40.9 *m.* (R. and L), extending from the lake along both sides of GOOSEBERRY RIVER, was created in 1933 and includes 638 acres. Visible just above the highway bridge is a WATERFALL, at the foot of which is a NATURAL SWIMMING POOL; below the highway are three lesser FALLS. Along the grassy ravine, parking spaces afford fine views of lake and river. There are substantial stone buildings with fireplaces, stoves, and tables. On the bluff above the lake are outdoor fireplaces, firewood, tables, benches, and drinking fountains.

SPLIT ROCK RIVER, 45.1 *m.*, so-called because of the rocky canyon at its mouth, flows into Lake Superior across a wide sand bar.

At 48.1 *m.* is the junction with a gravel road.

Right on this road is SPLIT ROCK LIGHTHOUSE (*open daily 8 a. m. to 5 p. m., July 1 to Sept. 1*), 0.3 *m.*, perched high on a cliff overlooking dangerous reefs. Its light is 168 feet above the level of Lake Superior. It is of great value to mariners, for magnetic rock formations in the area divert compass needles. An iron stairway leads from the top of the rock to the lake shore.

BEAVER BAY, 52.8 *m.* (602 alt., unincorporated) (*see Beaver Bay*), at the mouth of BEAVER RIVER.

At 58.1 *m.* is PALISADE HEAD, a massive headland of basalt.

Right on a winding gravel road is a lookout point, 0.5 *m.*, atop a 348-foot precipice that stands as it was when the walls of the crater crashed and formed the basin of Lake Superior (*see Geology*). From this and other vantage points boats far out on the lake are visible, and on clear days even the Apostle Islands, 30 miles distant, can be seen. There are picnic grounds with tables and fireplaces, but no water.

BAPTISM RIVER, 59.6 *m.*, called "Au Bapteme" by a French trader, has many falls and rapids and a deep canyon at its mouth; it is one of the best trout streams on the north shore.

CRYSTAL BAY, 60.4 *m.*, is noteworthy for several points of scenic and historic interest.

Left from the highway is a footpath leading to MOUNT MARY LOOKOUT, 1.5 *m.*, which offers an excellent view of lake and shore line. Right from the highway on a dirt road is the HUDSON'S BAY TRAIL, 0.1 *m.*, over which mail was carried from Two Harbors to Grand Portage. To the left of the pathway is a FLAGPOLE—remnant of the old log schoolhouse that was used by both Indians and whites until 1905. A footpath continues straight ahead to a promontory, 0.3 *m.*, overlooking the bay and the remains of a CORUNDUM MINE that operated from 1903 to 1906, when it was abandoned because of poor shipping facilities. At the northeastern end is CAVE OF WAVES, a natural rock formation through which a passage large enough for rowboats and canoes has been worn through by the action of the waves.

ILLGEN CITY, 60.7 *m.*, is at the junction with State 1 (*see Arrowhead Tour 4*).

MANITOU RIVER, 69.6 *m.*, in a deep gorge, is crossed on a high curving bridge. Rainbow and speckled trout are abundant, and a typical Northern flower, the white rock-saxifrage, grows on the cold wet rocks.

Left from the highway on a footpath is an 80-foot WATERFALL, 0.1 *m*. Right from the highway is a footpath leading to the lakeshore, 0.5 *m.*, where are high gray overhanging cliffs. At the base of one is a deep CAVE; it is possible to scramble down to the narrow beach, where sometimes a sand bar, ten to 15 feet wide, closes the river's mouth, forming a BAY into which the river plunges.

TWO ISLAND RIVER, 78.8 *m.,* so named because of two islands, GULL and BEAR, opposite its mouth, offers excellent lake trout fishing. Agates are found on the beach and occasionally thomsonites, imbedded semiprecious stones formed by mineral deposition in gas or steam bubbles of lava flows. Gulls nest on the ledges of the island cliffs.

At SCHROEDER, 80.8 *m.* (100 pop.), a small resort and fishing settlement, a bridge spans CROSS RIVER, named for FATHER BARAGA'S CROSS.

The original wooden cross, erected in 1846 by this Roman Catholic missionary after he had made a perilous journey across Lake Superior from La Pointe, has been replaced by a granite one that stands on the footpath leading R. from the highway. Frederic Baraga, "Apostle of the Chippewa," was born at Carniola, Austria, June 29, 1797; and, in 1830, after giving up a life of wealth to become a priest, came to this country. He spent the rest of his life ministering to the Indians of the Upper Great Lakes region. Baraga published the first grammar of the Chippewa language in 1850, and compiled a dictionary that was issued in 1853. In the same year he was consecrated a Bishop, the first to have episcopal jurisdiction over any part of the Minnesota Arrowhead. It has been told that once he walked 57 miles on snowshoes to baptize a dying infant. His example and persuasiveness brought some 20 other missionaries from his homeland to the wilderness regions of the New World (*see Arrowhead Tour 3*). He died in 1868 and was buried in the Cathedral at Marquette, Michigan. In 1930, when the centenary of his coming to America was celebrated in the Midwest, a movement for his beatification was started, a step toward canonization.

TEMPERANCE RIVER, 82.8 *m.,* received its name because it is the only north shore stream without a bar at its mouth. A public campground (L) contains tables and fireplaces.

Here the road passes between the lake (602 alt.) and CARLTON PEAK (1,529 alt.). A part of the Sawtooth Range, Carlton Peak is the highest point on the north shore this side of the border.

TOFTE, 84.3 *m.,* is at the junction with the Temperance River Road.

Left on the Temperance River Road to SAWBILL LAKE, 21.8 *m.* (*see Superior National Forest: Canoe Trip 6*).

ONION RIVER, 88.6 *m.,* owes its name to a Paul Bunyan legend. The river was formed—so the story goes—by tears the great logger and his crew shed while cutting timber in the vicinity, where wild onions grew in profusion.

At LUTSEN, 92 *m.* (700 alt., 50 pop.), a summer resort town, the POPLAR RIVER flows between vertical cliffs. At the bottom of the gorge are several pot holes.

CASCADE RIVER, 101.5 *m.*, named from a series of beautiful water-falls near its mouth, has Cascade, Little Cascade, Swamp, Eagle, and Zoo lakes, as well as the large Island Lake. It flows through 2,300-acre CAS-CADE STATE PARK where camping spots have been cleared, fireplaces, tables, and benches built, and trails cut along the gorge and lake shore. Here woods are sparse, cut-over and burned areas stretch far up into the hills, and only thin underbrush softens the rugged shore line.

GRAND MARAIS, 111.1 *m.* (616 alt., 855 pop.) (*see Grand Marais*): U. S. Coast Guard Station, Lighthouse. Boat service to Isle Royale.

ISLE ROYALE—declared a National Park in 1940—160 miles northeast of Duluth, is the largest island in Lake Superior, measuring about 45 miles in length and from five to eight miles in width. The island contains approximately 205 square miles. Isle Royale is reached by boat from Duluth, Grand Marais, Grand Portage and Port Arthur.

Its virgin forests of spruce and pine, its 32 lakes and four excellent harbors attract tourists, sportsmen, and nature lovers. The many inland lakes, open glades, magnificent coniferous and hardwood forests, and shore line broken with coves, add to the attractiveness of this rock-ribbed island. The rare combination of forest and inland waterways, together with its comparative inaccessibility, makes it a sanctuary for wild life—a choice place for the study of plants and animals.

Many commercial fishermen have settled along its shores, but few stay during winter months, when radio is the only means of communication with the mainland. Fishing is permitted on Isle Royale under the Michigan law. A State license is required. Fishing guides may be engaged.

Camping is permitted at several locations, and many organized parties and small groups come to the island with their own boats to spend a week camping and fishing. Camping parties should advise the National Park Service, Isle Royale headquarters, of their planned schedule.

As there are no roads on Isle Royale, travel is by foot trail and boat. Boats may be rented for short trips.

From June 15 through September 15, lodge rooms and guest cabins are available at Rock Harbor Lodge, Rock Harbor; Belle Isle Resort, Belle Harbor; and, by midsummer, limited facilities may be available at Washington Harbor.

Among other interesting features of the island are its ancient copper mines. Traces of mining camps, with the broken "hammer stones" used to crush the rock, indicate that Indians mined copper on the island. White men began to extract copper about 1850, apparently without profit, but the abandoned mines as well as evidences of Indian culture still remain. In 1921, the ruins of a prehistoric city were uncovered on the island's south shore.

The first known record of copper was that of Pierre Boucher in 1664. He described Isle Royale as he had heard of it from a group of traders who explored the lake in 1660. Nevertheless, the island—called "Minong" by the Indians—remained virtually unknown for almost 200 years, appearing on Jesuit maps as Isle Royale, in honor of the French Monarchy, but apparently considered of no importance. During the War of 1812, boats were hidden in coves along the shore line.

Given to Michigan in 1837, when that State was admitted to the Union, Isle Royale was opened to white men by a treaty with the Chippewa in 1843, and the next few years saw it overrun by prospectors and explorers. By 1855, however, the island was deserted, remaining practically uninhabited until vacationers chose it for summer homes and fishermen began to make a livelihood from its surrounding waters.

Approximately 15 miles northwest of McCargo's Cove, on the north side of Isle Royale, lies SILVER ISLET, a mere speck of land, yet once one of the world's richest little silver mines. During its ten years of operation, the mine produced $3,500,000 worth of the precious ore. In November, 1884, when the pumps ceased to function from lack of fuel, the mine became flooded, and silver mining on the island came to an end.

At Grand Marais is the junction with the GUNFLINT TRAIL (cor. Wisconsin St. and 2nd Ave. W.).

North on the Gunflint Trail, an improved road, narrow, winding, and steep in places, swings northwest into the heart of the SUPERIOR NATIONAL FOREST (*see Superior National Forest*), a rugged region of many lakes and towering, over-arching pines. Moose, bear, deer, wolves, foxes, porcupine, and other animals frequent this section. The adventurous canoeist can paddle through a maze of lakes and streams from Lake Superior to the western border of the Minnesota Arrowhead. Numerous resorts of every type offer ample accommodations at varying rates. The Federal Forest Service maintains campgrounds with tables, benches, fireplaces, tent and trailer sites, and water; some of the camp and picnic grounds have bathing beaches.

SOUTH BRULE RIVER CAMPGROUND (R), 14.4 *m.*

NORTH BRULE RIVER CAMPGROUND (R), 18.8 *m.*

SWAMPER LAKE CAMPGROUND (L), 25.1 *m.*

At 26.8 *m.* is the junction with a dirt road; R. on this road to EAST BEARSKIN LAKE CAMP AND PICNIC GROUNDS, 3 *m.* (*see Superior National Forest: Canoe Trip 2*).

At 29.2 *m.* is the junction with a dirt road; R. on this road to FLOUR LAKE CAMPGROUND, 2.5 *m.* (*see Superior National Forest: Canoe Trip 2*).

At 30.4 *m.* is the junction with a dirt road; R. on this road to WEST BEARSKIN LAKE CAMP AND PICNIC GROUNDS, 1.5 *m.* (*see Superior National Forest: Canoe Trip 2*).

At 31 *m.* the trail skirts POPLAR LAKE (*see Superior National Forest: Canoe Trip 3*).

There are two IRON LAKE CAMPGROUNDS, one (L) at 34.5 *m.*, on the west end of the lake, and the other (L), at 38.3 *m.*, on the east end.

At 39 *m.* is the junction with a dirt road; R. on this road to CRAB LAKE CAMP-GROUND, 1 *m.*

LOON LAKE CAMPGROUND (R), is at 41.3 *m.*

At 46.7 *m.* is the junction with a gravel road; R. on this road is the village of GUNFLINT (unincorporated), 1.9 *m.*, at the west end of GUNFLINT LAKE (*see Superior National Forest: Canoe Trip 1*). To the south is the GUNFLINT IRON RANGE, where Minnesota iron ore was first discovered. In 1850, J. G. Norwood, assistant geologist with the D. D. Owens Survey, collected samples here and sent them to the Smithsonian Institution; some were exhibited at the International Exposition in Paris. It was found that the ore contained too much titanium to make mining profitable.

At 48.6 *m.* is the junction with MAGNETIC ROCK TRAIL.

R. here to MAGNETIC ROCK, 1.9 *m.*, an ancient Indian landmark 24 feet high, whose location unknown for many years was only recently rediscovered. The rock is highly magnetic and causes compasses in the vicinity to function inaccurately.

At 52.3 *m.* is the junction with a dirt road; L. to ROUND LAKE, or Cross River, 2 *m.* (*see Superior National Forest: Canoe Trip 4*).

At 52.8 *m.* is the junction with a trail; L. to the site of the PAULSON MINE (R), 1 *m.*, which probably was opened during the height of the fever of exploration for iron ore. Its first owner was a man named Paulson. Later a group of interested Canadians built a railroad from Port Arthur. This road, the Port Arthur, Duluth and Western, commonly referred to as the P. D. & W., always was in financial difficulties and was known to railroad men as the Poverty, Distress, and Want. Paulson died and the mine was purchased first by a Minneapolis banker, then by a Detroit man, but finally, because of depression years, the venture was abandoned. Recently members of a Civilian Conservation Corps found an old warehouse near here, containing ten tons of dynamite, which, upon orders from Government officials, they destroyed.

SEA GULL LAKE CAMP AND PICNIC GROUNDS (L), 56.4 *m.* (*see Superior National Forest: Canoe Trips 4, 5*).

The trail ends at BIG SAGANAGA LAKE, 59.5 *m.* (*resorts, swimming, fishing, canoes; varying rates*) (*see Superior National Forest: Canoe Trips 1, 5*). Retrace to US 61.

The main tour continues from Grand Marais.

CHIPPEWA CITY, 112.7 *m.,* is inhabited by Indians and a few white men who have married into the tribe. Their dwellings are concealed in woods adjoining the highway.

KADUNCE (Diarrhoea) CREEK, 121.5 *m.,* a good trout stream, owes its name to mineral salts in the water.

ARROWHEAD RIVER, 126.7 *m.,* once called the Brule, was renamed to avoid confusion with the Brule River that flows through Wisconsin into southwestern Lake Superior.

HOVLAND, 131.2 *m.,* is at the junction of US 61 with the Arrowhead Trail.

Left on the Arrowhead Trail is McFARLAND LAKE, 16 *m.,* the starting point of the International Boundary Route (*see Superior National Forest: Canoe Trips 1, 2*). Retrace to US 61.

RESERVATION RIVER, 137.7 *m.,* flows through the GRAND POR-TAGE INDIAN RESERVATION (*see Cass Lake*), established in 1854 and now reduced to a small tract around Grand Portage. Approximately 400 Indians live in the area.

From this point US 61 swings inland.

MINERAL CENTER, 144.5 *m.* (715 alt., unincorporated), is the most northerly settlement on US 61.

Right from Mineral Center, 5.8 *m.,* on a dirt road is GRAND PORTAGE (700 alt., 100 pop.), oldest white settlement in Minnesota (*see Grand Portage*), though its population now is almost entirely Indian. The village on GRAND PORTAGE BAY was built at one end of the nine-mile "great portage" that skirted the falls at the mouth of the Pigeon River, and connected the canoe routes of the border waters with Lake Superior. The origin of this trail is lost in obscurity; when Vérendrye, the first white man to leave a record of the route, visited here in 1731, he found Indians using the trail. Increasing fur trade activities made the site of Grand Portage a logical location for a trading post. At the time of the Revolutionary War, it was the thriving center of a trade area, extending 2,000 miles northwest to Great Slave and Athabasca Lakes and 800 miles east to Montreal. The 20 years following the formal organization of the Northwest Company in 1784 witnessed the greatest fur-trading period in the region's history. Today, there are only a few cabins and houses and a general store and post office, although many old landmarks, including a stockade, have been restored. An old cabin, long used as a historical museum, was replaced in 1939 by a new museum building. At the northern edge of the village stands a wooden structure on the site of the first Catholic Mission School in the State, consecrated in 1838 by Father Pierz (*see Arrowhead Tour 3*). Indian handicraft products are for sale. There is regular launch service to Isle Royale during the summer. This region is one of the most rugged in Minnesota. Its rough hills, resulting from volcanic action, have been modified by a long period of erosion and glacial action. Retrace to US 61.

At 149.6 *m.,* US 61 crosses the GRAND PORTAGE TRAIL (marker R), recently cleared for hiking. The Webster-Ashburton Treaty of 1842, which fixed the international boundary, provided that the Grand Portage be free and open for use by citizens of both countries. A tale has been told of a New Hampshire man who homesteaded along the trail. It seems he had read literature sent to him by the Government and was impressed by the Grand Portage provision. Some time later, another settler filed a claim on adjoining land. Soon petty differences arose between the neighbours, so the newcomer built a fence between the two homesteads. Unfortunately for him, his fence crossed the Portage. The New Englander wrote to the Secretary of State demanding the treaty be upheld; the letter was referred in turn to the Attorney General, the U. S. District Attorney for Minnesota, and the U. S. Marshal, who sent a deputy to remove the obstruction.

Left along the trail is the site of FORT CHARLOTTE, 5 *m.*, an eighteenth-century fur-trading post. Only scattered mounds mark the locations of the buildings; there are a few remaining timbers of the dock that extended into the Pigeon River.

The INTERNATIONAL BORDER, 151 *m.*, is formed here by the PIGEON RIVER, crossed by a steel bridge. Tradition maintains that large flocks of the now extinct passenger pigeon frequented the region. Customs offices and hotels are at each end of the bridge (*see General Information: Border Regulations*). Across the border, the INTERNATIONAL HIGHWAY follows the Pigeon River for several miles through valleys walled by rugged cliffs.

MIDDLE FALLS, 155 *m.*, on Pigeon River, are a beautiful sight, with their rocky background. Public picnic grounds adjoin the river.

At 188 *m.* the tour passes MOUNT McKAY (1,587 alt.), which overlooks Fort William and the southwestern extremity of THUNDER BAY. LOCH LOMOND, on the promontory, is the source of Fort William's water supply. On the side of the mountain is a CROSS that is illuminated at night, a memorial to Indians who lost their lives in the World War.

FORT WILLIAM, 195 *m.* (608 alt., 26,000 pop.), is the largest city in the western part of the Province of Ontario. It is an important shipping point for grain from the Western provinces and is a railroad terminal serving a large area. Grain elevators, with a total capacity of 40,000,000 bushels, line the waterfront.

Great Lakes Paper Company, Ltd. (*open during summer, 11 a. m. to 4 p. m.*); Abitibi Power and Paper Company, Ltd. (*open daily except Sun. 9 a. m. to 3 p. m.*); Fort William Municipal Golf Course (*9 holes*); Fort William Country Club, Ltd. (*open to public*).

PORT ARTHUR, 199 *m.* (602 alt., 20,506 pop.), is a grain-shipping center; its 16 elevators have a total capacity of 52,500,000 bushels. Port Arthur and Fort William are the world's greatest wheat ports and the world's largest single-unit grain elevator, with a capacity of 7,000,000 bushels, is located at Port Arthur.

Provincial Paper, Ltd. (*open by permission from office, daily 9 a. m. to 5 p. m.*); Thunder Bay Paper Company, Ltd. (*open daily 10:30 a. m. to 2 p. m.*); Strathcona Golf Course (*municipal; 9 holes*); Port Arthur Shipbuilding Company; Provincial Government Fish Hatchery (*open daily 8 a. m. to 5 p. m., Oct. 1 to July 10*); Port Arthur Golf and Country Club (*private but open to public*); Waverly Lawn Bowling Green; Port Arthur Rowing Club.

Arrowhead Tour 2

(To See Open Pit Mines)

Duluth—Eveleth—Virginia—Hibbing—Grand Rapids—Floodwood—Proctor—Duluth; 206.9 m., US 53, US 169, US 2.

US 53 is paved from Duluth to Virginia; US 169 is paved to Grand Rapids; US 2 is bituminous-surfaced to Proctor, paved to Duluth.

This tour, running north from its junction with US 61 to Virginia, passes through open-pit mining country, swings southwest along the western Mesabi Range, and returns to Duluth from Grand Rapids. Good tourist facilities are available throughout; there are many summer resorts where fishing is excellent (*see General Information: Fishing and Hunting*).

DULUTH, 0 m. (cor. Superior St. and Piedmont Ave.) (602 alt., 101,065 pop.) (*see Duluth*).

Leaving Duluth, US 53 swings over the escarpment, 1.3 m., affording an excellent panoramic view of city and harbor.

The DULUTH HOMESTEADS PROJECT OF THE RESETTLEMENT ADMINISTRATION (L), 7 m., with houses built by the Works Progress Administration, covers 1,220 acres of rolling, tillable land, and is the only such undertaking in the Minnesota Arrowhead. Eighty-four houses, of four styles, have been erected on lots ranging from three and one-half to ten acres.

At 11.2 m. is the junction with an improved road.

Right on this road is PIKE LAKE, 0.9 m., where are located the DULUTH AUTOMOBILE CLUBHOUSE, unit of the A. A. A., and its nine-hole GOLF COURSE (*private*). Summer homes line the shores.

The CLOQUET RIVER, 27 m., is at the junction with State 33 (*see Arrowhead Tour 4*).

At COTTON, 37 m., the State Forestry Department maintains a RANGER STATION (L).

On the shores of HALF MOON LAKE (R), 52.6 m., is the DULUTH GIRL SCOUTS' CAMP, *Fanny Bailey Olcott,* given in 1931 by W. J. Olcott, Duluth mining man, in memory of his wife. The camp accommodates approximately 50 girls. Willis Hall, recreational headquarters, is equipped with a swimming pool, shower rooms, handicraft rooms and a dark room for photography enthusiasts.

The EVELETH PUMPING STATION is on ST. MARY'S LAKE, 56.8 m.

EVELETH, 57.3 m. (1,574 alt., 6,887 pop.) (*see Eveleth*): Adams-Spruce Open Pit Mine, Leonidas Underground Mine, Public Library, City Hall, Recreational Bldg.

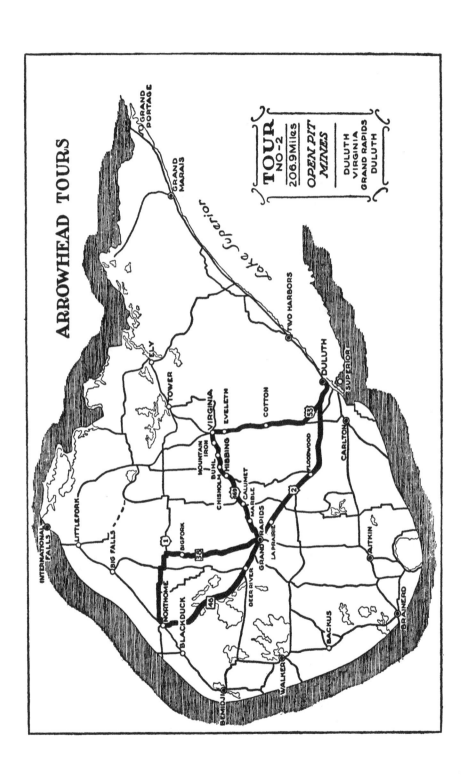

ARROWHEAD TOURS

TOUR
NO-2
206.9 Miles

OPEN PIT MINES

DULUTH
VIRGINIA
GRAND RAPIDS
DULUTH

VIRGINIA, 62.5 *m.* (1,438 alt., 12,264 pop.) (*see Virginia*): Missabe Mountain Mine, Memorial Bldg., Olcott Park, Schools.

The tour runs west on US 169.

At 65.7 *m.* is the junction with a county road.

Left on this road to the junction with another road, 0.25 *m.;* L. here to the WACOOTAH MINE, 0.45 *m.,* an active open pit.

MOUNTAIN IRON, 66.3 *m.* (1,510 alt., 1,492 pop.) (*see Mountain Iron*): Mountain Iron Mine, Granite Quarry, Schools, Public Library, Fiftieth Anniversary Monument.

At 72.3 *m.* is the junction with the Sherwood Road.

Right on the Sherwood Road is the KINNEY MINE (inactive), 1.5 *m.,* an open pit from which approximately 6,000,000 gross tons of ore have been shipped. KINNEY, 2 *m.* (1,500 alt., 462 pop.) (*see Kinney*).

BUHL, 74.2 *m.* (1,500 alt., 1,600 pop.) (*see Buhl*): Martin Hughes High School, Wabigon Mine, Fire Hall, Public Library.

FRASER, 77.6 *m.* (155 pop.), claims it is the world's smallest city. It grew around the Billings Mine (inactive), was organized as a village in 1923, and in 1931, to prevent annexation by Chisholm, incorporated as a city. It has a city hall but no stores; its one industry is mining.

At 79.2 *m.* is the junction with a county road.

Right on this road is located the SHENANGO MINE, 0.6 *m.,* an open pit 400 feet deep.

CHISHOLM, 79.9 *m.* (1,492 alt., 7,487 pop.) (*see Chisholm*): St. Vasselj Church, Schools, Public Library, Community Bldg., Godfrey Mine.

HIBBING, 87.8 *m.* (1,537 alt., 16,385 pop.) (*see Hibbing*): Hull-Rust-Mahoning Mine (world's largest open-pit iron-ore mine), Technical and Vocational High School, Memorial Bldg., Park School ("The Glass School"), Bennett Park, Village Hall.

East on US 169 (Howard St.) from the cor. of 1st Ave. to the junction with a dirt road, 6.7 *m.;* L. on this dirt road to the junction with Co. Rd. 464, 8.3 *m.;* R. on Co. Rd. 464 Sturgeon Lake Road, which crosses a WATERSHED where a figurative drop of rain would split into three parts, one flowing through the Mississippi to the Gulf of Mexico, the second through the Great Lakes to the Gulf of St. Lawrence, and the third through Rainy River to Hudson's Bay.
At 14.6 *m.* is the junction with Co. Rd. 5, which runs through sections wooded with virgin pine and areas dotted with lakes.
At 21.3 *m.* is the junction with Co. Rd. 753.
L. on Co. Rd. 753 to STURGEON LAKE (*resorts, cabins, boats, swimming*), 22.8 *m.,* one of the best fishing lakes in the region; muskellunge, pike, pickerel, bass, crappies, and perch can be caught. It is on the eastern border of the GEORGE WASHINGTON STATE FOREST, a 400,000-acre tract that was established by the State Legislature in 1932.

An alternate route from Hibbing to Floodwood via State 73 will shorten the tour 26.7 miles.

South on State 73 (1st Ave.) from the cor. of Howard St. The highway runs through a sparsely settled farming area and follows the FLOODWOOD RIVER, a tributary of the St. Louis, to their confluence at FLOODWOOD, 45.1 *m.*

The main tour continues west from Hibbing on US 169.
KEEWATIN, 96.8 *m.* (1,505 alt., 1,942 pop.) (*see Keewatin*): Mesabi Chief, St. Paul, Sargent, Mississippi No. 2, and Bennett Mines; Mesabi Chief and St. Paul Washing Plants.
At 97.3 *m.* is the junction with a county road.

Right on this road is the MESABI CHIEF MINE, 0.5 *m.*, an active open pit that has one of the range's most complete and modern plants for washing sand from ore (*see Coleraine*).

NASHWAUK, 101.4 *m.* (1,500 alt., 2,228 pop.) (*see Nashwauk*): Hawkins Mine, Washing and Jigging Plant, La Rue Mine, Washing Plant, Village Hall.
A MAGNETIC SEPARATING PLANT, 102.6 *m.*, frees ore from foreign material.
CALUMET, 108.3 *m.* (1,400 alt., 946 pop.) (*see Calumet*): Hill-Annex Mine, Crushing and Screening Plant, Village Hall.

North on Gary St. from the cor. of 5th Ave. (US 169) to the junction with a dirt road, 0.2 *m.;* R. on this road to the junction with another road, 0.5 *m.;* L. on this second road is the large HILL-ANNEX MINE, 1.3 *m.*

MARBLE, 110.3 *m.* (1,382 alt., 792 pop.) (*see Marble*); Hill-Trumbull Mine, Washing Plant.
At TACONITE, 113.1 *m.* (375 pop.), is the Holman-Cliffs Mine (inactive).
BOVEY, 115.3 *m.* (1,354 alt., 1,355 pop.) (*see Bovey*): Canisteo Mine, Danube Mine.
At 115.6 *m.* is the junction with a county road.

Left on this road is the TROUT LAKE WASHER (*open daily 7 a. m. to 6 p. m.*), 2.25 *m.*, the world's largest iron-ore concentration plant, which has served as a model for other plants of its type.

COLERAINE, 116 *m.* (1,343 alt., 1,325 pop.) (*see Coleraine*): Canisteo Mine, Schools.
GRAND RAPIDS, 123.2 *m.* (1,290 alt., 4,875 pop.) (*see Grand Rapids*): Paper Mill, Village Hall.

North on State 38 (3rd Ave. W.) from its junction with US 2 (4th St.) is the southeastern entrance to CHIPPEWA NATIONAL FOREST, 13.1 *m.* (*see Chippewa National Forest*). All parts of it are accessible by good roads, and within its confines are excellent beaches, good fishing, and recreational facilities of various kinds. Many historic spots in the area are connected with Indian legends.
BIG FORK, 32.9 *m.* (1,292 alt., 382 pop.), one of the oldest settlements in the timbered valley of the Big Fork River (*see Big Falls*), is at the junction of State 38 and Scenic Park Drive. It is a logging center from which timber in large quantities is moved by truck annually.
Right on Scenic Park Drive is SCENIC STATE PARK, 7 *m.*, which was set aside

in 1921 to preserve a stand of virgin pine, and now embraces 2,121 acres. Within its borders are several beautiful lakes, all stocked with bass, northern and wall-eyed pike, crappies, and blue gills; a well-equipped tourist camp; and cleared trails.

EFFIE, 40.2 *m.*, trade center for the Effie-Busti farming region, is at the junction with State 1; L. on State 1.

NORTHOME, 73.9 *m.* (1,451 alt., 343 pop.) (*see Northome*): Consolidated School.

This side tour continues southeast on State 46, cutting diagonally through the Chippewa National Forest and crossing the CONTINENTAL DIVIDE (the Hudson's Bay—Gulf of Mexico watershed). This district is a forest of Norway pine, where the State Conservation Department is carrying on pine-thinning experiments.

THE STATE FISH HATCHERY (*open*), 96.4 *m.*, annually stocks surrounding lakes with approximately 80,000,000 pike fry.

At 100.4 *m.* is the junction with INGER ROAD, which was built along an old four-mile portage between Little Cut Foot Sioux Lake and Bowstring River. Following the Continental Divide, it was used by the Indians for generations.

Left on Inger Road is the TURTLE AND SNAKE INDIAN MOUND (R), 2.5 *m.*, about which a legend has been woven. For years the area was coveted by both Sioux and Chippewa, until a battle in the 1740's ended in victory for the former. Jubilant, they built the turtle part of the mound with the head pointing north to signify the direction of the enemy's retreat. The Chippewa returned the following year and massacred the Sioux, then built the snake around the turtle with the head pointed south, as a warning to other hostile tribes and an indication of the future path of Chippewa conquest.

At 100.5 *m.* is the junction with a dirt road. Left on this road is LITTLE CUT FOOT SIOUX LAKE, 0.25 *m.* Like Cut Foot Sioux, this lake received its name from the legend. The morning after the massacre, squaws from the victorious tribe found and killed an unconscious Sioux warrior whose foot was almost severed.

At 107.9 *m.* is the junction with a dirt road. Right here to LAKE WINNIBI-GOSHISH (*see Bena*), 8 *m.*, an excellent pike-fishing lake with an area of more than 70 square miles.

At 119.1 *m.* is the junction with US 2; L. on US 2 to DEER RIVER, 120.4 *m.* (1,294 alt., 987 pop.) (*see Deer River*): Deer River School and Dormitory, Box Factory, State Forestry Station. At 134.3 *m.* is GRAND RAPIDS.

LA PRAIRIE, 124.2 *m.*, now a ghost town, was one of the first settlements in Itasca County. It developed with the lumber industry and, when platted, was boomed as the head of navigation on the Mississippi River. However, Grand Rapids became the steamboat center (*see Aitkin*) and absorbed the older village. The buildings have been removed, but the outlines of the streets are still visible.

SWAN RIVER, 142.4 *m.* (1,294 alt., unincorporated), is at the junction with State 65.

Left on State 65 is GOODLAND, 5.7 *m.*, a town in which all services are operated on a cooperative basis.

FLOODWOOD, 159.8 *m.* (1,257 alt., 571 pop.) (*see Floodwood*); Cooperative Creamery, School.

At 178.6 *m.* the highway crosses the historic ST. LOUIS RIVER, which flows into Lake Superior and furnishes electric power for Duluth (*see Duluth Tour 4*).

SAGINAW, 186.4 *m.*, is at the junction with State 53 (*see Arrowhead Tour 4*).

PROCTOR, 201.5 *m.* (1,236 alt., 2,468 pop.) (*see Proctor*): Railroad Shops and Classification Yards, Village Hall.

DULUTH, 206.9 *m.* (*see Duluth*).

Arrowhead Tour 3

(To see Border and Farms)

Duluth—International Falls—Bemidji—Brainerd—Duluth; 493.8 m., US 53, US 71, US 2, US 371, US 210, US 61.

US 53 is paved from Duluth to Virginia, hard-surfaced to International Falls; US 71 is graveled to Northome, hard-surfaced to Bemidji; US 2 is hard-surfaced to Cass Lake; US 371 is hard-surfaced to Brainerd; US 210 is paved to its junction with US 61; US 61 is paved to Duluth.

This tour runs north on US 53 from its junction with US 61 to the northern and western parts of the Minnesota Arrowhead, through sections opened up by the great logging industry of early days and by farming in the fertile bed of glacial Lake Agassiz (see Geology). From International Falls on the international border, the route swings southwest to Bemidji, thence southeast through beautiful lake country to Brainerd. Heading eastward, it passes through the Cuyuna Iron Range and returns to Duluth. Tourist facilities are good between Duluth and Virginia, fair between Virginia and International Falls, but limited between International Falls and Northome. Accommodations along the rest of the route are good. Most of the lakes and streams are stocked with a wide variety of fish (see General Information: Fishing and Hunting).

DULUTH, 0 m. (cor. Superior St. and Piedmont Ave.) (602 alt., 101,065 pop.) (see Duluth).

This tour duplicates Arrowhead Tour 2 as far as VIRGINIA, 62.5 m. (see Arrowhead Tour 2), whence it continues north on US 53.

US 53 crosses the GREAT LAURENTIAN HIGHLAND DIVIDE (marker R), 67 m., between the Atlantic and Arctic watersheds.

COOK, 86.1 m. (1,320 alt., 470 pop.) (see Cook): St. Louis County School 114, Flour Mill, Granite Quarries, Christmas Tree Processing Plants.

At 101.6 m. is the junction with a graded road.

Left on this road, which winds through groves of maple and birch, to PELICAN LAKE, 9.5 m., especially noted for its good duck hunting.

NETT LAKE, 16 m., is on the BOIS FORT INDIAN RESERVATION, a unit of the Consolidated Chippewa Indian Agency (see Cass Lake). The heavy timber that once covered the district and attracted many settlers has been cut. During the berry season, the Indians from miles around gather in swamps near the village to pick blueberries to sell. The wild rice that grows plentifully in Nett Lake also is harvested by Indians. One man paddles a canoe while a second threshes the rice heads into it. In camp, the rice is heated in large kettles over open fires to loosen the hulls. Stalks and foreign substances then are shaken or fanned out, and the rice goes into a wooden vat, where a boy wearing moccasins "jigs" the hulls from the grain with a peculiar tramping step. Once again the rice is fanned, then weighed. Wild rice, long a staple in the Indian diet, has become a luxury food throughout the country.

A short distance from shore in Nett Lake is SPIRIT ISLAND. Seemingly imbedded in the rocks are pictures with a reddish-brown film. Indians claim that when their ancestors first came to the lake they found the pictures and sometimes heard sounds like children playing. Knowing the island was uninhabited, they dared not venture near it at such times, attributing both pictures and sounds to spirits (*see Arrowhead Tour 4; Superior National Forest: Canoe Trip 1*).

ORR, 103.5 *m.* (1,305 alt., 234 pop.) (*see Orr*): St. Louis County School 142.

CUSSON, 106.6 *m.*, was headquarters for the Virginia and Rainy Lake Lumber Company (*see Virginia; Cook; Orr*) during the heyday of lumbering in northern Minnesota. Today, Cusson is virtually a ghost town with few inhabitants. It has a Civilian Conservation Corps Camp. The greatest activity occurs in the spring when the Indians make maple sugar.

INTERNATIONAL FALLS, 158 *m.* (1,124 alt., 5,626 pop.) (*see International Falls*): Paper Mills, Curio Collection. (*Before crossing border see General Information: Border Regulations.*)

East on 3rd St. from the junction of US 53 (3rd Ave.) and US 71 (3rd St.) to the junction with 2nd Ave., 0.1 *m.*; L. on 2nd Ave. are CUSTOMS OFFICES on International Bridge, 0.35 *m.*

At International Falls is the junction with State 11 (cor. 3rd St. and 3rd Ave.).

East on State 11, which follows the south shore of beautiful RAINY LAKE, named Lac la Pluie (lake of the rain) by the French. White men first visited it more than 200 years ago; Vérendrye navigated its waters in 1731 on his search for a passage to the Pacific. The lake, about 50 miles long and from 3 to 15 miles wide, has an area of approximately 325 square miles. With 1,600 islands, most of them heavily forested, its beauty is not surpassed in the State.

RANIER, 3.1 *m.* (228 pop.), at the point where the Duluth, Winnipeg and Pacific (Canadian National) crosses the international border, is the only American village on Rainy Lake, and one of the important northern ports of entry. Annually $500,000 in duties are collected here. Customs officials inspect and supervise boats on Rainy Lake and Rainy River, in addition to their usual duties.

West on Main St. is the STATE FISH HATCHERY, 0.1 *m.*, largest in the State; it hatches approximately 100,000,000 wall-eyed pike each season. Most of its stock is planted in Rainy Lake, but it also supplies eggs to the French River Hatchery (*see Arrowhead Tour 1*) and to stations where pike are raised with difficulty.

BLACK BAY, 12.7 *m.* (R), one of Rainy Lake's numerous inlets, is claimed to be among the best pike-fishing grounds in North America. The shore is heavily wooded, as are many near-by islands.

LITTLE AMERICAN ISLAND (*boat service, 25¢ per person*), 0.2 *m.*, was the scene of a gold rush in 1893-94 (*see Copper and Gold Exploration*). The locations of old drifts and test pits are still discernible.

RAINY LAKE CITY (*boat service, 50¢ per person*), 0.3 *m.*, is a ghost town on the mainland across the bay. At the time of the gold rush this was a booming mining town; remnants of its old buildings and stamp mill can be seen.

BUSHY HEAD ISLAND (*boat service, $1.00 per person*), 2.5 *m.*, has a cave and old mining shaft that are filled with water.

The tour continues southeast from International Falls on US 71.

LITTLEFORK, 176.5 *m.* (1,153 alt., 608 pop.) (*see Littlefork*): Potato Warehouse, Ranger Station.

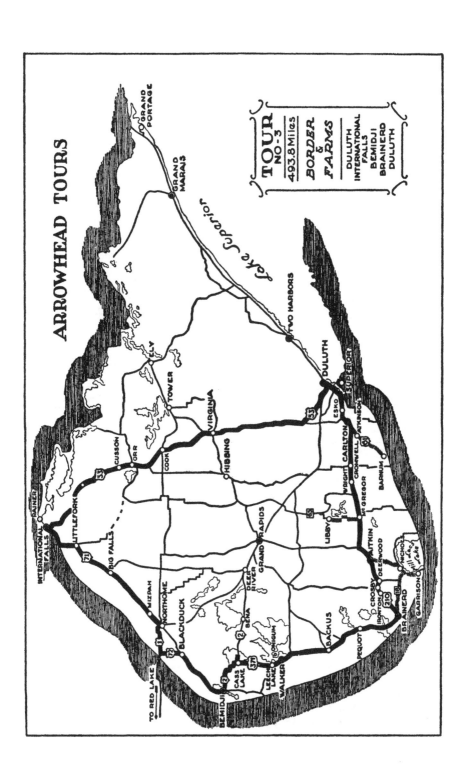

ARROWHEAD TOURS

TOUR
NO-3
493.8 Miles
BORDER
&
FARMS

DULUTH
INTERNATIONAL
FALLS
BEMIDJI
BRAINERD
DULUTH

BIG FALLS, 195.8 *m.* (1,240 alt., 509 pop.) (*see Big Falls*): Grade and High School.

US 71 runs southwest through MARGIE, 205.4 *m.*, and GEMMELL, 216.9 *m.;* from here to Bemidji, it follows the CONTINENTAL DIVIDE (Gulf of Mexico—Hudson's Bay watershed).

MIZPAH, 223 *m.* (173 pop.), is a farming village, whose Hebrew name means "watchtower."

NORTHOME, 226.9 *m.* (1,451 alt., 343 pop.) (*see Northome*); Co-operative Creamery, Consolidated School.

West on State 1 through a farming region drained by many small streams and rivers that offer good fishing.

At 15 *m.* State 1 crosses State 72.

At 30.3 *m.* is the junction with a newly constructed all-weather road; R. on this road that circles the eastern shore of LOWER RED LAKE. RED LAKE, the largest freshwater lake lying wholly within one State, consists of two sections, Upper and Lower, that have a total area of 441 square miles. Most of the shore line is sand and gravel. The greater part of the lake is within the boundaries of the Red Lake Indian Reservation, under the jurisdiction of the Red Lake Indian Agency at Red Lake on the south shore. Among early missionaries who attempted to Christianize the Chippewa was Father Lawrence Lautischar, a young Austrian priest who came to Minnesota in 1857 at the request of Father Pierz. Father Lautischar made the journey up the Mississippi, then was brought by Indian guides to this wilderness outpost. Despite the severe climate and unfriendly surroundings, he immediately began to minister to the natives while learning their language. Little more than a year after his arrival, he was frozen to death on the lake as he was returning from a visit to a sick Indian.

The village of PONEMAH, 52.8 *m.*, is inhabited by Indians who cling to their ancient religion and customs. Because of their unusual burial ritual, they often are referred to as pagans. Reluctant to use Christian graveyards, they have buried their dead in little houses near the road, placing food on a shelf for the spirits of the departed relatives. In summer, the Indians move out of their houses and live in tepees. These huts are not conical in shape, but are constructed with rounded tops, which make them more resistant to heavy winds.

Today fishing is almost the sole industry of both Indians and white men in the region.

At 58.8 *m.* is an INDIAN VILLAGE at RED LAKE NARROWS, a channel between Upper and Lower Red lakes. One of the finest forests of virgin pine in the State stands on this narrow point of land.

At 243.5 *m.* on US 71, the main tour, is BLACKDUCK (1,404 alt., 753 pop.) (*see Blackduck*): Cooperative Creamery, Independent School 60. At 245.6 *m.* is the junction with Blackduck Lake Road.

Right here to BLACKDUCK LAKE, 0.5 *m.*, largest in the vicinity, on whose shores is the site of a prehistoric village and Indian battlefield, where archeologists unearthed the well-known Blackduck pottery.

BEMIDJI, 270.4 *m.* (1,351 alt., 9,427 pop.) (*see Bemidji*): Fireplace of States Building, Statues of Paul Bunyan, his Blue Ox Babe, and Chief Bemidji, State Teachers College, Egg-packing Plant, Woodworking Plants, Hydroelectric Plant.

The tour follows US 2 southeast.

CASS LAKE, 290.3 *m.* (1,323 alt., 1,904 pop.) (*see Cass Lake*): Star Island, Armory, General Chippewa Hospital, U. S. Government Nursery.

An alternate route from Cass Lake to Duluth via US 2 will shorten the tour 65.7 miles.

From Cass Lake US 2 runs east through the heart of the CHIPPEWA NATIONAL FOREST (*see Chippewa National Forest; Arrowhead Tour 2*) and passes through SCHLEY, 11.7 *m.*, named for Winfield Scott Schley, who as rear admiral of the U. S. Navy during the Spanish-American War directed the naval battle off Santiago, Cuba.

BENA, 19.1 *m.* (1,311 alt., 319 pop.) (*see Bena*): Lake Winnibigoshish.

DEER RIVER, 38.9 *m.* (1,294 alt., 987 pop.) (*see Deer River*): Deer River Grade and High School and Dormitory, Box Factory, State Forestry Station.

From this point, this alternate tour follows the route of Arrowhead Tour 2 (*see Arrowhead Tour 2*) to Duluth, 137.8 *m.*

At 296.3 *m.*, US 371 skirts PIKE BAY, named for Zebulon M. Pike. On this southern extension of CASS LAKE, the Lake States Forest Experiment Station maintains a forest for the intensive study of tree growth.

LEECH LAKE, 305.9 *m.*, is named from an Indian legend that tells of a huge leech seen swimming in the lake. Third largest body of water in Minnesota, it is 40 miles wide and 175 square miles in area; wall-eyed and northern pike, bass, and blue gills are plentiful.

As early as 1785 the Northwest Company had a trading post on Otter-tail Point, and later the American Fur Company established one at Pine Point. Boutwell (*see Duluth*), who had accompanied Schoolcraft to Lake Itasca in 1832 (*see Cass Lake*), returned to Leech Lake the following year, to start a mission among the Pillager band of Chippewa, and remained here for four years. In 1836, he was visited by the eminent cartographer, Joseph N. Nicollet, who had been commissioned to survey the headwaters of the Mississippi. Another missionary, Reverend James Lloyd Breck, arrived at Leech Lake in 1856, hoping to Christianize the Pillagers, but left after eight months of disappointing labor. Later, the mission was abandoned.

Apparently much of the lake bed at one time was dry. In 1897, remnants of an oak forest on the lake bottom still were visible, but that year the ice loosened the stumps. Back from the shore is cut-over land, where groves of poplar and hardwood intersperse the remaining Norway and white pine.

The last battle between Indians and Federal troops took place on Sugar Point in 1898.

WALKER, 311.3 *m.* (1,336 alt., 939 pop.) (*see Walker*): Cass County Courthouse, Creamery, Museum, Tianna Farms, Village Hall.

At AH-GWAH-CHING, 314.3 *m.* (310 pop.), its name Chippewa for out-of-doors, is the MINNESOTA STATE SANATORIUM for tubercular patients. Its 35 buildings, on 881 acres of land overlooking the west shore of Leech Lake, serve 47 counties that have no sanatoriums.

At 315.7 *m.* is the junction with State 34.

Left on State 34 to the junction with Onigum Indian Road, 3.3 *m.*; L. on Onigum Indian Road is the "OLD AGENCY," 7.3 *m.*, once an Indian village that at the turn of the century was moved to Onigum. Father Pierz (*see Arrowhead Tour 1*) visited here in 1853, and somewhere in the near-by woods preached his first sermon to the Pillager Indians, thus establishing the ONIGUM INDIAN MISSION. This pioneer missionary, born in Carniola, Austria, November 20, 1785, had come to America in 1838 at the persuasion of Father Baraga (*see Arrowhead Tour 1*), and was called to the Minnesota diocese in 1852. His first mission was at Crow Wing, near what now is Brainerd, and at that time he was the only Roman Catholic missionary to the Indians in the territory that became Minnesota. He found converting and teaching the Pillager Indians around Leech Lake a well-nigh impossible task, for they were a troublesome band who strongly resented the white man's invasion of their territory.

The LOG CHURCH, built in 1892, was the first at the Onigum Mission. It was abandoned when the Mission was transferred to Onigum at the time the village was moved.

ONIGUM, 13.5 *m.*, on Agency Bay of Leech Lake is under the jurisdiction of the Consolidated Chippewa Indian Agency (*see Cass Lake*).

Near TEN MILE LAKE, 321.8 *m.*, on US 371, stood Lathrop, a railroad terminal that in 1895 had a population of 2,000. When the Minnesota and International Railroad was built to the north, the town was moved to the railroad line. Today, no trace of the old village remains. The lake was so named because of its distance from the Indian Agency at Leech Lake.

The tour winds southeast through a lake region with numerous resorts.

PEQUOT LAKES, 354.2 *m.* (514 pop.), is a dairying village with a hundred lakes in a ten-mile radius. Within 15 miles are 60 summer resorts ranging in size from the largest in the State to those with only a few housekeeping cabins. Pequot Lakes has a cooperative creamery, a pickle plant, and a cooperative shipping association.

At 372.8 *m.* is the junction with US 210, which the main tour follows (L).

BRAINERD, 374.9 *m.* (1,213 alt., 12,071 pop.) (*see Brainerd*): Railroad Shops, Paper Mill, Demanganization Plant, Crow Wing County Courthouse and Historical Society Museum, City Hall, Library.

South on US 371 (6th St. S.) from its eastern junction in Brainerd with US 210 to the junction with State 18 (Oak St.), 0.4 *m.;* L. on State 18 to junction with US 169, 20.7 *m.*, at GARRISON (211 pop.), one of numerous resort centers in the area.

Left on US 169 along the northwest shore of MILLE LACS LAKE, among the largest and most beautiful in Minnesota. Its many miles of shore line are wooded with birch, maple, and pine, and more than a thousand Indian mounds dot the region. Father Hennepin and his companions were held captive at a Sioux village on the southwest shore of Mills Lacs just prior to their rescue in 1680 by Du Lhut, who named the place Izatys, soon distorted to Kathio. Indian legends recount the frequent appearance here of spirits of warriors killed in the battle of Kathio (*see Aitkin*), insisting that white, shapeless forms move among the trees with low, sighing moans. Duck hunting is popular, and the lake—one of the best wall-eyed pike-fishing grounds in the Arrowhead—abounds in northern pike, bass, crappies, and sunfish. The many smaller streams feeding and draining it afford good bass fishing. One of these, Rum River, flowing southward to the Mississippi, once was an important logging waterway.

NICHOLS, 23.5 *m.*, is another resort settlement. To the right, between the highway and the lake, are several INDIAN MOUNDS.

The highway continues north past FARM ISLAND LAKE (L), 32.5 *m.*, and a few smaller lakes.

AITKIN, 41.1 *m.* (*see Aitkin*).

The main tour continues from Brainerd on US 210.

IRONTON, 388.9 *m.* (1,260 alt., 827 pop.) (*see Ironton*): Mines, Crushing and Screening Plant, Mahnomen Crushing Plant.

CROSBY, 390.2 *m.* (1,200 alt., 2,954 pop.) (*see Crosby*): Sintering Plant, Evergreen Mine, Armory, Junior College.

North on State 6 (3rd Ave. S.W.) from its junction with US 210 (Main St.) to the EVERGREEN MINE (*observation tower*), 0.5 *m.* At the other end of the pit is the MINNESOTA SINTERING COMPANY PLANT, one of three in the world, operated by the Evergreen Mines Company. Here the ore is beneficiated by washing, screening, and sintering to make it more adaptable to the mechanics of the blast furnace. The sintering machine has an over-all length of 240 feet and a capacity of 1,400 long tons in 24 hours.

DEERWOOD, 393.8 *m.* (1,291 alt., 570 pop.), on the east end of SERPENT LAKE, is a resort center with 30 lakes in the immediate vicinity. Deerwood is on the Cuyuna Iron Range, but there are no mines near the town, and farming and dairying are its main industries. A sanatorium for tubercular patients is supported by Aitkin and Crow Wing counties.

This village was the home of Cuyler Adams, discoverer of the Cuyuna Range (*see Crosby*).

On the north end of CEDAR LAKE, 402 *m.*, the Northwest Company had a fur-trading post in 1806.

AITKIN, 404.7 *m.* (1,230 alt., 2,063 pop.) (*see Aitkin*): Cooperative Creamery, Aitkin County Courthouse, Armory, St. James Catholic Church.

The highway parallels the MISSISSIPPI RIVER (L) to HASSMAN, 411.6 *m.* and McGREGOR, 426.7 *m.* (1,254 alt., 311 pop.) (*see McGregor*).

Left on State 65 to BIG SANDY LAKE, 13 *m.* Fur traders paddled across the lake on their journeys through the region (*see McGregor; Floodwood*). In 1794, the Northwest Company built a post on the western shore of the lake at what now is Brown's Point. This post was one of the most important in the Northwest until the American Fur Company bought out the British interests in 1816. Some time between 1820 and 1834, the post was moved to the confluence of the Mississippi and Sandy rivers, where the village of Libby stands. The first Indian mission in Minnesota was established in 1833 by Reverend Edmund F. Ely at Big Sandy Lake where, a year before, a fellow missionary, Frederick Ayer, had conducted the first school in the State.

WRIGHT, 442 *m.* (201 pop.), is a small farming community on the Northern Pacific. After leaving Wright, US 210 crosses the Cromwell terminal moraine that extends for several miles.

CROMWELL, 449.1 *m.* (214 pop.), is a typical farming village with a well-equipped consolidated school and a cooperative creamery.

SAWYER, 461.9 *m.*, is on the edge of the FOND DU LAC INDIAN RESERVATION (*see Cass Lake; Cloquet*).

At 465.8 *m.* is the junction with State 33.

Left on State 33 is the entrance to the STATE FORESTRY EXPERIMENT STATION, 1 *m.*, under the direction of the University of Minnesota. Its 3,000 acres comprise one of the most intensively developed forest areas in the country. Plant disease and insect control are studied, and demonstration projects, experiments, and formal instruction are carried on. All forestry students from the State University spend part of their training period here, as do students in game management and related courses.

At 468.3 *m.* is the junction with US 61, where US 210 ends.

Right on US 61, the road in places is cut through ridges of taconite, some of the oldest rock on the North American continent. The highway crosses OTTER CREEK, at 0.9 *m.*, and recrosses, at 2.5 *m.*, all that remains of one of the torrents through which glacial Lake Duluth drained into the Mississippi.

ATKINSON, 5 *m.*, and MAHTOWA, 9.1 *m.*, are farming communities producing high-grade potatoes.

BARNUM, 15.3 *m.* (1,122 alt., 327 pop.) (*see Barnum*): Creamery, Maplewood Farm, Big Hanging Horn Lake.

MOOSE LAKE, 20 *m.* (1,085 alt., 1,432 pop.) (*see Moose Lake*): Creamery, Tile and Pottery Company, State Hospital, Granite Shaft (monument).

The main tour continues on US 61 from Junction with US 210.

A wooden SIGN, 470.3 *m.,* marks the point at which construction of the Northern Pacific Railroad began (*see Carlton*).

CARLTON, 471.3 *m.* (1,084 alt., 700 pop.) (*see Carlton*): Carlton County Courthouse, Village Hall, Jay Cooke State Park (*see Duluth Tour 4*).

SCANLON, 474.1 *m.* (460 pop.), developed as a lumbering town, but with the depletion of the forests and the growth of Cloquet, the village has declined (*see Arrowhead Tour 4*).

The highway crosses the ST. LOUIS RIVER at 475.2 *m.* (*see Duluth Tour 4*).

ESKO, 477.2 *m.,* is a Finnish dairying community, which has a co-operative creamery with a branch in Duluth. As is characteristic of the Finns, most families in this district have a *sauna* (bathhouse), resembling a small cabin (*see Embarrass*). Suspicious farmers once accused the Finns of worshipping pagan deities and claimed that whole families, wrapped in white sheets, went to these small outbuildings to call upon their gods. Investigation proved the motive was not godliness, but cleanliness.

At 482.7 *m.* is a junction with a dirt road.

Right on this road is NOPEMING, 0.3 *m.,* the St. Louis County Tuberculosis Sanatorium, opened in 1912, which has accommodations for 230 patients. Its name is Chippewa for "out-in-the-woods." The 270 acres of improved woodland border the St. Louis River Valley, and the buildings are on a hill that affords a beautiful view.

REST POINT, 488.4 *m.,* is a fine vantage point from which to see the St. Louis River Valley and the city of Duluth. A bronze tablet set in the retaining wall describes the area and briefly relates its history.

DULUTH, 493.8 *m.* (*see Duluth*).

Arrowhead Tour 4

(To See Underground Mines)

Duluth—Illgen City—Ely—Virginia—Cloquet—Duluth; 247.2 *m.*, US 61, State 1, State 169, US 53, State 33, State 45.

US 61 is paved from Duluth to Two Harbors, hard-surfaced to Illgen City; State 1 is hard-surfaced to Ely, paved to Tower; State 169 is paved to Virginia; US 53 is paved to its junction with State 33; State 33 is graveled to Cloquet; State 45 is paved to its junction with US 61; US 61 is paved to Duluth.

This tour runs northeast on US 61 from its junction with US 53, swings northwest to the underground mining region of the Vermilion and eastern Mesabi iron ranges, then returns through cut-over forest areas. Good tourist facilities are available, with hotels in larger towns and numerous resorts and campsites throughout. Wild game is abundant, and lakes and streams are well stocked (*see General Information: Fishing and Hunting*).

DULUTH, 0 *m.* (cor. Superior St. and Piedmont Ave.) (602 alt., 101,065 pop.) (*see Duluth*).

This tour is identical with Arrowhead Tour 1 as far as ILLGEN CITY, 60.7 *m.* (*see Arrowhead Tour 1*), whence it follows State 1 (Ely-Finland Trail).

ILLGEN FALLS (L), 62.8 *m.*, are typical of the beautiful falls along the north shore (*see Arrowhead Tour 1*). The BAPTISM RIVER together with its upper tributaries is one of the most fished of the northern trout streams.

At 66 *m.* the trail passes through the little settlement of FINLAND, where the State Forest Service has DISTRICT HEADQUARTERS. Several obscure foot trails lead (R) from Finland toward the upper reaches of the Baptism River, some following old logging roads over decaying bridges that in many places are almost hidden by vegetation. The region, although cut-over, is uncultivated and partially wooded. The swamps are filled with black spruce, tamarack, cranberries, and bog flowers. In such setting grows the rare and exquisite moccasin flower— the Minnesota State flower—whose name *Cypripedium* means "slipper of Venus."

At 68.6 *m.*, the highway enters the famous SUPERIOR NATIONAL FOREST.

A STATE GAME AND FISH STATION (R), 76.6 *m.*, stands near the overhead crossing of an old logging railroad.

ISABELLA, 83.1 *m.*, a small village, gives the highway one of its names, Isabella Trail.

The KAWISHIWI RIVER, 112.2 *m.*, is a principal waterway for several canoe trips (*see Superior National Forest: Canoe Trips 6, 7, 8*). The short portages (averaging less than one-quarter mile) make this one of the finest canoe countries in the United States.

The SOUTH KAWISHIWI CAMP AND PICNIC GROUNDS (R) (*free picnic, tent and trailer sites, water*) are supervised by the Federal Forest Service, at whose DISTRICT HEADQUARTERS (L) visitors are welcome.

Pike fishing is excellent at BIRCH LAKE DAM CAMP AND PICNIC GROUNDS (R) (*free picnic sites; no water*), 114.6 *m.*, maintained by the Minnesota Power and Light Company. Most of these northern lakes are noted for their lake trout, pike, and pickerel. Bass are numerous in some of the lakes; brook and rainbow trout prefer the spring-fed creeks.

ELY, 124.8 *m.* (1,417 alt., 5,970 pop.) (*see Ely*): City Hall, Memorial High School, Community Center, South Slavonic Catholic Union, Pioneer (Shafts A and B), Sibley, and Zenith mines.

TO SEE MINES
(*Visitors by permission*)

North on Central Ave. from the junction of State 1 (Sheridan St.) and Co. Rd. 21 (Central Ave.) to the junction with the Chandler Location Rd., 0.1 *m.*, that branches (R) over the railroad tracks. At 0.2 *m.* on the Chandler Location Rd. is the junction with a narrow dirt road; R. on the dirt road to the PIONEER MINE (SHAFT B), 0.4 *m.* The Pioneer, a fully electrified mine with two shafts, is one of the largest underground mines in the State. It has shipped more than a million gross tons in one season. At 0.3 *m.* on the Chandler Location Rd. is the junction with a gravel road; R. on the gravel road to the PIONEER MINE (SHAFT A), 0.8 *m.*, and to the SIBLEY, 1.7 *m.*, which was opened in 1899 and was the last one on the Vermilion Range to operate by steam power. For ZENITH MINE (*see below*).

First alternate route from Ely to Virginia (Ely to Buyck, Cook, and Virginia) via Echo Trail, lengthening the tour 60.1 miles.

East on State 1 (Sheridan St.) from its junction with Co. Rd. 21 (Central Ave.).

At 1.3 *m.* is the junction with Co. Rd. 35; first alternate route continues L. on Co. Rd. 35. Right on Co. Rd. 35, at 2 *m.*, is the junction with a hard-surfaced road that leads to WHITE IRON LAKE, or Silver Rapids (*see Superior National Forest: Canoe Trip 8*). WINTON, 3.5 *m.* (224 pop.), on FALL LAKE (*see Superior National Forest: Canoe Trip 9*), is at the junction with the Fernberg Road. Right on the Fernberg Road to the junction with a dirt road at 15.3 *m.* Left on the dirt road to MOOSE LAKE, 2 *m.* (*see Superior National Forest: Canoe Trip 13*). On LAKE ONE, 19.5 *m.*, is FERNBERG LANDING (*see Superior National Forest: Canoe Trip 7*). Retrace to junction with Co. Rd. 35.

Left on Co. Rd. 35, first alternate route, to a junction with a dirt road at 1.6 *m.* Left on this dirt road to the ZENITH MINE, 0.2 *m.*, opened in 1892 and now completely electrified.

At 2.2 *m.* is the junction with Co. Rd. 88.

Left on Co. Rd. 88 to the junction with Co. Rd. 603, 4.3 *m.;* R. on Co. Rd. 603, the ECHO TRAIL, also called the Ely-Buyck Trail, that runs northeast, then swerves north, and continues northwest through the wilderness of the Superior National Forest. Much of this 12-foot road is built on solid rock, and the remainder is graveled; it is seldom impassable. Canoe routes in the area include that used by the Hudson's Bay Company and the famed Dawson Route (*see International Falls*)—both well known to fur traders—and others used for centuries by Indians. At the time of the first Riel Rebellion (in 1870), English troops moved through this territory from Port Arthur to Fort Garry (Winnipeg) in a hundred big canoes. The Federal Forest Service maintains

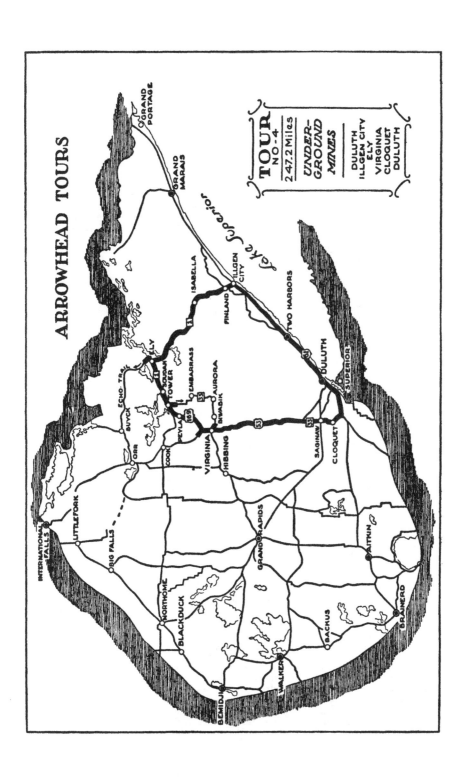

ARROWHEAD TOURS

TOUR
NO-4
247.2 Miles
UNDER-
GROUND
MINES

DULUTH
ILLGEN CITY
ELY
VIRGINIA
CLOQUET
DULUTH

campgrounds with tables, benches, fireplaces, tent and trailer sites, and water; also camp and picnic grounds that have bathing beaches.

NORTH ARM BURNTSIDE LAKE CAMP AND PICNIC GROUNDS (L), 9.3 *m.* (*see Superior National Forest: Canoe Trip 11*).

FENSKE LAKE CAMP AND PICNIC GROUNDS (R), 12.8 *m.* (*see Superior National Forest: Canoe Trip 10*).

NELS LAKE CAMPGROUND (R), 15.3 *m.*

SOUTH HEGMAN CAMP AND PICNIC GROUNDS (R), 17.3 *m.* INDIAN ROCK PAINTINGS were discovered recently on cliffs at the northeastern end of Hegman Lake. These ancient drawings include the figure of a man with five moons over his right shoulder and, below him, figures of moose and other game. A connecting line beneath the figures suggests this is a picture-story drawing. Several theories have been advanced concerning the origin and significance of these pictographs, but their interpretation still is questionable. They furnish interesting examples of the picture language of northern Minnesota tribes (*see Superior National Forest: Canoe Trip 1; Arrowhead Tour 3*).

SPRING CREEK CAMPGROUND (L), 19.3 *m.*

SECOND LAKE CAMPGROUND (R), 20.3 *m.* The trail skirts SECOND LAKE and winds upward around a cliff overhanging the lake, with a sharp, blind curve at the top.

BIG LAKE CAMP AND PICNIC GROUNDS (L), 24.3 *m.* (*see Superior National Forest: Canoe Trip 11*).

In some places the highway cuts through stands of virgin timber, where occasionally in early morning or late afternoon deer may be seen close to the road. The timid animals stand, with ears pricked for the slightest sound, and dart off into the forest when a car approaches.

PORTAGE RIVER CAMPGROUND (L), 26.8 *m.*

MOOSE RIVER CAMPGROUND (R), 29.5 *m.* (*see Superior National Forest: Canoe Trip 12*).

MEANDER LAKE CAMP AND PICNIC GROUNDS (R), 32.5 *m.*

The trail, winding through fine stands of white, Norway, and jack pine, is one of the most beautiful forest roads in Minnesota. Game is abundant throughout the area, particularly deer, bear, and smaller animals; moose often are seen.

SIOUX RIVER CAMPGROUND (R and L), 36.1 *m.* (*see Superior National Forest: Canoe Trip 14*).

LAKE JEANNETTE CAMP AND PICNIC GROUNDS (R), are at 41 *m.*

HUNTING SHACK CAMPGROUND (L), 45.1 *m.,* is the last campsite on the trail. At 53.8 *m.* is the junction with Co. Rd. 24.

1. Right to the junction with a dirt road, 0.5 *m.* Right on this dirt road to ECHO LAKE, 0.3 *m.* (*resort, cabins, boats, swimming*). CRANE LAKE, 8.5 *m.,* is the west end of the International Boundary Route (*see Superior National Forest: Canoe Trips 1, 15*).

2. Left on Co. Rd. 24 to BUYCK, 55.8 *m.,* a small settlement that once was a half-way point for prospectors en route to Rainy Lake during the gold rush (*see Arrowhead Tour 3*).

At 57.8 *m.,* the road crosses VERMILION RIVER (*see Superior National Forest: Canoe Trip 15*), which originates in Lake Vermilion to the south.

At 58.1 *m.* is the junction with Co. Rd. 23, which leads (R) to ORR (*see Orr; Arrowhead Tour 3*).

At 71.3 *m.* on Co. Rd. 24 is the junction with a dirt road.

Right on this road to VERMILION DAM, 0.2 *m.* (*see Superior National Forest: Canoe Trip 15*), on Vermilion River. COOK is at 94.2 *m.* (1,320 alt., 470 pop.) (*see Cook; Arrowhead Tour 3*); and VIRGINIA at 110.7 *m.*

Second alternate route from Ely to Virginia (Ely to Embarrass, Aurora, Biwabik, Virginia via County Road 21 and State 35, lengthening the tour 6 miles).

South on Co. Rd. 21 (Central Ave.) from the junction with State 1 (Sheridan St.). (One of the most successful early forest plantations in the lake states is located 15 miles south of Ely on the southwest side of Birch Lake. It is known as the Birch Lake Plantation and can be easily reached from the Ely-Babbitt Road.)

EMBARRASS is at 29 *m.* (1,427 alt., unincorporated) (*see Embarrass*). At 30.6 *m.* is the junction with State 35; L. on State 35 to AURORA, 40.6 *m.* (1,478 alt., 1,528 pop.) (*see Aurora*); and BIWABIK, 45.8 *m.* (1,448 alt., 1,304 pop.) (*see Biwabik*): Biwabik Mine.

South on Co. Rd. 4 (Shaw Ave.) from its junction with State 35 (Main St.) to the junction with the Esquagama Lake Road, 4.7 *m.,* R. to the log 4-H CLUBHOUSE on ESQUAGAMA LAKE, 5.1 *m.,* a prize awarded to the St. Louis County organization for nationally outstanding club work.

GILBERT, 53.1 *m.* (1,593 alt., 2,504 pop.) (*see Gilbert*): Village Hall, Library, Schools.

VIRGINIA, 56.6 *m.*

The main tour continues west from ELY on State 1. At the junction with Co. Rd. 88, 127.9 *m.,* is the site of the old QUARRY AND ROCK-CRUSHING PLANT of the Emeralite Surfacing Company (R).

Right on Co. Rd. 88 is BURNTSIDE LAKE (*resorts, fishing, swimming, canoeing, launches, garage facilities*), 2.8 *m.,* one of the most popular lakes in the region. It is seven miles long and seven miles wide with numerous islands and an irregular, wooded shore line (*see Superior National Forest: Canoe Trips 10, 11, 12, 14*).

At 143.3 *m.* JASPER PEAK (1,650 alt.), composed largely of red jasper, is visible (L). Atop it is a FOREST SERVICE LOOKOUT TOWER; a footpath leads to the tower, from which the view of the surrounding country is excellent.

At SOUDAN (1,500 alt.) is a MONUMENT (R), 144.3 *m.,* that commemorates the fiftieth anniversary of the first shipment of iron ore from the SOUDAN MINE (*see Tower*) and from Minnesota (*see Two Harbors*).

TOWER, 146.5 *m.* (1,367 alt., 820 pop.) (*see Tower*): Lake Vermilion, Lake Vermilion Indian Reservation, McKinley Monument.

From PEYLA, 151 *m.* (1,435 alt.), a small settlement near the head of PIKE BAY on LAKE VERMILION, State 169 runs southwest through a farming region into the Mesabi Iron Range.

At 169.5 *m.* is the junction with US 53; L. on US 53.

VIRGINIA, 175.4 *m.* (1,438 alt., 12,264 pop.) (*see Virginia*): Missabe Mountain Mine, Memorial Bldg., Olcott Park, Schools.

The tour continues south on US 53 (*see Arrowhead Tour 2*) to the CLOQUET RIVER, 210.9 *m.,* and the junction with State 33; R. on State 33, which runs through the farming district of the Cloquet River Valley.

SAGINAW, 219.4 *m.,* at the junction with US 2 (*see Arrowhead Tour 2*), was first settled by timber workers from Saginaw, Michigan. The story has been told that during the boisterous lumbering days of the village, the reversed spelling of its name was chosen to designate a brand of whiskey.

The FOND DU LAC INDIAN HOSPITAL, 226.5 *m.,* a Federal institution, is a two-story building on an 80-acre tract. Between 500 and 600 Indians are treated each year. Originally it served only the Fond du Lac Reservation, on which it is located, but when seven Minnesota Chippewa reservations were placed under control of the Consolidated Chippewa Indian Agency (*see Cass Lake*), the hospital was opened to surgical cases from all Agency territory. Hospitalization is free to all Indians who are members of the Agency, except tubercular patients.

CLOQUET, 227.2 *m.* (1,189 alt., 7,304 pop.) (*see Cloquet*): Wood Conversion Plant, Paper Mills, Saw and Planing Mills.

Left on State 45 to SCANLON, 230.5 *m.* (460 pop.), at the junction with US 61, which the tour follows (*see Arrowhead Tour 3*) to DULUTH, 247.2 *m.* (*see Duluth*).

PART V

Appendices

Industrial and Commercial Data

INDUSTRIAL STATISTICS

(*1939 figures*)

General:	(Retail)*	(Wholesale)*
Stores	5,307	523
Proprietors	4,935	355
Employees	12,007	3,811
Sales	$116,287,000	$118,569,000
Payroll	$ 11,685,000	$ 6,140,000
Manufacturing: **		
Establishments		393
Wage earners		9,382
Wages		$ 9,436,342
Cost of materials, fuel, power		$ 33,925,754
Value added by manufacture (including wages and overhead)		$ 27,991,655
Value of products		$ 61,917,409

* Figures represent all Carlton, Cass, Cook, Itasca, Lake, St. Louis Counties; 9/10 Aitkin, Koochiching; 2/3 Crow Wing.

** No figures are available on Cook County; Koochiching is included only in number of establishments and wage earners, no data on wages, value of products, etc., being available.

AGRICULTURAL STATISTICS *

(United States Census of Agriculture, 1940)

Arrowhead acreage	13,350,784
Total acreage in farms	2,088,168
Percentage in farms	15.6
Average acreage of farms	93.18
Average value of forms	$2,348
Average value per acre	$25.20
Number of farms	22,411
Value of farms (land and buildings)	$52,622,802
Livestock (Apr. 1, 1940):	
Horses and colts	26,329
Cattle and calves	158,774
Sheep and lambs	56,631
Swine	15,447
Chickens over 4 months old	502,481
Turkeys over 4 months old	12,539
Livestock products (1939):	
Milk produced (gallons)	51,871,918
Eggs produced (dozens)	3,673,488
Crops (1939):	
Winter wheat, threshed (bushels)	32,635
Spring wheat, threshed (bushels)	24,789
Oats, threshed (bushels)	1,397,498
Barley, threshed (bushels)	138,408
Rye, threshed (bushels)	73,537
Mixed grains, threshed (bushels)	70,580
Flax, threshed (bushels)	56,345
All hay, and sorghum for forage (tons)	507,734
Corn for grain (bushels)	516,096
Irish potatoes (bushels)	1,878,577
Forest products sold (1934: latest available figure)	$370,358

* Figures represent all Carlton, Cass, Cook, Itasca, Lake, St. Louis Counties; 9/10 Aitkin, Koochiching; 2/3 Crow Wing; 1/10 Beltrami, Hubbard.

HARBOR STATISTICS
(1939)

Exports and imports:	Duluth-Superior (short tons)	Two Harbors (short tons)	Grand Marais (short tons)
I. Volume			
Shipments......	29,936,618	9,602,477	19,863
Receipts........	8,111,788	127,961	1,070
Totals	38,048,406	9,730,438	20,933
II. Value			
Shipments......	$243,590,808	$35,145,066	$142,604
Receipts........	99,472,006	538,432	25,004
Totals	$343,062,814	$35,683,498	$167,608

III. Harbor tonnages: (a) Duluth-Superior

Shipments—	Volume	Value
Animals and animal products:		
Butter (tons)	65,969	$ 34,171,942
Cheese (tons)	1,396	469,056
Eggs (tons)	9,505	2,809,088
Poultry, dressed (tons)...........	5,315	2,009,070
All other (tons)	5,589	757,426
Vegetable food products:		
Canned food products (tons)......	13,237	1,747,284
Flour, wheat (barrels)..........	1,938,804	9,306,259
Flour and meal (tons)	21,622	1,219,042
Grains:		
Barley (bushels)	6,855,083	3,111,412
Corn (bushels)	13,810,928	6,864,326
Oats (bushels)	15,525,500	5,211,954
Rye (bushels)	4,422,000	2,295,018
Wheat (bushels)	40,679,067	35,040,989
Mill products (tons)	46,165	830,970
Sugar (tons)	9,430	886,420
All other (tons)...............	16,838	1,622,564
Vegetable products, inedible:		
Flaxseed (bushels)	4,664,821	8,718,550
All other (tons)	825	54,465
Textiles:		
Bags and bagging (tons)	45	12,825
Wool (tons)	11,373	7,119,498
Wood and paper:		
Lumber and shingles (tons)	37,197	1,133,161
Paper (tons)	801	53,298
All other (tons)	239	11,110
Nonmetallic minerals:		
Coal, bunker (tons)	24,654	103,547
Coke (tons)	19,645	139,480
Fuel oil (barrels)	29,360	73,044
All other (tons)	879	7,136

HARBOR STATISTICS (*Contd.*)

Ores, metals, and manufactures of:

Copper ingots (tons)	13,448	2,877,872
Iron ore (tons)	26,673,842	97,259,774
Iron and steel, manufactured (tons)	49,863	3,623,262
Iron and steel, unmanufactured (tons)	69,559	1,883,802
Scrap iron (tons)	309,844	4,054,304
Zinc (tons)	23,070	2,445,420
All other (tons)	11,620	4,016,336

Machinery and vehicles:

Automobiles (units)	65	43,810
All other (tons)...............	259	110,633
Chemicals (tons)	68	10,384

Unclassified:

Miscellaneous (tons)	7,500	1,486,277

Total shipments		$243,590,808

Receipts—

Animals and animal products:

Fish, fresh (tons)	740	$ 36,601
Fish, salt, dried and canned (tons)	562	111,557
All other (tons)	1,032	216,673

Vegetable food products:

Barley (bushels)................	347,583	102,349
Beverages (tons)	3,500	3,038,816
Canned goods (tons)	13,917	1,837,044
Confectionery (tons)	3,649	1,032,667
Grain screenings (tons)	35,816	32,771
Sugar (tons)	1,878	176,532
All other (tons)	15,263	1,274,983

Vegetable products, inedible:

Flaxseed (bushels)	104,250	113,996
Rubber and tires (tons)	7,815	2,980,176
All other (tons)	319	530,127

Textiles:

Linoleum (tons)	5,641	1,548,455
Twine and cordage (tons)	5,749	930,547
All other (tons)	1,947	623,135

Wood and paper:

Paper (tons)	5,132	625,456
Woodpulp (tons)	7,085	236,147
All other (tons)	739	100,224

Nonmetallic minerals:

Coal, anthracite (tons)	183,267	1,667,730
Coal, bituminous (tons)	6,278,864	26,371,229
Coke (tons)	25,188	178,835

HARBOR STATISTICS (*Contd.*)

Fuel oil (barrels)	921,207	2,291,853
Gasoline (gallons)	194,035,455	15,239,545
Gravel and sand (tons)	28,054	21,634
Kerosene (gallons)	11,720,286	635,415
Limestone and limestone products (tons)	364,972	1,057,625
Lubricating oils (gallons)	1,523,784	545,307
Stone (tons)	9,993	14,747
Sulphur (tons)	3,882	128,494
Tar, coal (tons)	18,472	295,552
All other (tons)	40,920	1,105,183
Ores, metals, and manufactures of:		
Dolomite (tons)	14,000	56,000
Iron and steel, manufactured (tons)	56,182	4,814,771
All other (tons)	9,681	624,111
Machinery and vehicles:		
Automobiles and trucks (units)....	21,163	14,263,862
All other (tons)	5,281	2,922,096
Chemicals:		
Creosote oil (tons)	6,148	227,476
Soda ash (tons)	11,295	237,195
All other (tons)	6,578	920,859
Unclassified:		
Miscellaneous (tons)	51,849	10,304,231
Total receipts		$99,472,006

(b) Two Harbors

Shipments—	Volume	Value
Iron ore (tons).................	9,602,477	$35,145,066
Receipts—		
Coal, bituminous (tons)..........	127,939	537,344
Fish, fresh (tons)	22	1,088
Total receipts (tons).............	127,961	$ 538,432

(c) Grand Marais

Shipments—	Volume	Value
Pulpwood (tons)	19,863	$ 142,604
Receipts—		
Fish (tons)	345	17,064
Coal, bituminous (tons)	700	2,940
Miscellaneous (tons)	25	5,000
Total receipts (tons)	1,070	$ 25,004

Note: Tons in this table are *short tons* = 2,000 pounds.

DOCKS AND TERMINALS

I. Duluth-Superior
>   Docks
>>   21 coal (capacity 13,013,000 tons)
>>   7 iron ore (length 3 miles; capacity 819,000 tons)
>>   25 grain
>>   4 cement, lime, salt
>>   42 miscellaneous
>>   ——
>>   99 docks, with a frontage of 49 miles
>   Terminals
>>   9 warehouses (floor space 1,730,000 sq. ft.; capacity 18,637,000
>>   cu. ft.)
>>   25 grain elevators (capacity 46,925,000 bushels)
>>   1 cement (capacity 114,000 barrels)
>>   ——
>>   35 terminals

II. Two Harbors
>   Docks
>>   3 iron ore (length .75 mile; capacity 168,800 tons)
>>   1 coal (capacity 125,000 tons)
>>   1 merchandise (draft insufficient for commercial craft)
>>   ——
>>   5 docks

SHIPS AND THEIR LANGUAGE

The larger Great Lakes boats are about 600 feet long, have a crew of 35, and cost about $700,000; package freighters cost about $300,000, and Standard Oil tankers with Diesel engine about $1,500,000.

The average boat travels 12 miles per hour with load and 14 miles when light; a round trip is made in about 11 or 12 days.

Regulations (Duluth-Superior Harbor):

I. Speed
>   Not to exceed 8 miles in dredged channels
>   Must be reduced when vessel approaches drawspan, to enable full
>   stop if draw fails to open

II. Anchorage
>   The Corps of Engineers, U. S. A., and U. S. Harbor Inspector,
>   or authorized representatives, have jurisdiction over position
>   and arrangement of vessels at anchor in basin
>   Mooring at U. S. piers not permitted

III. Lights
>   White light not over 40 ft. high, visible 5 miles on clear night
>   from bow
>   Green light (not visible from port side), visible 2 miles on star-
>   board bow
>   Red light (not visible from starboard), visible 2 miles on port bow
>   White light visible 3 miles on line with keel and not more than
>   75 ft. abaft bow light

Signals:
  General
    1 blast (whistle)—I am directing my course starboard (right)
    2 blasts—I am directing my course port (left)
    1 long blast—I am approaching blind curve, or backing from dock
    1 short blast—I am overtaking you, passing on starboard
    2 short blasts—I am overtaking you, passing on port
    3 blasts repeated at 1 minute intervals—fog signal
    5 or more short blasts—Danger, or I do not understand your
      signal
    3 long, 2 short blasts—Courtesy to foreign or visiting craft, first
      or last vessel of season
    All signals are answered in kind, except danger signal
    No vessel overtakes another in channel less than 500 ft. wide with-
      out permission of second
    Steam vessels must avoid sailing vessels
Bridges:
  Duluth Lift ....3 long blasts
  Interstate ....1 long, 1 short, 1 long
  Minnesota Draw (N. P.) ....1 long, 2 short
  Wisconsin Draw (N. P.) ....2 long, 2 short
  Grassy Point ....2 short, 1 long
  Arrowhead ....3 long
  Lamborn Avenue ....3 short
  (Long blast should not exceed 3 seconds, short blast 1 second)
  Signal should be given when vessel is .5 mile distant
  Bridges answer in kind; if unable to open, signal is 5 short blasts
  Vessels are given precedence over highway, railway traffic. Except
    at Duluth Lift Bridge, those of 100 net registered tons or less may
    be held a short time if trains carrying U. S. mails, or 4 street cars
    from one direction, are ready to cross.

Glossary

Artifact: In archeology, anything made or modified by human workmanship as distinguished from a natural object.

Basalt: A heavy, dark-colored and fine-grained igneous rock.

Beneficiation: In mining, the reduction, or concentration, of iron ore, as by washing or jigging, drying, crushing, screening, magnetism, sintering or fusion.

Boom: In logging, a chain of floating logs or timbers fastened together end to end to keep logs from floating away.

Brig: A square-rigged vessel having two masts.

Bunyan, Paul: A legendary lumberjack capable of performing superhuman feats.

Canoe Tilting: A contest on water in which men in canoes, with long poles padded at one end, try to overbalance one another.

Chippewa, or *Ojibway:* A tribe of Indians of Algonquian stock living in the regions near the Great Lakes.

Coureur de Bois: An unlicensed trapper or hunter, usually French or French-Canadian.

Crushing: In mining, a process of beneficiation whereby iron ore is broken up in order to facilitate the removal of silica.

Curling: A game played on level ice in which two teams composed of four players each slide curling stones toward a mark at either end called the tee.

Cut-Over Land: Land from which salable timber has been removed.

Drift: In mining, a passage in a mine, horizontal, or nearly so, which follows the vein.

Drying: In mining, a process of beneficiation whereby excess moisture in iron ore is removed by revolving ovens.

Escarpment: The steep face or slope of a ridge.

Esker, or *Eskar:* A narrow ridge of glacial sand and gravel.

Factor: The agent in control of a post of the Hudson's Bay Company, who in addition supervises the surrounding area.

Gabbro: A coarse, igneous rock.

Gill Net: A net set upright in the water that catches fish by their gills.

Grain Elevator: A building for the elevation, storage and distribution of grain.

Hopper-Bottomed Car: A railroad car with an open top, used for coal, ore, etc., with hoppers in the bottom to discharge the contents.

Intendant: During the French regime in Canada, the highest administrative officer under the governor.

Livre: A former French coin, which was equivalent to 19½ cents in United States currency.

Loading Pocket: The bin on an ore dock from which iron ore is discharged into the hold of a vessel.

Log Drive, or *Drive:* The floating of logs down a river.

Log Rolling: A contest in which competitors on a floating log attempt to dislodge each other by rapidly rotating the log with their feet.

Low-Grade Ore: In the Arrowhead mining regions, ore containing less than 50% iron is considered low grade.

Magnetism: In mining, a process of beneficiation whereby iron oxide is extracted from the ore by magnetic attraction.

Mallet Engine: An articulated type of locomotive used for heavy freight.

Mine Shaft: In mining, an opening in underground mines, vertical or nearly so, through which ores are hoisted, supplies let down, water pumped, and the mine ventilated.

Ore Body: A mass of earth containing ore.

Ore Car: A car of the hopper type used for hauling iron ore.

Outcrop, or *Outcropping:* In mining, the exposure at the surface of a vein, or stratum, of ore.

Paying Lode: A deposit of ore large and rich enough to warrant its extraction.

Portage: The land route between navigable bodies of water over which goods, supplies and boats are carried; transportation over such a route.

Pot Hole: A pit formed in the bed of a river by water whirling stones in an eddy.

Pre-Emption: A right of preference in the purchase of Government land legally accorded to actual settlers.

Raft Piloting: In lumbering, the floating of log rafts down the larger streams in the earlier days.

Raise: In mining, an opening, vertical or nearly so, which connects one level (passageway) with another one.

"Roll": A slang term for the robbing of a person when he is either asleep or drunk.

Saulteurs: A Chippewa Indian tribe formerly living around Sault Ste. Marie.

Schooner: A fore-and-aft rigged vessel originally having two masts, but now often more.

Screening: In mining, a process of beneficiation whereby some of the silica is removed from the iron ore by sifting.

Set Line: A line on which single hooks hung by short lines are fastened for catching fish.

Silica: A silicon dioxide found in its crystalline form as quartz.

Sintering, or *Fusion:* In mining, a process of beneficiation whereby fine, powdery iron ores are fused through the application of heat, thus removing impurities and making the ore an acceptable charge for a blast furnace.

Sioux, or *Dakota:*   An extensive family of Indians, many tribes of which inhabit the plains west of the Mississippi River.

Skijoring: A winter sport in which a horse draws a person on skis over ice or snow.

Skip: A large-sized bucket run up and down a mine shaft for hoisting purposes.

Slag: The refuse, or dross, of the smelting process.

Slalom Skiing: Skiing downhill on a zigzag course between upright obstacles, usually flags.

Sloop: A fore-and-aft rigged vessel having one mast and carrying a mainsail and jib.

Stock Pile: In mining, the ore stored at the surface.

Strippings: In the open-pit method of mining, the surface, or overburden, stripped to expose the ore body; mining excavations or diggings.

Subscriber: A signer of a document, as one who signs papers of occupation.

Taconite: On the Mesabi Range, iron-bearing rock formations.

Test Pit: In mining, a miniature shaft sunk to determine ore deposits (obsolete).

Till Plain: Unstratified level land of glacial origin.

Timber Cruiser, or *Cruiser:*   One who estimates timber on forest lands.

Tote Sleigh: In lumbering, a sleigh on which supplies are hauled.

Trillium: A flower of the lily family.

Veinstone: In mining, the valueless material around ore.

Voyageur: In early fur-trading days, licensed fur traders in the Northwest, later restricted to boatmen.

Washing, or *Jigging:*   In mining, a process of beneficiation whereby silica, gangue and other extraneous materials are removed from iron ore through the action of water.

Chronology

At the insistence of Benjamin Franklin, England ceded the region to the United States in the Treaty of Paris, which brought the Revolutionary War to an end.

1784   The Northwest Company was organized by dissatisfied traders of eastern Canada.

1787   The Continental Congress passed an ordinance for the purpose of putting unoccupied territory under government. In 1796 it was applied to the Northwest Territory, including the Arrowhead.

1793   Jean Baptiste Perrault built Fort St. Louis, a fur-trading post, on the Wisconsin side of what is now the Duluth-Superior Harbor.

1794   The Jay Treaty between the United States and Great Britain stipulated the withdrawal of British garrisons from American soil before June 1, 1796.

1801–1804   The trading posts of the great fur companies were removed from Grand Portage to the present site of Fort William.

1806   Lieutenant Zebulon M. Pike visits the Sandy Lake, Leech Lake, and Cass Lake posts of the Northwest Company.

1808   The American Fur Company was founded by John Jacob Astor.

1816   Congress excluded foreigners from trading in the Arrowhead.

1820   Territorial Governor Lewis Cass of Michigan traveled 4,000 miles through Indian country, including the Arrowhead.

1821   The Northwest and Hudson's Bay Companies united under the latter's name.

1823   Major Stephen H. Long and William H. Keating, by order of the Federal Government, made a survey of the International Boundary.

1825   David Thompson made the first scientific survey in St. Louis County.

1826   By the Treaty of Fond du Lac, the Chippewa gave white men permission to explore any part of their country for metals and minerals, and to carry them away.

1831   William A. Aitkin, a fur trader, takes charge of the Fond du Lac department of the American Fur Company at Sandy Lake.

1832   Schoolcraft discovers the source of the Mississippi in Lake Itasca, after his expedition had passed through the Arrowhead region.
Frederick Ayer started the first missionary school in the Arrowhead at Sandy Lake and completed there an Ojibway spelling book.

1833   Reverend Edmund F. Ely succeeded Frederick Ayer as missionary at Big Sandy Lake. In June, 1834, the mission school was removed to Fond du Lac.
Reverend William Thurston Boutwell established a mission at Leech Lake.

1834   John Jacob Astor withdrew from the American Fur Company and Ramsay Crooks took it over.

1836   Joseph N. Nicollet began his explorations in Minnesota, and spent the late summer with Boutwell at Leech Lake.

1842   The Webster-Ashburton Treaty fixed the present International Boundary between the United States and Canada.
The American Fur Company collapsed.

1843   Nicollet's large map of the Northwest was published. It was a con-
        tribution of first importance to American geography.
1845   Steamer *Independence* was the first steamboat on Lake Superior.
1846   Father Baraga made his famous journey across Lake Superior from
        La Pointe, Wisconsin, to Cross River, Cook County, in a canoe
        during a storm.
1847   Reuben B. Carlton, after whom Carlton County was later named,
        arrived at Fond du Lac.
1849   The Territory of Minnesota was created and organized. Alexander
        Ramsey was the first governor.
1850   Itasca County, established in 1849 and then embracing all of north-
        eastern Minnesota, had a population of 97 persons, excluding the
        Indians.
1851   Cass County created.
1852   George R. Stuntz, a government surveyor, arrived at the head of the
        lakes—Duluth's first permanent settler. He prepared the region for
        settlement.
1854   The Treaty of La Pointe, Wisconsin, opened the north shore of
        Lake Superior to white settlement. The cession of one square mile
        of land to Chief Buffalo subsequently had detrimental bearing on
        Duluth realty.
1855   There was a rush to the north shore for copper.
        The first frame house in Duluth built by Robert Emmet Jefferson
        on Lake Avenue.
        The Arrowhead's first sawmill was established at Duluth.
        Lewis H. Merritt and his oldest son, Napoleon, arrived by steamer
        at the head of the lakes.
        The *Superior Chronicle,* first published on June 12, was the first
        newspaper at the head of the lakes.
1856   A big boom in north shore lands, caused by rumors of copper de-
        posits, resulted in the platting of numerous town sites.
        Duluth was platted. The name was suggested by Reverend Joseph
        G. Wilson.
        St. Louis County established and first elections held.
        Lake, Morrison, and Pine Counties established.
        First public school on north shore was held at Oneota, now a part of
        Duluth. Jerome Merritt was the teacher.
        The site of Beaver Bay, Lake County, was occupied by William H.
        Newton and Thomas Clark.
        The Military Road was cut from St. Paul to the head of the lakes.
        First temperance society on north shore organized.
        A famine prevailed at the head of the lakes during the winter of
        1855-56. Flour sold as high as 60 cents a pound.
1857   A national money panic was almost calamitous to the head of the
        lakes region. The population fell from 3,000 to about 750.
        The first land office in the Arrowhead was established at Buchanan,
        one mile west of the mouth of Knife River.
        Duluth was incorporated as a village.

The first frame schoolhouse in northeastern Minnesota was built at Oneota.

The Arrowhead's first newspaper, *The North Shore Advocate,* was published at Buchanan.

Aitkin, Carlton, Crow Wing, and Mille Lacs Counties established.

1858   Minnesota was admitted as a State into the Union.

1859   First agricultural society in St. Louis County organized at Oneota.
The first brewery in Duluth was started near Washington Avenue and First Street, on Brewery Creek.

1860   The Arrowhead region, including several adjoining counties, had a population of 2,016, of which number 406 were in St. Louis County. A topographical survey of the bays, rivers, and shores of Lake Superior was made. General Meade was in charge.

1861   Luke Marvin and Sidney Luce were appointed officers of the U. S. Land Office at Portland. They were influential in making Duluth, in 1870, the northern terminus of the first railroad to Lake Superior (see 1865).

1862   The total valuation of personal property in St. Louis County was $5,000.
A Catholic missionary, Reverend Francis Pierz, prevented the Chippewa from joining the Sioux in their uprising.

1864   St. Louis County tax contribution to the State was $725.05.

1865   Rumors of gold caused a "rush" to Lake Vermilion.
George R. Stuntz discovered iron ore on the Vermilion Range. His location was the first iron ore bed later to be worked in Minnesota, the Breitung Mine.
Henry H. Eames, the State Geologist, and his brother Richard found large deposits of iron ore near Lake Vermilion.
Christian Wieland, a civil engineer, discovered iron ore near Babbitt, on the eastern Mesabi Range.
The Vermilion Trail was cut from Duluth to Tower.
The total enrollment of children of school age in St. Louis County was 87.
Commodore H. Saxton and the Hon. Thomas Clark examined and surveyed the route for the first railroad between St. Paul and Duluth. Ansel Smith and John M. Gilman did much to make Duluth the northern terminal (see 1861).

1866   Beltrami County established.

1867   Jay Cooke, the eastern financier, paid his first visit to Duluth. He made Duluth, in 1870, the eastern terminal of the Northern Pacific Railroad.

1869   The first Duluth newspaper, *The Duluth Minnesotian,* was first published on April 24. Dr. Thomas Foster was the editor.

1870   Duluth received a city charter. Colonel Joshua B. Culver was the first mayor.
Federal Census shows a population of 3,131 for Duluth, and 4,561 for St. Louis County. Other counties in or adjacent to the Arrowhead region show the following figures: Aitkin, 178; Beltrami, 80;

Carlton, 286; Cass, 380; Crow Wing, 200; Itasca, 96; Kanabec, 93; Lake, 135; Mille Lacs, 1,109; Morrison, 1,681; Pine, 648.

First issue of *Duluth Tribune*, a weekly paper, appears on May 4; publisher Robert C. Mitchell.

The Arrowhead's first railroad, the Lake Superior and Mississippi, reaches Duluth from St. Paul.

Work on the Northern Pacific Railroad begins February 15 at N. P. Junction, now the location of Carlton.

Duluth Chamber of Commerce first organized; Henry A. Gould first president (see 1880).

1871 The Duluth Ship Canal was dug.
The first grain elevator was built in Duluth.
Peter Mitchell explores the eastern end of the Mesabi Range for an Ontonagon (Michigan) Syndicate. This aroused the interest of eastern financiers in Minnesota iron ore deposits.

1872 *The Duluth Evening Tribune*, a daily paper, established on May 15 by Robert C. Mitchell.

1873 *The Duluth Daily Herald* founded by Robert D'Unger in the spring of this year.
The failure of Jay Cooke caused a nation-wide panic, dealing an almost mortal blow to the development of the area.
The Duluth Ship Canal was reconstructed and taken over by the U. S. Government.

1874 Cook County established.

1875 Professor Albert H. Chester explores the eastern end of the Mesabi and also the Vermilion Range for iron ore (see 1880).

1877 The village of Duluth is created out of a part of the bankrupt city.

1878 W. S. Woodbridge establishes the *Weekly Lake Superior News*. This paper, in 1886, became a daily, and, in 1892, by consolidation, the *News-Tribune* came into being.

1879 A public library established in Duluth (see 1890).

1880 United States Census figures for the following counties, within or adjacent to the Arrowhead region, are: Aitkin, 366; Beltrami, 10; Carlton, 1,230; Cass, 486; Cook, 65; Crow Wing, 2,319; Itasca, 124; Kanabec, 505; Lake, 106; Mille Lacs, 1,501; Morrison, 5,875; Pine, 1,365; St. Louis, 4,504.
Professor Albert H. Chester leads a second expedition to the Vermilion Range with George R. Stuntz as guide.
The Duluth Chamber of Commerce established (see 1870).

1881 State Legislature imposes a tax of one cent a long ton on iron ore.
The Duluth Street Railway Company was granted a franchise.
First telephone exchange established in Duluth.

1882 The town sites of Tower and Soudan are surveyed by George R. Stuntz.
In December, the Minnesota Iron Mining Company was formed by Tower, Breitung, Lee, Stuntz, and Stone.
St. Luke's Hospital in Duluth was founded.

Robert C. Mitchell changes the *Duluth Evening Tribune* to a morning paper.

A thirty year franchise is granted to the Duluth Gas and Water Company (see 1898).

1883   Hubbard County established.

1884   The Arrowhead's first iron ore was shipped from the Soudan Mine, Vermilion Range, to Agate Bay (now Two Harbors) over the Duluth and Iron Range Railroad.

1885   The site of the Pioneer Mine at Ely discovered.

R. E. Denfeld, a graduate of Amherst, becomes superintendent of Duluth public schools.

Duluth has a population of 18,036.

1886   Cloquet has a population of 1,500, Tower 3,000.

The Duluth and Iron Range Railroad was completed from Two Harbors to Duluth.

The site of the Chandler Mine at Ely discovered.

David T. Adams discovers iron ore near Grand Rapids.

The Old Settlers' Association of the Head of Lake Superior organized.

Duluth gets its first regular fire department.

22,000,000 bushels of grain and 700,000 tons of coal were handled at Duluth Harbor.

1887   Captain Griffith made iron ore explorations on the Mesabi Range.

Ely organized as a village.

Duluth reincorporated as a city on March 2.

The Duluth population estimated at 30,000.

1888   Two Harbors, incorporated as a village, becomes county seat of Lake County, succeeding Beaver Bay.

John Mallman, Frank Hibbing, and Captain Elisha Morcom explore different sections of the Mesabi Range for iron ore.

St. Mary's Hospital in Duluth was founded.

Duluth has epidemic of typhoid fever, caused by contaminated water.

The Imperial Mill was built in Duluth; daily capacity of 3,000 was later increased to 8,000 barrels.

City Hall at Second Avenue East was built in Duluth and completed January 30, 1889.

1889   The "Nelson Bill," for the relief and civilization of all Chippewa Indians in Minnesota, becomes law.

A census of Chippewa Indians in Minnesota shows a total number of 8,304 of whom 1,708 were in Lake Superior bands.

John McCaskill dug the first test-pit in iron ore on the Mesabi Range.

Captain Alexander McDougall invented a new type of Lake freighter (see 1893).

1890   United States Census figures for the following counties, within or adjacent to the Arrowhead region, are: Aitkin, 2,462; Beltrami, 312; Carlton, 5,272; Cass, 1,247; Cook, 98; Crow Wing, 8,852; Hubbard,

1,412; Itasca, 743; Kanabec, 1,579; Lake, 1,299; Mille Lacs, 2,845; Morrison, 13,325; Pine, 4,052; St. Louis, 44,862.

Duluth begins to use electricity, instead of mules, to run streetcars.

The Merritts discover iron ore (Mountain Iron Mine, Mesabi Range) and organize the Mountain Iron Company with Leonidas Merritt as first president.

The Duluth Public Library opened August 1 (see 1879).

Duluth has a population of 33,115.

1891   Duluth Incline Railway has first trial run on October 2 (see 1939).

Ely becomes a city.

Grand Rapids incorporated as a village.

1892   The first iron ore was shipped on October 17 from the Mesabi Range (Mountain Iron Mine).

The first passenger train was run over the Duluth, Missabe and Northern Railroad from Stony Brook to Mountain Iron in August.

The Lake Superior Iron Company was organized. It became the operating company for many holdings of Hibbing, Trimble, and Alworth.

Henry W. Oliver, of Pittsburgh, made the Mesabi Range what it is today—he made the market for its ore. He founded, in 1892, the Oliver Iron Mining Company. The same year the Carnegie Steel Company took over one half of the stock of the Oliver against a loan of $500,000. In 1901 the Oliver became a subsidiary of the newly formed United States Steel Corporation. Most of the Minnesota mining properties passed eventually to the Oliver Iron Mining Co. (see 1896).

Duluth was almost completely buried under snow and cut off from the world from March 9 to March 11.

Villa Sancta Scholastica founded by the Sisters of St. Benedict.

The Duluth Central High School building completed.

A normal training school, forerunner of the State Normal School, was started in Duluth by Denfeld.

The Duluth News-Tribune came into being by consolidation (see 1878).

Virginia, Biwabik, McKinley, and Mountain Iron were organized as villages.

1893   Rainy Lake was the scene of a "gold rush."

Eveleth organized as a city.

Hibbing became a municipality.

Proctor, just outside the Duluth city limits, was organized under the name Proctorknott. This was coincidental with the establishment of storage yards and engine shops by the Duluth, Missabe and Northern Railroad.

The Duluth, Missabe and Northern Railroad completes its line from Mountain Iron to Duluth, and makes connections with Virginia, Biwabik, and Hibbing.

Disastrous fire at Virginia June 18.

Great financial panic (see 1890).

The first wooden ore dock in Duluth completed in October; the first steamer loaded from its pockets the same month.

Lake Superior Consolidated Iron Mines Company organized by Rockefeller and the Merritt brothers (see 1894).

Captain Alexander McDougall's "immense passenger boat" *Christopher Columbus* was in service at the World's Fair in Chicago (see 1889).

Jay Cooke visits Duluth for the last time.

1894 Collapse of the Merritt brothers enterprises. They live in history as the "Seven Iron Men." Rockefeller men became directors and officials of the Lake Superior Consolidated Iron Mines Company (see 1893).

Virginia incorporated as a city.

Forest fires destroy Hinckley and Sandstone in Pine County.

Township of Stuntz, richest in St. Louis County, organized. It contributes almost twice as much to the county revenue as Duluth.

1895 Congress designated the harbors of Duluth and Superior as one— the Duluth-Superior Harbor.

Duluth ranks second in country in flour production with ten flour mills of 19,000 barrels daily capacity.

1896 The Oliver Iron Mining Company leased the properties of the Lake Superior Consolidated Iron Mines Company—the Rockefeller interests—on a royalty basis of twenty-five cents a ton for fifty years, 1,200,000 tons to be shipped annually over the Rockefeller railroads. Control of the Oliver Iron Mining Company passed to the Carnegie Steel Company with the shifting of an additional one-third of the Oliver mining stock to Carnegie, thus making the holdings of Carnegie five-sixths of the total stock. The capital was then $1,200,-000 (see 1892).

Beltrami County organized. Bemidji, the county seat, incorporated.

1898 Duluth takes over water and gas plants, which are henceforth operated as municipal utilities (see 1882).

Indian uprising at Leech Lake.

1900 United States Census figures for the following counties, within or adjacent to the Arrowhead region, are: Aitkin, 6,743; Beltrami, 11,030; Carlton, 10,017; Cass, 7,777; Cook, 810; Crow Wing, 14,250; Hubbard, 6,578; Itasca, 4,573; Kanabec, 4,614; Lake, 4,654; Mille Lacs, 8,066; Morrison, 22,891; Pine, 11,546; St. Louis, 82,932.

The cut of lumber in the Duluth district amounted to 675,000,000 board feet.

The Alger-Smith Mill in West Duluth considered the largest white pine sawmill in the world.

1902 A Federal Reserve was established in the western part of the Arrowhead region, which, in 1908, became the Minnesota National Forest and, in 1928, the Chippewa National Forest.

1903 Aurora and Chisholm, both in St. Louis County, incorporated as villages.

1906 Koochiching County established.

The Thomson Dam in the Cloquet River, near Carlton, completed.

1907 Two Harbors, Lake County, incorporated as a city.

1908 State Sanatorium for Consumptives opens at Ah-Gwah-Ching, near Walker, on Leech Lake.

Ore Dock No. 6, first steel ore dock in the United States, completed at Two Harbors.

1909 The Superior National Forest was established.

1910 United States Census figures for the following counties, within or adjacent to the Arrowhead region, are: Aitkin, 10,371; Beltrami, 19,337; Carlton, 17,559; Cass, 11,620; Cook, 1,336; Crow Wing, 16,861; Hubbard, 9,831; Itasca, 17,208; Kanabec, 6,461; Koochiching, 6,431; Lake, 8,011; Mille Lacs, 10,705; Morrison, 24,053; Pine, 15,878; St. Louis, 163,274.

1911 The first iron ore was shipped from the Cuyuna Range (Kennedy Mine).

1913 Duluth adopts new city charter, changing from aldermanic to commission form of government.

1914 The plant of the Minnesota Steel Company was completed in Duluth.

1916 Iron, steel, and Portland cement plants begin large scale production at Duluth.

The world's first Insulite mill was opened by the Minnesota and Ontario Paper Company at International Falls.

1917 Act passed to regulate commercial fishing on Lake Superior.

1918 A forest fire devastated more than 1,500 square miles in the Arrowhead region with a death toll of 432 persons.

1919 The village of Hibbing was moved because rich deposits of iron ore were found underneath its streets.

State Normal School at Bemidji opens.

1920 United States Census figures for the following counties, within or adjacent to the Arrowhead region, are: Aitkin, 15,043; Beltrami, 27,079; Carlton, 19,391; Cass, 15,897; Cook, 1,841; Crow Wing, 24,566; Hubbard, 10,136; Itasca, 23,876; Kanabec, 9,086; Koochiching, 13,520; Lake, 8,251; Mille Lacs, 14,180; Morrison, 25,841; Pine, 21,117; St. Louis, 206,391.

1922 St. Louis County Historical Society organized by its first president, the Hon. William E. Culkin.

1923 The Hibbing Technical and Vocational High School—a "Monument to Education"—completed at a cost of $3,800,000.

1924 The Minnesota Arrowhead Association was formed.

1929 The world's largest white pine mill—owned by The Virginia and Rainy Lake Lumber Company—was closed at Virginia.

Record shipment of 51,531,748 short tons of iron ore from Minnesota mines—44,141,805 tons from the Duluth-Superior Harbor, 7,393,943 tons from Two Harbors.

1930 The Duluth lift bridge was completed.

United States Census figures for the following counties, within or adjacent to the Arrowhead region, are: Aitkin, 15,009; Beltrami,

20,707; Carlton, 21,232; Cass, 15,591; Cook, 2,435; Crow Wing, 25,627; Hubbard, 9,596; Itasca, 27,224; Kanabec, 8,558; Koochiching, 14,078; Lake, 7,068; Mille Lacs, 14,076; Morrison, 25,442; Pine, 20,264; St. Louis, 204,596.

1934 The Duluth Civic Symphony Association was formed.

1935 The $30,000 4-H Clubhouse, a prize awarded to the St. Louis County organization for nationally outstanding club work, was dedicated at Esquagama Lake (near Biwabik).

1937 The completion of the Duluth Civic Center is celebrated.
St. Louis County library service begun through contract with County Board of Commissioners.

1939 Crown Prince Olav and Crown Princess Martha of Norway visit the Arrowhead region and dedicate Enger Memorial Tower in Duluth.
Duluth Incline Railway discontinues service and is dismantled.

1940 The thirty-second annual National Governor's Conference was held at Duluth.
Fiftieth Anniversary of the discovery of iron ore at the site of Mountain Iron, on the Mesabi Range, is celebrated at Mountain Iron.
A new sewage disposal system was completed at Duluth at a cost of more than $1,850,000.
United States Census figures for the following counties, within or adjacent to the Arrowhead region, are: Aitkin, 17,865; Beltrami, 26,107; Carlton, 24,212; Cass, 20,646; Cook, 3,030; Crow Wing, 30,226; Hubbard, 11,085; Itasca, 32,996; Kanabec, 9,651; Koochiching, 16,930; Lake, 6,956; Mille Lacs, 15,558; Morrison, 27,473; Pine, 21,478; St. Louis, 206,917.

Bibliography

Adams, Charles C. *An Ecological Survey of Isle Royale, Lake Superior.* 1909. Hallenbeck Crawford Co. Lansing, Mich.

Agassiz, Louis. *Lake Superior: Its Physical Character, Vegetation, and Animals, Compared with Those of Other and Similar Regions.* 1850. Gould, Kendall and Lincoln. Boston.

Anderson, Parker O. *Trees and Tree Planting.* 1936. Webb Book Publishing Co. St. Paul.

Andrews, C. C. *Minnesota and Dacotah: In Letters Descriptive of a Tour Through the North-West, in the Autumn of 1856.* 1857. Robert Farnham. Washington.

Arnold, John B. *A Story of Grand Portage and Vicinity.* 1923. Harrison and Smith Co. Minneapolis.

Bain, James (editor). *Travels and Adventures in Canada and the Indian Territories, Between the Years 1760 and 1776.* 1901. Little, Brown, and Co. Boston.

Beasley, Norman. *Freighters of Fortune.* 1930. Harper and Brothers. New York.

Bill, Ledyard. *Minnesota: Its Character and Climate.* 1871. Wood and Holbrook. New York.

Bishop, Harriet E. *Floral Home; or, First Years of Minnesota.* 1857. Sheldon, Blakeman and Co. New York.

Blegen, Theodore C. *Minnesota; Its History and Its People.* 1937. The University of Minnesota Press. Minneapolis.

Bond, J. Wesley. *Minnesota and Its Resources.* 1853. Redfield. New York.

Brown, Elton T. *The History of the Great Minnesota Forest Fires.* 1894. Brown Brothers and Kingsley. St. Paul.

Bryce, George. *The Remarkable History of the Hudson's Bay Company.* 1900. Sampson Low, Marston and Co., Ltd. London.

Burnham, Guy M. *The Lake Superior Country in History and in Story.* 1930. The Ashland Daily Press. Ashland, Wis.

Burnquist, Joseph A. A. (editor). *Minnesota and Its People.* 4 volumes. 1924. The S. J. Clarke Publishing Co. Chicago.

Butterfield, Consul Willshire. *History of Brule's Discoveries and Explorations, 1610-1626.* 1898. The Helman-Taylor Co. Cleveland.

Channing, Edward, and Lansing, Marion Florence. *The Story of the Great Lakes.* 1909. The Macmillan Co. New York.

Christianson, Theodore. *Minnesota, the Land of Sky-Tinted Waters.* 5 volumes. 1935. The American Historical Society, Inc. Chicago, New York.

Clements, Frederic E., Rosendahl, C. Otto, and Butters, Frederic K. *Minnesota Trees and Shrubs.* 1912. The University of Minnesota, Minneapolis.

Coffin, Charles Carleton. *The Seat of Empire.* 1871. James R. Osgood and Co. Boston.

Cooley, Jerome Eugene. *Recollections of Early Days in Duluth.* 1925. Published by author. Duluth.

Copway, G. *The Traditional History and Characteristic Sketches of the Ojibway Nation.* 1851. Benjamin B. Mussey and Co. Boston.

Coues, Elliott (editor). *New Light on the Early History of the Greater Northwest.* 3 volumes. 1897. Francis P. Harper. New York.

Crowell and Murray. *The Iron Ores of Lake Superior.* 1923. The Penton Press Co. Cleveland.

Culkin, William E. *North Shore Place Names.* 1931. Scott-Mitchell Publishing Co. St. Paul.

——— *St. Louis County, Minnesota, Chronology from the Earliest Times to and Including the Year 1900.* 1924. St. Louis County Historical Society. Duluth.

Davis, Mary Dabney (editor). *The Story of Duluth.* 1923. The Board of Education. Duluth.

De Kruif, Paul. *Seven Iron Men.* 1929. Harcourt, Brace and Co. New York.

Duluth and Iron Range Rail Road Company. *Transportation of Iron Ore.* 1927. Duluth and Iron Range Rail Road Co. Duluth.

Ensign, J. D. *History of Duluth Harbor.* No date; no publisher.

Flandrau, Charles E. *The History of Minnesota and Tales of the Frontier.* 1900. E. W. Porter. St. Paul.

Folsom, W. H. C. *Fifty Years in the Northwest.* 1888. Pioneer Press Co. St. Paul.

Folwell, William Watts. *A History of Minnesota.* 4 volumes. 1921-1930. Minnesota Historical Society. St. Paul.

——— *Minnesota, the North Star State.* 1908. Houghton Mifflin Co. Boston, New York.

Fountain, Paul. *The Great North-West and the Great Lakes Region of North America.* 1904. Longmans, Green, and Co. London, New York, Bombay.

Gates, Charles M. (editor). *Five Fur Traders of the Northwest.* 1933. The University of Minnesota Press. Minneapolis.

Geological and Natural History Survey of Minnesota. Annual and Final Reports, Bulletins, Publications.

Geological Survey of Michigan. Volume 6. 1898. Lansing, Mich.

Hall, Christopher Webber. *Geography and Geology of Minnesota.* 1903. The H. W. Wilson Co. Minneapolis.

Hall, Christopher Webber, and Lehnerts, Edward M. *Dodge's Geography of Minnesota.* 1911. Rand, McNally and Co. Chicago, New York, London.

Havighurst, Walter. *Upper Mississippi, A Wilderness Saga.* 1937. Farrar and Rinehart, Inc. New York.

Haworth, Paul Leland. *Trailmakers of the Northwest.* 1921. Harcourt, Brace and Co. New York.

International Boundary Commission. *Joint Report upon the Survey and Demarcation of the Boundary Between the United States and Canada from the Northwesternmost Point of Lake of the Woods to Lake Superior.* 1931. Government Printing Office. Washington.

Jaques, Florence Page. *Canoe Country.* 1938. The University of Minnesota Press. Minneapolis.

Johnson, Horace. *Gold Rush to the Vermilion and Rainy Lake Districts of Minnesota and Ontario in 1865 and 1894.* 1926. Duluth and Iron Range Rail Road Co. Duluth.

Kappler, Charles J. (editor). *Indian Affairs. 3 volumes.* 1904-1913. Government Printing Office. Washington.

Kellogg, Louise Phelps. *The British Regime in Wisconsin and the Northwest.* 1935. State Historical Society of Wisconsin. Madison, Wis.

—— *The French Regime in Wisconsin and the Northwest.* 1925. State Historical Society of Wisconsin. Madison, Wis.

—— (editor). *Early Narratives of the Northwest, 1634-1699.* 1917. Charles Scribner's Sons. New York.

Kenton, Edna (editor). *The Jesuit Relations and Allied Documents.* 1925. Albert and Charles Boni. New York.

Kohl, J. G. *Kitchi-Gami.* 1860. Chapman and Hall. London.

Lanman, Charles. *A Summer in the Wilderness; Embracing a Canoe Voyage up the Mississippi and Around Lake Superior.* 1847. D. Appleton and Co. New York.

Laut, Agnes C. *The Conquest of the Great Northwest.* 2 volumes. 1908. The Outing Publishing Co. New York.

—— *Pathfinders of the West.* 1914. The Macmillan Co. New York.

Leggett, William F., and Chipman, Frederick J. *Duluth and Environs: An Historical, Biographical, Commercial and Statistical Record from the Wilderness to the Present Time.* 1895. Nugent and Brown. Duluth.

Lindquist, Maude L., and Clark, James W. *Community Life in Minnesota.* 1933. Charles Scribner's Sons. New York, Chicago.

Longstreth, T. Morris. *The Lake Superior Country.* 1924. The Century Co. New York, London.

McClung, J. W. *Minnesota As It Is In 1870.* 1870. Published by author. St. Paul.

MacElwee, Roy S., and Ritter, Alfred H. *Economic Aspects of the Great Lakes-St. Lawrence Ship Channel.* 1921. The Ronald Press Co. New York.

MacKay, Douglas. *The Honourable Company.* 1936. The Bobbs-Merrill Co. Indianapolis, New York.

MacLean, R. B., and Flynn, H. E. *Minnesota and the Junior Citizen*. 1936. Webb Book Publishing Co. St. Paul.

Macmillan, Conway. *Minnesota Plant Life*. 1899. The Pioneer Press. St. Paul.

Mattoon, Wilbur R., and Anderson, Parker. *Forest Trees of Minnesota*. 1930. The University of Minnesota. Minneapolis.

Maxwell, Hu., and Harris, John T. *Wood Using Industries of Minnesota*. 1913. Minnesota State Forestry Board. St. Paul.

Merrill, James A. *The Wonderland of Lake Superior*. 1936. Burgess Publishing Co. Minneapolis.

Minnesota Geological Survey. Bulletins 12, 13, 15, 16, 19, 20, 21, 22, 23, 24 and 26. University of Minnesota. Minneapolis.

Minnesota Historical Society, Collections of the. 17 volumes. 1872-1920. Minnesota Historical Society. St. Paul.

Minnesota History (formerly *Minnesota History Bulletin*). 18 volumes. 1915-1937. A quarterly magazine published by the Minnesota Historical Society. St. Paul.

Minnesota School of Mines Experiment Station. *Bulletins 1, 2, 3, and 5.* University of Minnesota. Minneapolis.

Mussey, Henry Raymond. *Combination in the Mining Industry: A Study of Concentration in Lake Superior Iron Ore Production*. 1905. The Columbia University Press. New York.

Neill, Edward Duffield. *The History of Minnesota: From the Earliest French Explorations to the Present Time*. 1858. J. B. Lippincott and Co. Philadelphia.

Nute, Grace Lee. *The Voyageur*. 1931. D. Appleton and Co. New York, London.

Oliphant, Laurence. *Minnesota and the Far West*. 1855. William Blackwood and Sons. Edinburgh, London.

Parker, Nathan H. *The Minnesota Handbook, for 1856-7*. 1857. John F. Jewett and Co. Boston.

Phelps, H. H. *Personal Recollections of Forty-five Years at and Around the Bar in Minnesota*. 1928. Published by author. Glendale, Calif.

Phelps, William F. (editor). *A Vast Empire and Its Metropolis*. 1896. Rand, McNally and Co. Chicago.

Piper, W. S. *The Eagle of Thunder Cape*. 1924. The Knickerbocker Press. New York.

Pitezel, John K. *Lights and Shades of Missionary Life: Containing Travels, Sketches, Incidents, and Missionary Efforts, During Nine Years Spent in the Region of Lake Superior*. 1862. Western Book Concern. Cincinnati.

Primmer, George Henry. *The Influence of Location on the Evolution of Duluth, Minnesota*. 1933. Duluth.

Ritchie, James S. *Wisconsin and Its Resources: with Lake Superior, Its Commerce and Navigation*. 1858. Charles DeSilver. Philadelphia.

Robinson, Edward Van Dyke. *Early Economic Conditions and the Development of Agriculture in Minnesota*. 1915. The University of Minnesota. Minneapolis.

Roy, Pierre-Georges (editor). *Rapport de L'Archiviste de la Province de Quebec.* 9 volumes. 1922-1930. Province of Quebec, Canada.

St. John, John R. *A True Description of the Lake Superior Country: Its Rivers, Coasts, Bays, Harbours, Islands, and Commerce.* 1846. William H. Graham. New York.

Sakolski, A. M. *The Great American Land Bubble.* 1932. Harper and Brothers. New York, London.

Schoolcraft, Henry R. *Narrative of An Expedition Through the Upper Mississippi to Itasca Lake, the Actual Source of This River.* 1834. Harper and Brothers. New York.

—— *Summary Narrative of An Exploratory Expedition to the Sources of the Mississippi River, in 1820: Resumed and Completed, by the Discovery of Its Origin in Itasca Lake, in 1832.* 1855. Lippincott, Grambo, and Co. Philadelphia.

—— *The American Indians.* 1851. Wanzer, Foot and Co. Rochester.

Scull, Gideon D. (editor). *Voyages of Peter Esprit Radisson.* 1885. The Prince Society. Boston.

Seymour, E. S. *Sketches of Minnesota, the New England of the West.* 1850. Harper and Brothers. New York.

Stafford, Sara. *The Keeper of the Gate or the Sleeping Giant of Lake Superior.* 1903. (No publisher given.)

State Bureau of Immigration. *Minnesota by Counties.* (No date of publication.) State Board of Immigration. St. Paul.

State of Minnesota Department of Conservation. *State Parks of Minnesota.* Conservation Commission of the State of Minnesota.

State of Minnesota Department of Drainage and Waters. *Gazetteer of Meandered Lakes of Minnesota.* 1928.

Stewart, Lillian Kimball. *A Pioneer of Old Superior.* 1930. The Christopher Publishing House. Boston.

Surber, Thaddeus. *The Mammals of Minnesota.* 1932. Minnesota Department of Conservation. St. Paul.

Thwaites, Reuben Gold (editor). *The Jesuit Relations and Allied Documents.* 73 volumes. 1896-1901. The Burrows Brothers Co. Cleveland.

United States Geological Survey. Bulletins 274 and 678; Twenty-first Annual Report. 1901.

Upham, Warren, Holcombe, Return I., Holmes, Frank R., and Hubbard, Lucius F. *Minnesota in Three Centuries.* 4 volumes. 1908. The Publishing Society of Minnesota. New York.

Van Brunt, Walter (editor). *Duluth and St. Louis County, Minnesota.* 3 volumes. 1921. The American Historical Society. Chicago, New York.

Van Cleef, Eugene. *A Geographic Study of Duluth.* 1912. American Geographical Society. New York.

—— *Trade Centers and Trade Routes.* 1937. D. Appleton-Century Co., Inc. New York, London.

Vandiveer, Clarence A. *The Fur-Trade and Early Western Exploration.* 1929. The Arthur H. Clark Co. Cleveland.

Verwyst, P. Chrysostomus. *Life and Labors of Rt. Rev. Frederic Baraga,*

First Bishop of Marquette, Mich. 1900. M. H. Wiltzius and Co. Milwaukee.

Walker, Irma M., et. al. *The Story of the Arrowhead Country from the Age of Stone to. the Age of Steel.* 1929. Hibbing Branch of the American Association of University Women. Hibbing, Minn.

Warren, George Henry. *The Pioneer Woodsman As He Is Related to Lumbering in the Northwest.* 1914. Hahn and Harmon Co. Minneapolis.

Wilkinson, William. *Memorials of the Minnesota Forest Fires in the Year 1894.* 1895. Norman E. Wilkinson. Minneapolis.

Willard, Daniel E. *The Story of the North Star State.* 1922. Webb Publishing Co. St. Paul.

Winchell, N. H. *The Aborigines of Minnesota.* 1911. Minnesota Historical Society. St. Paul.

Winchell, N. H., Neill, Edward D., Williams, J. Fletcher, and Bryant, Charles S. *History of the Upper Mississippi Valley.* 1881. Minnesota Historical Co. Minneapolis.

Wirth, Fremont P. *The Discovery and Exploitation of the Minnesota Iron Lands.* 1937. The Torch Press. Cedar Rapids, Iowa.

Wisconsin, Collections of the State Historical Society of. 28 volumes. 1903-1920. Published by the Society. Madison, Wis.

Woodbridge, Dwight E., and Pardee, John S. (editors). *History of Duluth and St. Louis County.* 2 volumes. 1910. C. F. Cooper and Co. Chicago.

Wrong, Hume. *Sir Alexander Mackenzie.* 1927. The Macmillan Co. of Canada, Ltd. Toronto.

Suggestions for Further Reading

Banning, Margaret Culkin. *Mesabi*. New York: Harper & Row, 1969. Fiction.

Blacklock, Les, and Craig Blacklock. *Our Minnesota*. Photographs by the authors. 1978. Expanded ed. Bloomington: Voyageur Press, 1981.

Blegen, Theodore C. *Minnesota: A History of the State*. 1963. Reprint. Minneapolis: University of Minnesota Press, 1975.

Bogue, Margaret Beattie, and Virginia A. Palmer. *Around the Shores of Lake Superior: A Guide to Historic Sites, Including a Color Tour Map Showing Lake Superior's Historic Sites*. Madison: University of Wisconsin, Sea Grant College Program, 1979.

Bolz, J. Arnold. *Portage into the Past, by Canoe along the Minnesota-Ontario Boundary Waters*. Illustrations by Francis Lee Jaques. Minneapolis: University of Minnesota Press, 1960.

Carroll, Francis M. *Crossroads in Time: A History of Carlton County, Minnesota*. Cloquet: Carlton County Historical Society, 1987.

Davis, Edward W. *Pioneering with Taconite*. St. Paul: Minnesota Historical Society, 1964.

Densmore, Frances. *Chippewa Customs*. 1929. Reprint. Introduction by Nina Marchetti Archabal. St. Paul: Minnesota Historical Society Press, Borealis Books, 1979.

Ellis, William Donohue. *Land of the Inland Seas: The Historic and Beautiful Great Lakes Country*. Great West Series. Palo Alto, Calif.: American West Pub. Co., 1974.

Federal Writers' Project, Minnesota. *The WPA Guide to Minnesota*. 1938 (as *Minnesota: A State Guide*, American Guide Series). Reprint. Introduction by Frederick Manfred. St. Paul: Minnesota Historical Society Press, Borealis Books, 1985.

Fritzen, John. *Historic Sites and Place Names of Minnesota's North Shore*. Duluth: St. Louis County Historical Society, 1974.

Gebhard, David, and Tom Martinson. *A Guide to the Architecture of Minnesota*. Minneapolis: University of Minnesota Press, 1977.

Gilman, Carolyn. *Where Two Worlds Meet: The Great Lakes Fur Trade*. Museum Exhibit Series, no. 2. St. Paul: Minnesota Historical Society, 1982.

Hagg, Harold T. *The Mississippi Headwaters Region: Scenes from the Past.* Bemidji: Beltrami County Historical Society, 1986.

Hanft, Robert M. *Red River: Paul Bunyan's Own Lumber Company and Its Railroads.* Chico, Calif.: Center for Business and Economic Research, California State University, Chico, 1980.

Hatcher, Harlan. *The Great Lakes.* New York: Oxford University Press, 1944.

Havighurst, Walter. *The Long Ships Passing: The Story of the Great Lakes.* New York: Macmillan Co., 1942; rev. ed., 1975.

_____. *Upper Mississippi: A Wilderness Saga.* Rivers of America. New York: Farrar & Rinehart, 1937; rev. ed., 1944.

History of Koochiching County: Where Trees Make the Difference. Compiled and edited by the History Book Committtee. Dallas, Tex.: Taylor Pub. Co., 1983.

Hoffman, Daniel. *Paul Bunyan: Last of the Frontier Demigods.* 1952. Reprint. Lincoln: University of Nebraska Press, Bison Books, 1983.

Holling, Holling Clancy. *Paddle-to-the-Sea.* Illustrations by the author. Boston: Houghton Mifflin Co., 1941. Fiction for young people.

_____. *Minn of the Mississippi.* Illustrations by the author. Boston: Houghton Mifflin Co., 1951. Fiction for young people.

Holmquist, June Drenning, ed. *They Chose Minnesota: A Survey of the State's Ethnic Groups.* St. Paul: Minnesota Historical Society Press, 1981.

_____, and Jean A. Brookins. *Minnesota's Major Historic Sites: A Guide.* 1963. 2d ed., rev. St. Paul: Minnesota Historical Society Press, 1972.

_____, Sue E. Holbert, and Dorothy Drescher Perry, comps. *History Along the Highways: An Official Guide to Minnesota State Markers and Monuments.* Supplement, 1967-72, comp. Dorothy Perry Kidder and Cynthia Matson. Minnesota Historic Sites Pamphlet Series, no. 3; 6. St. Paul: Minnesota Historical Society, 1967; 1973.

Hoover, Helen. *The Long-Shadowed Forest.* New York: Thomas Y. Crowell Co., 1963.

In Our Own Back Yard: A Look at Beltrami, Cass and Itasca Counties at the Turn of the Century. Bemidji: North Central Minnesota Historical Center, 1979.

Jaques, Florence Page. *Francis Lee Jaques: Artist of the Wilderness World.* Garden City, N.Y.: Doubleday & Co., 1973.

_____. *Snowshoe Country.* Illustrations by Francis Lee Jaques. Minneapolis: University of Minnesota Press, 1944.

Kerfoot, Justine. *Woman of the Boundary Waters: Canoeing, Guiding, Mushing, and Surviving.* Introduction by Les Blacklock. Grand Marais: Women's Times Pub., 1986.

King, Frank A. *Minnesota Logging Railroads: A Pictorial History of the Era When White Pine and the Logging Railroad Reigned Supreme.* San Marino, Calif.: Golden West Books, 1981.

Kohl, Johann Georg. *Kitchi-Gami: Life Among the Lake Superior Ojibway.* Translated by Lascelles Wraxall. 1860. Reprint. Introduction by Robert E. Bieder. Additional translations by Ralf Neufang and Ulrike Böcker. St. Paul: Minnesota Historical Society Press, Borealis Books, 1985.

Larson, Agnes M. *History of the White Pine Industry in Minnesota.* Minneapolis: University of Minnesota Press, 1949.

Lass, William E. *Minnesota: A Bicentennial History.* The States and the Nation Series. New York: W. W. Norton & Co., 1977.

_____. *Minnesota's Boundary with Canada: Its Evolution since 1783.* St. Paul: Minnesota Historical Society Press, 1980.

Marling, Karal Ann. *The Colossus of Roads: Myth and Symbol along the American Highway.* Minneapolis: University of Minnesota Press, 1984.

Nute, Grace Lee. *Caesars of the Wilderness: Médard Chouart, Sieur des Groseilliers and Pierre Esprit Radisson, 1618-1710.* 1943. Reprint. St. Paul: Minnesota Historical Society Press, 1978.

_____. *Lake Superior.* American Lakes Series. Indianapolis: Bobbs-Merrill Co., 1944.

_____. *The Voyaguer.* 1931. Reprint. St. Paul: Minnesota Historical Society, 1955.

_____. *The Voyaguer's Highway: Minnesota's Border Lake Land.* St. Paul: Minnesota Historical Society, 1941.

Ojakangas, Richard W., and Charles L. Matsch. *Minnesota's Geology.* Minneapolis: University of Minnesota Press, 1982.

Olsenius, Richard. *Minnesota Travel Companion: A Unique Guide to the History along Minnesota's Highways.* Wayzata: Bluestem Productions, 1982.

Olson, Sigurd F. *The Hidden Forest.* Photographs by Les Blacklock. New York: Viking Press, 1969.

_____. *Listening Point.* Illustrations by Francis Lee Jaques. New York: Alfred A. Knopf, 1958.

_____. *Open Horizons.* New York: Alfred A. Knopf, 1969.

_____. *The Singing Wilderness.* Illustrations by Francis Lee Jaques. New York: Alfred A. Knopf, 1956.

_____. *Sigurd F. Olson's Wilderness Days.* New York: Alfred A. Knopf, 1972.

O'Meara, Walter. *Daughters of the Country: The Women of the Fur Traders and Mountain Men.* New York: Harcourt, Brace & World, 1968. Fiction.

_____. *The Grand Portage: A Novel.* Indianapolis: Bobbs-Merrill Co., 1951. Fiction.

_____. *Minnesota Gothic: A Novel.* New York: Henry Holt and Co., 1956. Fiction.

_____. *Tales of the Two Borders.* Indianapolis: Bobbs-Merrill Co., 1952. Fiction.

_____. *The Trees Went Forth: A Novel.* New York: Crown Publishers, 1947; reprint, 1982. Fiction.

_____. *We Made It Through the Winter: A Memoir of Minnesota Boyhood.* St. Paul: Minnesota Historical Society Press, 1974.

Raff, Willis H. *Pioneers in the Wilderness: Minnesota's Cook County, Grand Marais, and the Gunflint in the 19th Century.* Grand Marais: Cook County Historical Society, 1981.

Rounds, Glen. *Ol' Paul the Mighty Logger: Being a True Account of the Seemingly Incredible Exploits and Inventions of the GREAT PAUL BUNYAN...* Illustrations by the author. 1949. Reprint. New York: Holiday House, 1976. Fiction for young people.

Rottsolk, James E. *Pines, Mines, and Lakes: The Story of Itasca County, Minnesota.* Grand Rapids: Itasca County Historical Society, 1960.

Sandvik, Glenn N. *Duluth: An Illustrated History of the Zenith City.* Woodland Hills, Calif.: Windsor Publications, 1983.

Sansome, Constance J. *Minnesota Underfoot: A Field Guide to the State's Outstanding Geologic Features.* Bloomington: Voyageur Press, 1983.

Searle, R. Newell. *Saving Quetico-Superior: A Land Set Apart.* St. Paul: Minnesota Historical Society Press, 1977.

Treuer, Robert. *The Tree Farm.* Boston: Little, Brown and Co., 1977.

_____. *Voyageur Country: A Park in the Wilderness.* Minneapolis: University of Minnesota Press, 1979.

Umhoefer, Jim. *Guide to Minnesota's Parks, Canoe Routes, and Trails.* Madison, Wis.: Northword, 1984.

Vizenor, Gerald. *The People Named the Chippewa: Narrative Histories.* Minneapolis: University of Minnesota Press, 1984.

Walker, David A. *Iron Frontier: The Discovery and Early Development of Minnesota's Three Ranges.* St. Paul: Minnesota Historical Society Press, 1979.

Warren, William W. *History of the Ojibway People.* 1885. Reprint. Introduction by Roger Buffalohead. St. Paul: Minnesota Historical Society Press, Borealis Books, 1984.

Waters, Thomas F. *The Streams and Rivers of Minnesota.* Minneapolis: University of Minnesota Press, 1977.

_____. *The Superior North Shore.* Minneapolis: University of Minnesota Press, 1987.

Wheeler, Robert C., Walter A. Kenyon, Alan R. Woolworth, and Douglas A. Birk. *Voices from the Rapids: An Underwater Search for Fur Trade Artifacts, 1960-73.* St. Paul: Minnesota Historical Society, 1975.

Zapffe, Carl A. *Oldtimers—Stories of Our Pioneers: 57 Essays Presenting a Carefully Researched Account of Our Early Lake Region History.* Pequot Lakes: Echo Pub. Co.; Brainerd: Historic Heartland Association, 1987.

Index

Knife Falls, 95
see Cloquet
Knife River, 162
Knott, J. Proctor, 149, 150
Komoko, 90
Koochiching county, 3, 134, 140, 147

Labor, 106-197
Lachmund, Ernest, 28
Lac la Pluie (Rainy Lake), 176
Lake county, 3, 75, 152, 153, 162
Lakes:
Ada, 57; Agamok, 55; Agassiz, 4, 20, 175; Agnes, 63, 64; Ahmakose, 54, 65; Alder, 52; Aldon, 56; Alice, 58; Alpine, 54, 55; Bald Eagle, 59; Ball Club, 39; Bass, 64; Basswood, 51, 60, 61; Bear, 54, 56; Bemidji, 41, 77-78, 79; Beth, 56; Big, 62, 186; Big Hanging Horn, 75, 182; Big Knife, 50; Big Rice, 39; Big Saganaga, 55, 167; Big Sandy, 71, 125, 140, 141, 181; Big Sletten, 61; Birch, 16, 50, 60, 64, 184, 186; Blackduck, 83, 178; Bonnie, 65; Boot, 61; Bottle, 51; Bowstring, 39; Boy, 39; Brule, 53; Buck, 66; Burntside, 61, 62, 63, 65, 66, 67, 186, 187; Canoe, 52; Cap, 54; Caribou, 41, 53; Carp, 50, 64; Carson, 131; Cass, 39, 40, 41, 42, 43, 78, 92, 93, 178, 179; Cedar, 181; Cedar Island, 126; Cherokee, 48, 53, 56, 57; Chippewa, 61; Clear, 60; Clearwater, 52; Colby, 74; Copper, 54, 56; Cove, 50; Crab, 63, 66, 67, 167; Crane, 51, 68, 186; Crooked, 51, 54, 56, 61, 62; Cut Foot Sioux, 39, 41, 174; Cross Bay, 56; Crystal, 129; Cummings, 63, 67; Cypress, 50; Daniels, 50, 52; Deer, 101; Dora, 41; Duck, 51; Duluth, 3, 119, 182; Dumbell, 46; Duncan, 50, 52;

Lakes (*Continued*)
East Bearskin, 52, 167; East Pike, 50, 52; East Twin, 61; Echo, 186; Eddy, 54; Elk, 92; Elton, 54, 56; Embarrass, 82; Ensign, 64; Esquagma, 74, 82, 187; Eugene, 66; Everett, 47, 61; Fairy, 61; Fall, 60, 184; Farm, 59; Farm Island, 180; Fenske, 61, 186; Flour, 52, 167; Fly, 64; Four, 58; Fourtown, 61; Frazer, 54, 65; Gabbro, 59; Gabmichigami, 48, 55; Gaskin, 53; Ge-be-on-e-quet, 64; Gerund, 54, 65; Glenmore, 66; Gneiss, 50; Gordon, 53, 56; Grace, 56; Grassy, 61; Green, 64; Greenwood, 15; Gun, 61, 66, 141; Gunflint, 50, 167; Half Moon, 170; Ham, 54; Hazel, 56; Hegman, 186; Henson, 53; Hoe, 54; Horse, 61, 62; Horseshoe, 53; Hub, 57; Hudson, 58; Hug, 57; Hungry Jack, 52; Ima, 64; Insula, 58; Iron, 51, 167; Isabella, 59; Island, 39, 147; Itasca, 43, 78, 92, 179; Jasper, 54; Jeanette, 186; John, 49; Jordan, 64; Karl, 56; Kavendeba, 56; Kawasachong, 48, 58; Kawishiwi, 58; Kekekabic, 48, 54, 65; Kelso, 57; Kiskadinna, 53; Knife (or Big Knife), 50, 54, 65; Koma, 56, 58; Korb, 63, 67; Lac La Croix, 49, 51, 63, 64, 66; Lake Thirteen, 40; Lake of the Woods, 45, 80, 148; Ledge, 54; Leech, 39, 40, 43, 116, 157, 179, 180; Lily, 53; Little Crab, 63, 66, 67; Little Cut Foot Sioux, 174; Little Gunflint, 50; Little John, 49; Little Knife, 50; Little Moose, 143; Little Saganaga, 54, 55, 56, 57; Little Sagus, 54; Little Sletten, 61; Little Trout, 65; Little Vermilion, 51; Lizz, 53; Loch Lomond, 169; Long, 42; Long

www.ingramcontent.com/pod-product-compliance
Lightning Source LLC
Jackson TN
JSHW020017141224
75386JS00025B/565